T0202907

Communications
in Computer and Information Science
1853

Rationale

The CCIS series is devoted to the publication of proceedings of computer science conferences. Its aim is to efficiently disseminate original research results in informatics in printed and electronic form. While the focus is on publication of peer-reviewed full papers presenting mature work, inclusion of reviewed short papers reporting on work in progress is welcome, too. Besides globally relevant meetings with internationally representative program committees guaranteeing a strict peer-reviewing and paper selection process, conferences run by societies or of high regional or national relevance are also considered for publication.

Topics

The topical scope of CCIS spans the entire spectrum of informatics ranging from foundational topics in the theory of computing to information and communications science and technology and a broad variety of interdisciplinary application fields.

Information for Volume Editors and Authors

Publication in CCIS is free of charge. No royalties are paid, however, we offer registered conference participants temporary free access to the online version of the conference proceedings on SpringerLink (http://link.springer.com) by means of an http referrer from the conference website and/or a number of complimentary printed copies, as specified in the official acceptance email of the event.

CCIS proceedings can be published in time for distribution at conferences or as postproceedings, and delivered in the form of printed books and/or electronically as USBs and/or e-content licenses for accessing proceedings at SpringerLink. Furthermore, CCIS proceedings are included in the CCIS electronic book series hosted in the SpringerLink digital library at http://link.springer.com/bookseries/7899. Conferences publishing in CCIS are allowed to use Online Conference Service (OCS) for managing the whole proceedings lifecycle (from submission and reviewing to preparing for publication) free of charge.

Publication process

The language of publication is exclusively English. Authors publishing in CCIS have to sign the Springer CCIS copyright transfer form, however, they are free to use their material published in CCIS for substantially changed, more elaborate subsequent publications elsewhere. For the preparation of the camera-ready papers/files, authors have to strictly adhere to the Springer CCIS Authors' Instructions and are strongly encouraged to use the CCIS LaTeX style files or templates.

Abstracting/Indexing

CCIS is abstracted/indexed in DBLP, Google Scholar, EI-Compendex, Mathematical Reviews, SCImago, Scopus. CCIS volumes are also submitted for the inclusion in ISI Proceedings.

How to start

To start the evaluation of your proposal for inclusion in the CCIS series, please send an e-mail to ccis@springer.com.

Sander Münster · Aaron Pattee · Cindy Kröber ·
Florian Niebling
Editors

Research and Education in Urban History in the Age of Digital Libraries

Third International Workshop, UHDL 2023
Munich, Germany, March 27–28, 2023
Revised Selected Papers

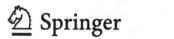 Springer

Editors
Sander Münster [ID]
Friedrich-Schiller-Universität Jena
Jena, Germany

Aaron Pattee
Ludwig-Maximilians-Universität München
Munich, Germany

Cindy Kröber
Friedrich-Schiller-Universität Jena
Jena, Germany

Florian Niebling
Fulda University of Applied Sciences
Fulda, Germany

ISSN 1865-0929   ISSN 1865-0937 (electronic)
Communications in Computer and Information Science
ISBN 978-3-031-38870-5   ISBN 978-3-031-38871-2 (eBook)
https://doi.org/10.1007/978-3-031-38871-2

This Springer imprint is published by the registered company Springer Nature Switzerland AG
The registered company address is: Gewerbestrasse 11, 6330 Cham, Switzerland

Preface

Urban and architectural history are key areas in digital humanities and digital heritage. While digital heritage refers to tangible and intangible cultural heritage objects and their preservation and use in education and research (e.g. UNESCO, 2003), the digital humanities focus on the application of digital technologies to support research in the humanities. Besides the aspect of general relevance, there are many commonalities in this central area, as both fields share concepts such as the idea of spatialization, extensive information about an object as a basis for research, and a strong connection to the creation and perception of visualization and imagery. Digital repositories are a core component of many approaches and meet a wide variety of demands, ranging from research in humanities and information technologies, to museum contexts, and library studies to tourist applications. Among the functions included in these digital repositories are the hosting of digitized historical sources as texts, images, audio-visual material, or representations of physical and virtual models as digital files. These repositories also store and integrate research data and results, in addition to curating further developing methodologies. Due to the wide field of possible research due to the digital turn, different approaches, methods, and technologies have emerged – and continue to emerge.

These digital libraries and repositories often function as the main facilitators of such projects, enabling researchers to digitize a large number of relevant documents and make these available to the public. Although the digitization process is currently accelerated by large-scale endeavours, such as the 3D digitization campaign in the EU Digital Space for Cultural Heritage, there has been a shift towards data-based analysis and integration—particularly with regard to statistical analysis, computer vision, or multimodal data. Although available technology and data are both important drivers and present possible constraints, the question as to whether the research is primarily data-driven or data-led often remains open. In this changing context, the question arises as to how research and education in urban history can be supported by digital libraries.

The primary objective of the 3rd Workshop on Research and Education in Urban History in the Age of Digital Libraries, held during March 27th–28th, 2023 in Munich, Germany, was to provide a full picture with regards to epistemics, technology, and framework conditions for digital projects. This book not only presents major findings and aims to highlight crucial challenges for further research, but was also compiled in order to encourage debate between the sciences. We showcase contributions on theoretical and methodological issues, application scenarios, as well as novel approaches and tools.

The 33 submissions to the event were reviewed by a joint program committee in a double-blind reviewing process, through which 15 papers were selected for the revised volume. These selected papers cover the following five research areas:

- Theory, Methods, and Systematization
- Data Handling and Data Schemes
- Machine Learning and Artificial Intelligence

- Visualization and Presentation
- Education in Urban History

1. Theory, Methods, and Systematization
   Digital humanities research as an inherently interdisciplinary field has created a high demand for critically reflected methods, techniques, valid strategies, classifications, and quality standards. But do computing methods also lead to new and ground-breaking research questions, approaches, or insights into architectural and urban cultural heritage research? In most cases, the use of computing simply extends non-digital possibilities, without much change to the pre-digital approaches and research questions. Nevertheless, digitalization has dramatically altered research qualities, quantities, and workflows. This section includes three articles about a methodology for 3D reconstruction and digitization, as well as usage scenarios for browser-based tools.

2. Data Handling and Data Schemes
   The immense effort invested in digitization and the rapid changes in technology and data formats has greatly increased the importance of data standards. Long-term data storage, availability of models, and the interoperability of data formats are major challenges to existing digital infrastructures. This section includes three articles focusing upon databases, data organization, and multi-modal indexing.

3. Machine Learning and Artificial Intelligence
   Throughout the past few years, various new technological opportunities have arisen from big data, Semantic Web technologies, and the exponential growth in data accessible via digital libraries such as Europeana. Data-driven supervised and unsupervised classification approaches have been used to acquire high-level semantic concepts—especially from the interconnection of different types of data. Interdisciplinary collaborations between computer science and humanities disciplines are essential in developing methods and workflows to enable cultural heritage research to capitalize on machine learning approaches. This section contains one article particularly dealing with computer vision and historical imagery.

4. Visualization and Presentation
   Historians in cultural heritage research today are encouraged to explore new research directions due to the availability of multitudes of digitized historical photographs in image repositories. Moreover, novel approaches such as the photogrammetric reconstruction of historical buildings from image databases allow for contextualization and intuitive access to data. The typical motivations for accessing such archives and repositories are scientific research, pedagogical applications, and the study of historical sites. These areas require advances in methods for visualization and presentation of data to support the different target groups. Four articles are compiled within this section, showcasing projects and investigations from urban history. These discuss visualizations and presentations of spatial data, as well as novel interdisciplinary approaches, such as combining musicology and computer visualization.

5. Education in Urban History

   Education supported by digital libraries plays an ever-increasing role within the study of urban heritage, which has direct effects upon the repositories targeting different user groups and scenarios of formal and informal learning and teaching. Consequently, the five articles in this section cover a large variety of educational scenarios for teaching urban history supported by digital methods, ranging from school education to city-scale virtual tourism experiences.

We would like to acknowledge the important work done by the chapter reviewers. We also thank the sponsors, program committee members, supporting organizations, and volunteers for making the joint event held in Munich in March 2023 a success. Without their efforts, the event would not have been possible.

Sander Münster
Cindy Kröber
Aaron Pattee
Florian Niebling

Organization

Organizing Committee

Sander Münster	Friedrich Schiller University Jena, Germany
Aaron Pattee	Ludwig Maximilian University of Munich, Germany
Cindy Kröber	Friedrich Schiller University Jena, Germany
Florian Niebling	Fulda University of Applied Sciences, Germany

Programm Committee

Fabrizio Apollonio	Università di Bologna – Alma Mater Studiorum, Italy
Clemens Beck	Friedrich Schiller University Jena, Germany
Jonas Bruschke	Julius-Maximilians-Universität Würzburg, Germany
Valerie Gouet-Brunet	Univ. Gustave Eiffel/IGN, France
Ning Gu	University of South Australia, Australia
Stephan Hoppe	Ludwig Maximilian University of Munich, Germany
Marinos Ioannides	Cyprus University of Technology, Cyprus
Thomas Köhler	TU Dresden, Germany
Piotr Kuroczyński	Hochschule Mainz – University of Applied Sciences, Germany
Ferdinand Maiwald	Friedrich Schiller University Jena/TU Dresden, Germany
Heike Messemer	TU Dresden, Germany
Gustavo Nogueira	Friedrich Schiller University Jena/Temporality Lab, The Netherlands
Ramon Reyes Rodriguez	Universidad de Guadalajara, Mexico
Heather Richards-Rissetto	University of Nebraska-Lincoln, USA
Fulvio Rinaudo	Politecnico di Torino, Italy
Ying Sun	Friedrich Schiller University Jena/Mediadesign Hochschule Berlin, Germany
Rosa Tamborino	Politecnico di Torino, Italy

Ronja Utescher	University of Bielefeld, Germany
Alex Yen	China University of Technology, Taiwan, Republic of China
Sina Zarrieß	University of Bielefeld, Germany

Contents

Theory, Methods, and Systematization

An Experimental Methodology for the 3D Virtual Reconstruction of Never Built or Lost Architecture

Fabrizio Ivan Apollonio ⓘ, Federico Fallavollita ⓘ, and Riccardo Foschi(✉) ⓘ

Department of Architecture, Alma Mater Studiorum University of Bologna, Via Dell'Università 50, 47521 Cesena, Italy
{fabrizio.apollonio,federico.fallavollita,
riccardo.foschi2}@unibo.it

Abstract. This paper proposes a methodology to rationalize the process of reconstruction of no more existing or designed but never built architectures. The methodology focuses on the following aspects of the hypothetical digital 3D reconstructions: sources (e.g., gathering, use, documentation), representation method (e.g., geometry, scale, segmentation, 3D modelling), and visualization (e.g., textures, light, point of view, projection method). The method was thought to be as objective, clear, transparent, and reproducible as possible, and it aims to generate 3D digital reconstructions of comparable quality and reusable in various scenarios. It was put to test for several years at the architectural drawing courses of the University of Bologna; one hundred students per class each academic year. The methodology presented is based on an iterative process of calibration of input and outputs based on annual trials. The 3D models constructed were archived in a repository and the retrospective annual assessment fostered critical observations. On the one hand, the method produces, in most cases, comparable, traceable, and reusable models for various purposes (e.g., visualization, semantic analysis, geometrical study, historical study, 3D printing, virtual exploration, etc.). On the other hand, the methodology aims to improve learning and foster architectural cultural heritage knowledge.

Keywords: 3D Modelling Reconstruction · Virtual Heritage · Higher Education · Standardization · C.N. Ledoux · M. Guidi

1 Introduction

Digital 3D reconstructions have been used as knowledge carriers, research tools and means of representation in architectural history research for more than thirty years [1, 2]. The amount of 3D digital reconstructions has continuously increased in the past years, and they show different technical, graphical, and content-related qualities [3]. In many cases neither the processes of creation nor the quality of the underlying research works is transparent. While a diversity of models and tools is desirable, especially due to the plurality of issues that are investigated, the question of criteria and approaches to evaluate and validate the use of these tools as well as the resulting findings arises.

S. Münster et al. (Eds.): UHDL 2023, CCIS 1853, pp. 3–18, 2023.
https://doi.org/10.1007/978-3-031-38871-2_1

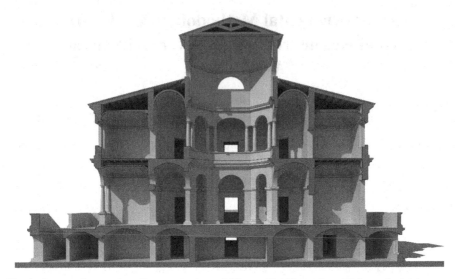

Fig. 1. Perspective section. Reconstruction of Mauro Guidi's project "Palazzo isolato per un nobile" Atlante 46, Carta 193 [4].

In this context, numerous research projects emerged with the common aim of systematizing and rationalizing the various issues identified by the scientific community. One of the most prominent and ambitious objectives was the definition of shared good practices as possible standards of reference for the academic/scientific community. The "Arbeitsgemeinschaft Digitale Rekonstruktion des Digital Humanities im deutschsprachigen Raum (DhD) e.V." ("Digital 3D Reconstruction working group" emerged from the 1st Annual Conference of Digital Humanities in German-speaking countries) at the end of 2014 [5] brought together scholars who deal with the topic from the perspective of architecture, archaeology, construction and art history as well as computer graphics and computer science. From this experience, the project "DFG Research Network: Digital 3D Reconstructions as Tools of Architectural Historical Research" (2018–2022) was born. The project aimed to publish a "Handbook of Scientific Digital 3D Reconstruction" that synthesized the topics that arose from the previous initiative [6].

As a direct consequence of the DFG project, the ongoing CoVHer Erasmus + project (Computer-based Visualization of Architectural Cultural Heritage, 2022–2025) can also be mentioned [7, 8]. The project is fostering collaboration between seven international partners from all over Europe, whose main purpose is to support the digital capabilities of the higher education sector and stimulate innovative learning and teaching practices. The project strives to define applicable standards and methods for the 3D hypothetical reconstruction, to create a repository of 3D models of CH and to disseminate those outcomes in academic activities, create teaching modules of university courses dedicated exclusively to the virtual reconstructions of CH, and jointly raising awareness among the academic world and the public on the possibility of scientifically reconstructing the past. The department of architecture of the University of Bologna played an active role in both projects.

We believe that research and teaching should be developed in parallel. A methodology can become standard only if it can be easily transmitted and assimilated by the scientific community. The search for an effective and clear methodology, to be shared at an international level, must therefore be tested in smaller contexts, for example with fellow scholars and/or with students. For several years we have been experimenting with a possible methodology in the Lab-based Course on Architectural Drawing (second academic year) of the five-year Architecture Degree course at the University of Bologna. From a didactic point of view, the integration of this experience/methodology in a second-year course of a five-year-long degree in architecture aims to develop skills in the fields of:

- advanced 3D modelling of architecture.
- digital representation, presentation, and visualization of architecture.

Concerning the consolidation of already mastered skills, this didactic experience aims to strengthen:

- the student's capability to perform scientifically valid and transparent documental research and analysis;
- the student's capability to develop an architectural 3D project reconstruction in its entirety.

Fig. 2. Indoor rendered views. Reconstruction of Mauro Guidi's project "Palazzo isolato per un nobile" Atlante 46, Carta 193 [4].

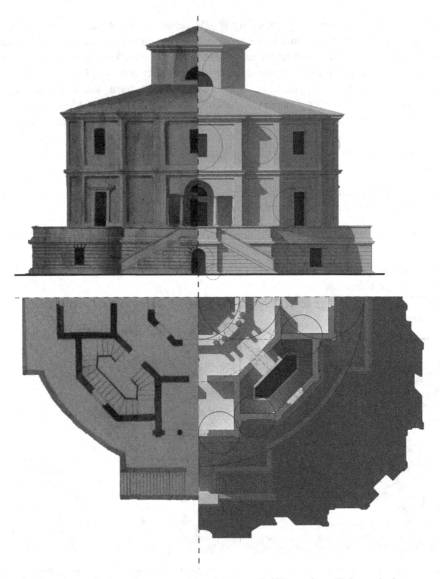

Fig. 3. Elevation and plan. Reconstruction of Mauro Guidi's project "Palazzo isolato per un nobile" Atlante 46, Carta 193 [4].

2   The Research and its Application

The experimental Methodology was proposed for the Lab-based Course on Architectural Drawing [9]. In this course, the students are required to build 3D models of lost or designed but never built architectures starting only from graphical or textual sources, while documenting the reconstruction process carefully (In Fig. 1, Fig. 2, Fig. 3, Fig. 4, Fig. 5, Fig. 6, Fig. 9 you can see an extract from the work presented by the students M.

Fig. 4. Cutaway drawing. Reconstruction of Mauro Guidi's project "Palazzo isolato per un nobile" Atlante 46, Carta 193 [4].

Barchi and M. J. Davey). Each year the seminar course focuses on a particular architect. For example, in recent years, the case studies proposed were the unrealized projects by Claude-Nicolas Ledoux (1736–1806), and Mauro Guidi (1761–1829). The architectural drawings of these two authors, children of the ideas of the French Enlightenment, are perfect sources of study for the objectives of the experimentation. Both sets of projects are composed of a multitude of different architectures, but with similar complexity and style, most of the architectures in these sets are never realized but are graphically represented in a wealth of detail.

They deal with different and well-defined typologies and experimental/practical use of the classical language of architecture. These graphical sources sometimes present inconsistencies and missing parts which foster critical thinking and require dealing with the topic of uncertainty and subjective additions. Both authors are known to be utopian and among the multitude of designs that they produced, only a minority was realized. Ledoux gathered and published numerous of his neoclassical designs in the book "*L'Architecture considérée sous le rapport de l'art, des mœurs et de la legislation*" [10]. Guidi, similarly, produced a multitude of projects (more than a thousand), civil and religious buildings, monuments and colonic houses, which mostly remained unrealized. All these projects, collected into eleven "*Atlanti*" now preserved at the Biblioteca Malatestiana in Cesena [11], document his ambitious dream to realize a new urban renewal of Cesena and Cesenatico cities which he was never able to realize.

The experimentation, carried out also in form of didactic activities, has allowed us to evaluate the progress and the results achieved concerning two main topics:

- the Applied Methodology for the virtual reconstruction of 3D models of architectures from the past;
- some Theoretical Aspects aimed at defining virtual 3D reconstruction as an autonomous discipline.

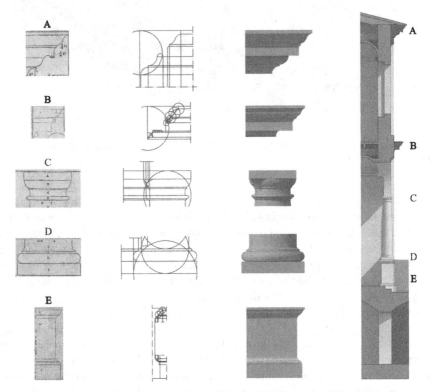

Fig. 5. Architectural details. Reconstruction of Mauro Guidi's project "Palazzo isolato per un nobile" Atlante 46, Carta 193 [4].

3 The Methodology

The course is aimed at second-year architecture students. After completing the course, students acquire the knowledge to analyse, decompose and represent the complexity of architectural projects through drawing. This acquired knowledge will allow students to use representation methods as graphic languages aimed at guiding the creative process of architectural design from its implementation phase to its execution.

The course includes one hundred hours of teaching: about a half dedicated to theoretical and practical lectures and the other half dedicated to laboratory work: in which students independently work on the assigned topics, assisted by teachers and tutors. The theoretical and practical lessons are dedicated to two fundamental topics: the first is descriptive geometry and the second deals with the theme of virtual reconstructions. The former is necessary to acquire the theoretical and practical concepts to control and visualize geometric shapes in 3D space (3D modelling is an integral part of this first topic); the latter is aimed at understanding the theoretical and practical aspects of the world of virtual reconstructions.

From a research point of view, the important aspect (onto which also the didactic is focused) is the systematization of the main concepts that can help to share 3D models as scientific products. The innovation of this research, therefore, does not consist in the methodology itself but in the analysis of the theoretical and practical aspects of the discipline. Virtual reconstruction is a mature enough field that could and should start to be considered as an autonomous discipline, but a systematization and rationalization effort should be made and should be shared at the international level.

The methodology used for the virtual reconstructions of the 3D model is divided into various phases of which the main four are:

- gathering, analysis and 2D redrawing of the main sources;
- critical virtual reconstruction of the 3D model;
- analysis and visualization of the 3D virtual reconstruction;
- documentation of the reconstruction process.

The first phase is dedicated to the analysis and redrawing of the 2D sources (see next paragraph). In the case studies addressed, the main sources are the digital reproductions of the original drawings of the projects. The digital images are obtained directly from the original sources: in the case of Mauro Guidi the sources are digital photographs of the original drawings conserved in the Malatestiana Library in Cesena [11]; in the case of Claude-Nicolas Ledoux the sources are the digital scans of the tables of the projects reported in the book *"L'architecture"* [10]. Whenever possible, it is advisable to obtain digital reproductions of the sources directly from the original drawings to avoid interpretation errors due to the scarce quality of digital reproductions or unknown eventual mistakes committed by the operator during the acquisition phase.

The 2D redrawing is performed with the method of continuous/mathematical representation (see next paragraph). The study and construction of the plans and elevations from the original drawings are carried out using the author's original construction module and the original most plausible reference historic units of measurement, however, this 2D critical redrawing is later transferred into the contemporary metric system right before starting modelling. This allows both to check the dimensions of the architecture in a system more comprehensible nowadays and to produce models that are easily comparable since they all have the same measurement system and scale.

The 3D model is reconstructed from this preliminary 2D redrawing. Sometimes the drawn references can be incomplete; e.g., plans or elevations may be entirely missing; or a section, a façade, or a plan might not be finished properly. Furthermore, the drawings are often not consistent with each other; e.g., there may be inconsistencies between the plan and the elevation: some dimensions may be different, or the plan may show windows that are not present in the elevation, etc. The most relevant problems are generally found in the design of the stairs, vaults and roofing. For example, both Ledoux and Guidi, in their projects often report the position of the stairs in plan and section without developing properly their features and correctly dimensioning them; or they do not show the design of the vaults or the roofs in elevation. These missing or inaccurate parts must be redesigned to make the 3D reconstruction coherent and functional.

The 3D model is semantically organized [12] by building each 3D element that makes up the architecture as independent geometries (e.g., column, architrave, tympanum, wall, roof, etc.) Furthermore, the various elements, when the sources allow it, are divided into sub-elements (e.g., the column consists of base, shaft and capital, etc.). The semantic organization is essential because it allows any user of the model to analyse and design the construction of the 3D model rationally and makes it possible to recognize the elements of the architecture without ambiguity. To improve the analysis possibilities and versatility of use, these elements must be watertight 3D models without self-intersections and assembled without overlapping (see next paragraph).

The Documentation/Visualization process [13] consists of describing textually the process of reconstruction and presenting visually the 3D outcomes of such process by producing graphical outputs such as images, mock-ups, videos, or interactive experiences. In the experimentation with the students, they were required to produce several graphical outputs where they had to present visually the 3D models and explain clearly, synthetically, and unambiguously the reconstruction process starting from the study of the sources, up to the reverse engineering of the details and the documentation of the subjective interpretations. In this last step, the use of abstract shading techniques such as the colouring of the surfaces with false colours was recommended to communicate visually various types of information such as the type of sources used to reconstruct each element or to estimate the level of uncertainty of the reconstruction (see next paragraph).

For visualization, the NURBS mathematical model can be projected into a plane to extract wireframe technical drawings or can be tessellated and transformed into a MESH polygonal model to make rendered views. An important part, therefore, is dedicated to the coherent and critical use of traditional and digital methods of representation which, for lack of space, we omit to describe here.

4 Theoretical Aspects

Concerning historical sources, the methodology proposes a first classification, and in the course, the students deal with the following two types: paper documents (e.g., the autographed original architectural drawings or written testimonies of the time, etc.); or real remains (e.g., the column of a specific reference building by the same author, etc.). In the case studies presented, the primary sources are the digital reproductions of the architects' original drawings: the unrealized projects by Ledoux and the unrealized projects for the cities of Cesena and Cesenatico by Guidi. For both types of sources, it is necessary to preliminary acquire them digitally.

4.1   Raw Model and Informative Model

Concerning the acquisition step, it is important to mention a novel classification: the Raw Models (RM), and the Informative Models (IM). RMs are digital models obtained through quasi-automatic procedures that process raw data captured from real sources (digital photogrammetry or laser scanning technology). In the first case, the raw model would be a 3D model (i.e., a point cloud or a textured mesh model). In the second case, the raw model would be a bidimensional object (i.e., a Raster image at a certain resolution). The IM is a 3D digital model that is enriched with information processed and interpreted by an author.

The main difference is conceptual: the RM represents only physical data transformed into digital raw data. The IM, on the other hand, represents the complex process of the interpretation of the sources. The IM is a model obtained through a reverse engineering operation. In this sense, the RM is used as a source for the latter operation: it represents the digitization of real sources (whether they are real archaeological remains or paper documents).

Concerning the generation of the IM, the method takes into consideration several formal aspects:

- the scale (level of detail);
- the semantic segmentation (a subdivision of the model into nominable sub-elements);
- the level of discretization of the geometry (approximation of continuous curve surfaces with a certain amount of flat faces);
- the study and use of the composition rules (e.g., the modularity, the presence of axes of symmetry, the presence of ratios or geometrical constructions, etc.);
- the use of historical units of measurement.

4.2   Semantic Segmentation

The semantic segmentation aspect is a fundamental step for the creation of a scientifically sound reconstruction. The organization of the model must comply with the analysis and construction of the various architectural elements that compose the 3D model to make them easily identifiable and univocally nominable (Fig. 6). The level of detail of these elements is linked to the concept of the scale of the model. The architectural elements, therefore, can be made up of doors, windows, walls, beams, roofs, etc., or more specific elements such as pillars, columns, lintels, tympanums, frames, etc. Each element or sub-element must consist of non-self-intersecting and watertight 3D models; for example, if the 3D digital method used is the NURBS mathematical method, the individual elements must be made up of manifold closed poly-surfaces.

4.3   Digital Representation Methods

The concepts of "Digital Representation Methods" and "3D Digital Modelling Techniques" are often used as synonyms, however, in the presented method these aspects are differentiated into two distinct families. The formers (namely, NURBS and mesh modelling, etc.), according to some authors [14], are related to the concepts of traditional methods of representations (axonometric projections, perspective projections, double

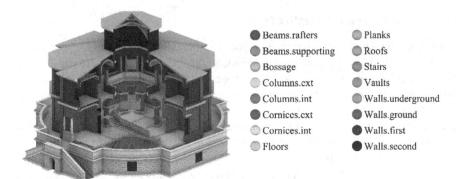

● Beams.rafters	○ Planks
● Beams.supporting	○ Roofs
○ Bossage	● Stairs
○ Columns.ext	● Vaults
● Columns.int	○ Walls.underground
● Cornices.ext	● Walls.ground
○ Cornices.int	● Walls.first
○ Floors	● Walls.second

Fig. 6. Semantic segmentation. Reconstruction of Mauro Guidi's project "Palazzo isolato per un nobile" Atlante 46, Carta 193 [4].

orthogonal projections, topographic terrain projections), thus they can be considered as representation languages. On the contrary, the latter are all those practical processes that are used to produce a 3D model by using specific tools (e.g., parametric modelling, hand-made direct modelling, algorithmic computational modelling, automatic reality-based modelling, etc.) and are comparable to the traditional drawing techniques (e.g., ruler and compass, free-hand pencil drawing, watercolour painting, etc.).

There are several ways to classify Digital Representation Methods. Figure 7 shows some possible classifications of architectural reconstructive 3D models, it shows their classification into the RM and the IM; the classification based on their Configuration Space; the classification based on the 3D Modelling Techniques and Representation Methods.

The Digital Representation Methods concern the intrinsic mathematical/geometrical nature/language of the 3D models and are the following:

- continuous methods: the geometry is described in a non-discrete way with continuously defined mathematical equations, the Mathematical/Surface Modelling is part of this category (for example NURBS modelling, Bezier modelling, Spline modelling, etc.);
- discrete methods: the curve geometry is approximated with a finite amount of non-curved elements (points, segments, planar faces), thus it is described numerically, not with equations, but with points identified by their coordinates (vertices), lines (edges), and planar faces (triangles/polygons); the Numerical/Polygonal Modelling is part of this category (for example Mesh modelling, Point Cloud modelling, Voxel modelling, etc.).

3D models can also be generated with Hybrid Methods (i.e., a model can be made of continuous and discrete surfaces at the same time). This also happens in traditional representation methods: for example, in the perspective section where the section is in true form (as in double orthogonal projections) and coexists with the perspective view of the inside space. All methods have a specific vocation, and one might be more effective than another only in some contexts. That is why they should all be mastered properly and chosen case by case.

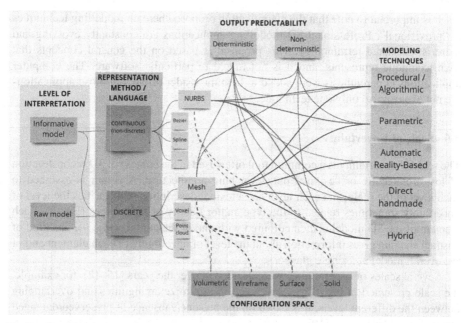

Fig. 7. Classification of different types of 3D modelling, in the field of 3D hypothetical architectural reconstructions.

4.4 3D Modelling Techniques

The 3D Modelling Techniques are those practices, processes and norms that are used to create the models. To make an analogy with traditional drawing: the watercolour technique, for example, can be used to draw and add a shading effect (chiaroscuro) to scenes that follow the rules of perspective projections, axonometric views, or double projections. Analogously, the direct handmade modelling technique or the procedural modelling technique, for example, can be used to generate models described by different Digital Representation Methods, such as Mesh and NURBS.

Given this assumption, the following approaches can be considered modelling techniques:

- procedural/algorithmic modeling (Rhinoceros + Grasshopper, Revit + Dynamo, Blender + Geometry Nodes…);
- parametric modelling (Inventor, Catia, Creo Parametric…);
- automatic reality-based modelling (Agisoft Metashape, Reality Capture…);
- direct handmade modelling (Rhinoceros, Autocad, Zbrush, Blender, 3Dmax, C4D…);
- hybrid modelling (Almost all commercial software packages nowadays support hybrid modelling);

Some 3D digital modelling well-known techniques that do not appear in the list (e.g., digital sculpting, subdivision surface modelling, etc.) aren't mentioned here because they can be considered as sub-groups of already mentioned techniques (e.g. both sculpting and subdivision surface can be subgroups of direct handmade modelling).

It is important to note that the classification proposed here on modelling techniques is "provisional". Professional 3D modelling applications are constantly evolving and there is no shared terminology. This proposal is based on the general concepts that each technique represents, and it is not linked to particular software. The computer applications in parenthesis were added to help the reader orient, but those applications are not exclusive to only one technique.

4.5 Scale of Uncertainty

The scale of uncertainty is a common tool often used in the context of 3D reconstruction of lost architecture or designed but never built architecture. A colour is assigned to each level of the scale, and each level has a textual description that clarifies the level of uncertainty sometimes related to the type and/or quality of the sources (Fig. 8). Each element of the 3D model is then coloured with one of the colours (Fig. 9), this kind of abstract shading gives information about the level of uncertainty of each element and of the overall model at a single glance.

Several scales of uncertainties were developed over the years [15–18], for example, the scale presented in Fig. 8 was developed to minimize ambiguities and overlapping between the different levels, it is based on the presence/absence of preserved/damaged sources and their authors [19].

Real object	Direct \ Primary sources		Secondary sources		Uncertainty
	Clear \ Consistent	Damaged \ Unclear	Same author\s	Other author\s	
1 √ available	\	\	\	\	Reality (objective)
2 X unavailable	√ available	\	\	\	Conjecture (reliable)
3 X unavailable	X unavailable	√ available	√ available	\	Conjecture
4 X unavailable	X unavailable	√ available	X unavailable	√ available	Conjecture
5 X unavailable	X unavailable	X unavailable	√ available	\	Conjecture
6 X unavailable	X unavailable	X unavailable	X unavailable	√ available	Conjecture
7 X unavailable	X unavailable	√ available or X unavailable	X unavailable	X unavailable	Conjecture (subjective)
\	\	\	\	\	Abstention

Fig. 8. Example of a scale of uncertainty where the uncertainty is measured from the type and authorship of the reference sources [19].

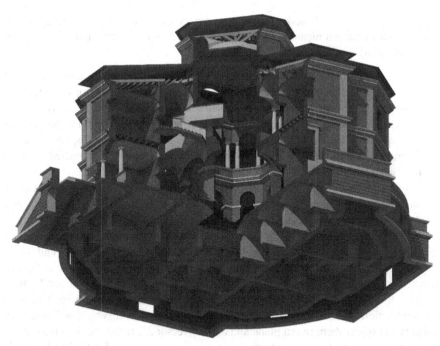

Fig. 9. False-colour shading representing the level of uncertainty of each element of the 3D model. Reconstruction of Mauro Guidi's project "Palazzo isolato per un nobile" Atlante 46, Carta 193 [4].

5   Iterative Improvement of the Methodology

The experimental methodology was proposed as a didactic tool at the academic level for more than ten years and the results of each year were assessed and rediscussed iteratively year after year to improve the methodology itself, i.e., to limit eventual errors by the students and various problems concerning readability, shareability and reusability of the archived 3D models as much as possible.

The results were evaluated based on several aspects:

- formal geometrical accuracy (geometry, scale, level of detail, etc. had to comply with the good practices taught, this would guarantee interoperable 3D models for various uses);
- description of the methodology adopted (Description of the design process to create the 3D model, including technical indications such as the method of digital representation used, etc.);
- clear and transparent documentation (all the sources used had to be clearly reported and related to the relative elements);

- visualization of the 3D model (creation of images, animated videos or interactive navigations to communicate the formal aspects and other information of the virtual reconstruction).

The students were required to present their 3D models through bidimensional visual outputs carefully designed (e.g., orthogonal views, perspective projections, renderings, etc.) proving to a commission that they followed a scientifically sound process of reconstruction. The reconstructed 3D models and the appended documentation were archived in a local repository (following the assigned archival guidelines) and inspected one by one by a trained commission. After a few years, some models were inspected again to see if they were still comprehensible and reusable in different contexts.

The retrospective annual assessment fostered critical observations. If a particular iteration of the method did not guarantee the 3D models to be: comparable, traceable, and reusable for various purposes the reconstruction method taught was adjusted accordingly.

In the first few yearly iterations for example the students were allowed to use any type of digital representation method to build the models (NURBS or Mesh) and it was observed that mesh models were hardly reusable for other applications at different scales unless heavy manual modifications were carried out (because the tessellation level wasn't always modifiable from the provided files). Furthermore, mesh models weren't suitable for the extraction and backtracking of the original generative curves, this limited the possibility to project them into a plane and extract vector 2D technical drawings of the models and thus it limited the geometrical analysis opportunities. Lastly Mesh models were much heavier to archive. The NURBS modelling was adopted as a better option to make more versatile reconstructions reusable in different contexts.

Another improvement carried out over the years regarded the adoption of non-self-intersecting watertight volumes, because these types of 3D models were necessary for 3D printing, and, most important, helped the scholars and the students to understand the three-dimensional relations of the architectural elements.

This research could produce some appropriate insights in terms of the analytical approach adopted to systematise the reconstruction process for a specific purpose aimed at producing a clear and transparent sharing of knowledge.

This systematisation effort should be a focus for all the research environments that aim to produce and archive comparable reusable and scientifically valid 3D reconstructions. Not every 3D modelling methodology returns the same level of overall quality concerning, geometry, documentation, traceability, and interoperability. Rising awareness about this aspect would help to start building an autonomous discipline for 3D reconstruction at the international level, and maybe it could set the basis for the standardization of the reconstruction processes according to various contexts and needs.

6 Conclusions

The proposed methodology aims to rationalize and systematise the 3D hypothetical reconstruction and sharing process of lost or designed but never realized architectures. The method, tested in a higher education architectural drawing course, proved to be an effective didactic experience that encouraged the students to focalize their attention on crucial aspects such as geometry, semantics, topology, and historical aspects; bringing forward the knowledge of the manufacts and fostering critical thinking about architectural composition. In a more general research context, it also proved to be effective in the production of uniform, transparent, comparable, interoperable, reproducible, and reusable 3D outputs for various needs.

The novelty of this experience does not consist in the methodology itself but in the analysis and systematisation effort of the theoretical and practical aspects of the discipline. This could help to share 3D hypothetical reconstructions as scientific products and could contribute to rise awareness that not every methodology produces results suitable for every type of scientific use. The presented discussion could foster and encourage standardization for scientific 3D reconstructions at the international level and would contribute to defining the 3D reconstruction of architectural models of the past as an autonomous discipline.

Acknowledgement. Some figures (Fig. 1, Fig. 2, Fig. 3, Fig. 4, Fig. 5, Fig. 6, Fig. 9) were extracted (and elaborated) from the case study curated by the students Matilde Barchi and Molly Jade Davey of the University of Bologna.

CoVHer (Computer-based Visualisation of Architectural Cultural Heritage) is an Erasmus Plus Project (ID KA220-HED-88555713) [7, 8]. It is a 36 monthly project and it started in February 2022. There are seven principal partners from five different European countries. The partners are University of Bologna (Bologna, Italy), Hochschule Mainz University of Applied Sciences (Mainz, Germany), Politechnika Warszawska (Waraw, Poland), Universidade Do Porto (Porto, Portugal), Universitat Autonoma de Barcelona (Barcelona, Spain), Tempesta Media SL (Barcelona, Spain), Interessengemeinschaft für semantische Datenverarbeitung e.V (München, Germany). The scholars currently involved in the project are (the order of persons follows the institution to which they belong): Fabrizio Ivan Apollonio, Federico Fallavollita, Riccardo Foschi, Irene Cazzaro, Piotr Kuroczyński, Jan-Eric Lutteroth, Igor Bajena, Krzysztof Koszewski, Franczuk Jakub, Karol Argasiński, Joao Pedro Sampaio Xavier, Clara Pimenta do Vale, Hugo Pires, Juan Antonio Barceló Álvarez, Evdoxia Tzerpou, Marc Hernández Güell, Raquel Garcia, Pol Guiu and Mark Fichtner.

References

1. Münster, S.: Digital 3D technologies for humanities research and education: an overview. Appl. Sci. **12**(5), 2426 (2022)
2. Münster, S., Köhler, T., Hoppe, S.: 3D modeling technologies as tools for the reconstruction and visualization of historic items in humanities. a literature-based survey. In: Traviglia, A. (eds.) Across Space and Time. In: Papers from the 41st Conference on Computer Applications and Quantitative Methods in Archaeology. Perth, 25–28 March 2013, pp. 430–441. Amsterdam University Press, Amsterdam (2015)
3. Kuroczyński, P., Pfarr-Harfst, M., Münster, S. (eds.): Der Modelle Tugend 2.0: Digitale 3D-Rekonstruktion als virtueller Raum der architekturhistorischen Forschung. Heidelberg University Press, Heidelberg (2019)
4. Guidi, M.: Carta 193, Atlante 46, Pianta di un sepolcro a guisa di tempio. Biblioteca Malatestiana, Cesena (1755)
5. AG Digital 3D Reconstruction homepage. https://dig-hum.de/ag-digitale-3d-rekonstruktion. Accessed 14 Dec 2022

6. DFG Research Network Webpage: Digital 3D Reconstructions as Tools of Architectural Historical Research. https://www.gw.uni-jena.de/en/faculty/juniorprofessur-fuer-digital-humanities/research/dfg-netzwerk-3d-rekonstruktion. Accessed 14 Dec 2022

7. CoVHer Project official website. www.CoVHer.eu. Accessed 14 Dec 2022

8. CoVHer Erasmus+ official page. https://erasmus-plus.ec.europa.eu/projects/search/details/2021-1-IT02-KA220-HED-000031190. Accessed 14 Dec 2022

9. 70116 - Lab-based Course on Architectural Drawing, Academic Year 2022/2023, Course official webpage. https://www.unibo.it/en/teaching/course-unit-catalogue?codiceMateria=70212&annoAccademico=2022&codiceCorso=9265&single=True&search=True

10. Ledoux, C.N.: L'architecture considérée sous le rapport de l'art, des moeurs et de la législation. Tome premier. Perronneau, Paris (1804)

11. Guidi, M.: Pensieri d'architettura. Ms., Biblioteca Malatestiana, Cesena (1790)

12. Apollonio, F.I.: From text and drawing to model. 3D virtual reconstruction, 3D semantic segmentation, C. N. Ledoux, knowledge representation. In: Kuroczyński, P., Pfarr-Harfst, M., Münster, S. (eds.) Der Modelle Tugend 2.0: Digitale 3D-Rekonstruktion als virtueller Raum der architekturhistorischen Forschung, pp. 433–446. Heidelberg University Press, Heidelberg (2019)

13. Koszewski, K.: Visual representations in digital 3D modeling/simulation for architectural heritage. In: Niebling, F., Münster, S., Messemer H. (eds.) Research and Education in Urban History in the Age of Digital Libraries, Cham, 2021, pp. 87–105. Springer International Publishing (2022). https://doi.org/10.1007/978-3-030-93186-5_4

14. Migliari R.: Geometria Descrittiva - vol. 1 - Metodi e costruzione. CittàStudiEdizioni, Italy (2009)

15. Georgiou, R., Hermon, S.: A London Charter's visualization: The ancient hellenistic-roman theatre in Paphos (2011)

16. Landes, T., Heissler, M., Koehl, M., Benazzi, T., Nivola, T.: Uncertainty visualization approaches for 3D models of castles restituted from archeological knowledge. Int. Arch. Photogramm. Remote. Sens. Spat. Inf. Sci. **42**, 409–416 (2019)

17. Lengyel, D., Toulouse, C.: Visualization of uncertainty in archaeological reconstructions. Virtual Palaces, Part II. Lost Palaces and their Afterlife, pp. 103–117 (2016)

18. Apollonio, F.I.: Classification schemes for visualization of uncertainty in digital hypothetical reconstruction. In: Münster, S., Pfarr-Harfst, M., Kuroczyński, P., Ioannides, M. (eds.) 3D research challenges in cultural heritage II. LNCS, vol. 10025, pp. 173–197. Springer, Cham (2016). https://doi.org/10.1007/978-3-319-47647-6_9

19. Apollonio, F.I., Fallavollita, F., Foschi, R.: The critical digital model for the study of unbuilt architecture. In: Niebling, F., Münster, S., Messemer, H. (eds.) Research and Education in Urban History in the Age of Digital Libraries. UHDL 2019. Communications in Computer and Information Science, vol. 1501, pp. 3–24. Springer, Cham (2022). https://doi.org/10.1007/978-3-030-93186-5_1

Historical Construction Research Based Upon 3D Digital Documentation of the Baroque Palais im Grossen Garten in Dresden

Aaron Pattee[1](✉), Matteo Burioni[1], Stephan Hoppe[1], John Hindmarch[2], and Mona Hess[2]

[1] Institute for Art History, LMU Munich, 80539 Munich, Germany
{aaron.pattee,matteo.burioni,Stephan.hoppe}@lmu.de
[2] Digital Technologies in Heritage Conservation, Institute of Archaeology, Heritage Sciences and Art History, University of Bamberg, 96047 Bamberg, Germany
{john.hindmarch,mona.hess}@uni-bamberg.de

Abstract. This paper explores the construction research of a recent 3D imaging campaign and resulting documentation of the 17th century Palais im Grossen Garten in Dresden, Germany. Both *Structure from Motion* (SfM) Photogrammetry and *Terrestrial Laser Scanning* (TLS) were employed for the recording process, from which the resulting 3D models provided the basis for the ensuing construction research. This represents only one example of six buildings located in Germany and France intended for digital recording as part of the multi-institutional and international PLAFOND-3D project. The emphasis of this paper is upon the interdisciplinary approach toward recording a high resolution model with the aim of collaboratively researching the construction history using digital assets. It is a streamlined process, beginning with an innovative procedure for recording a large structure with methods from engineering metrology, thus guaranteeing an accurate and empirical documentation.

Keywords: Baroque Architecture · Structure from Motion (SfM) · Laser Scanning · Construction Research

1 Introduction

The interpretation of a building's construction history, and the provenance of its materials, is not only subject to, but rather entirely dependent upon the quality of the underlying data. The primary source of information is the tangible and material evidence of the building itself [1], which can often cause complications in the research provided the state of a building and, at times, limited access to specific walls or rooms under investigation. In addition to these constraints, rehabilitation efforts including restorations, preservation measures, and even reconstructions can alter one's understanding of a building's history via the presentation of asynchronous architectural features in the contemporary exhibition of a site. For this reason, the individual elements must be attended to with a keen eye addressing alterations, and a special attention upon masonry joints. The purpose of

S. Münster et al. (Eds.): UHDL 2023, CCIS 1853, pp. 19–31, 2023.
https://doi.org/10.1007/978-3-031-38871-2_2

such a detailed approach is to provide a basis for interpreting the construction history and process of a site. This is essential for understanding the role that a building played within the larger architectural scene of a city, for exploring the expression of stylistic elements over time, and evaluating a building's structure for cultural preservation efforts. For this project, the Palais im Grossen Garten in Dresden, Germany, was selected not only for its special role within Dresden's architectural history, but also for the fact that very little has been published regarding its construction history.

1.1 Historical Background

The Palais im Grossen Garten is a casino type garden structure designed by the Saxonian court architects Wolf Casper von Klengel and Johann Georg Starcke beginning in 1679. However, the importance of Starcke's predecessor, Wolf Caspar von Klengel, as court architect and head of the electoral building administration in relation to his contribution to the design of the Palais has still to be better assessed [2, 3]. Provided the chronology of the construction, Starcke was clearly responsible for the site, though Klengel could has influenced the design given his extensive travels throughout several European countries in which he gathered novel architectural ideas [4]. The Palais was used as a place for festive gatherings, and provided at its time the most innovative and up-to-date interior space for the Electorate Court of Dresden. The exterior and interior decorations of the Palais display themes of hunting and pleasure, but the representations of the state are exhibited in paintings of the apotheosis of the elector in the hall alongside Greek gods, as well as along as a series of emperors on the facade. In the ground floor, or vestibule, there was also a representation of the zodiac signs. Nevertheless, the functional relation of the hall in the Palais to the residence in Dresden has still to properly ascertained [5]. Besides its role as a casino, the political themes in its decoration underscore the role of the building as a kind of satellite of the residence, taking over certain functional and courtly requirements that could not be properly housed in the residence. Its shape resembles an 'H' featuring a central structure orientated along horizontal axis, flanked on either side by structures along a vertical axis with additional chambers at their proximities. These chamber structures form the risalits on the southeastern and northwestern sides of the Palais, between which are two grand staircases that obscure the ground floor, directing one's attention toward the ball room floor (Fig. 1).

Evidence indicating that the structure was complete by 1683 is provided by delivery receipts of water reeds for applying plaster. The plaster and stucco decoration of the interiors presumably began soon thereafter, which was followed by the copper decoration of the roof, as indicated by additional payments in 1685. The final payments for the painter Samuel Bottschild and Heinrich Fehling were made in 1692, suggesting that the various paintings had been completed the year prior [6]. The central ballroom displays an array of peculiarities as it features various rehabilitation campaigns since its destruction in World War II. The interior decoration with stucco and ceiling paintings can be only ascertained on pre-World War II photographs. Both Samuel Bottschild and Heinrich Christoph Fehling worked as painters throughout the building, but the stucco of the great hall was done by Giacomo Botta de Merebillia. The ceiling paintings by Bottschild and Fehling in the 1680s depicted the apotheosis of the prince electors of Saxony, with the coats of arms of Saxony and the double swords of the office of the Arch-Marshal of

Fig. 1. View of the northwestern facade of the Palais im Grossen Garten. Note the side risalits and the grand staircase between them. Image Source: Prof. Stephan Hoppe.

the Holy Roman Empire flanked on all sides by virtues, and featured ceiling paintings of Merkur and Flora as well as a hunting Diana. The general theme of the apotheosis surrounded by virtues of good government in the ceiling painting was the first time this topic had been introduced in Dresden, before the ceiling painting by Louis Silvestre in the parade rooms of Dresden residence at the beginning of the 18 century [7]. Tragically, all of the paintings were utterly lost to the incendiary bombs of the Second World War in February 1945 that ravaged the city and erased the monumental work of art (Fig. 2).

Fig. 2. Comparison of the pre-World War II state of the ballroom and the immediate aftermath of the bombing. Note the loss of the various priceless ceiling paintings. Image Source: Deutsche Fotothek in Dresden (SLUB).

From 1963 until 1970, the building was incrementally stabilized including a temporary roof cover and ceiling of vaulted concrete, later replaced in the early 1990s and adorned with copper decorations. At the turn of 1970, a corner of the inner ballroom—the most exquisite and famous room of the palace—was fully restored as a sample guided by historical photographs, with stucco-work and painted columns (Fig. 3). In the early 1980s, the stucco of the vaulted ground floor was completely restored to its pre-war condition, and in 2005 other portions of plaster and stucco were repaired and preserved throughout the building. In 2008, Harmut Olbricht undertook an archeological investigation of the building that revealed a complex construction procedure. The results of this investigation were never published, but were graciously provided by Stefan Hertzig.

Nevertheless, the ceiling remains a bleak cement reminder of a brutal past and much of the masonry is still uncovered. However, it is precisely in this state that the palace offers one of the premier examples of baroque architectural construction, including a multitude of materials ranging from bricks, to stone ashlars, to metal anchors for the wooden columns. It was this opportunity to examine the building materials and techniques of the baroque period that re-awakened the palace from its quiescent state, and to conduct a scientific building investigation (*Bauforschung*) as used in heritage conservation and archaeology [8].

Fig. 3. The reconstructed corner of the ball room. Image Source: Aaron Pattee.

1.2 Previous Investigations

The current hypothesis is that Johann Georg Starcke had been the sole architect of the Palais, bringing in a *Style classique* from the realm of the French architectural influence, upon succeeding Wolf Caspar von Klengel as the *Oberlandbaumeister* (chief architect) of the Electorate of Saxony [6]. However, it is evident that Klengel had already drafted plans and ideas for a garden palace for the prince elector while he held the position [4]. Additionally, Klengel had worked with the painter Heinrich Christoph Fehling, who even painted his portrait at Moritzburg castle [9]. Together with Samuel Bottschild, he had designed medals and coins [10], indicating that Klengel was in contact with both painters of the Palais prior to its construction. With the exception of the various preservation, rehabilitation, and reconstruction efforts described in the previous section, scientific investigations regarding the development of the site's construction and the composition of its materials was largely left wanting until the last 10 years. The reason for this analytic dormancy is not least due to the ideological constraints imposed by the former GDR that hamstrung most efforts to explore elite architecture except when a case could be made to promote its connection to the proletariat.

Cultural implications and context necessarily influence both the construction and preservation of architecture. Thus, it must be mentioned the Palais im Grossen Garten was by all means the antithesis to the agenda of the communist GDR as it represented a lavish expenditure of the prince electors for their own personal use. Other sites of elite architecture were not so fortunate, such as the *Stadtschloss* in Berlin that had been damaged by the bombings of the Second World War, but certainly not obliterated. Despite the potential for its reconstruction—or at least preservation of the remains as was done at the Kaiser Wilhelm Memorial Church in former West Berlin—the authorities of East Berlin decided to demolish all that remained of the *Stadtschloss*, including all of the priceless ceiling paintings. In contrast to the densely urban environment of the *Stadtschloss* of Berlin, the grand garden surrounding the Palais in Dresden presented a scenic area to be enjoyed by the common people during the GDR, which is the most likely reason as to why the building was not simply done away with after the war. This, in turn, explains why only the façade was restored, though the GDR was in no hurry to repair the interior despite their ever-relaxing attitude toward scientific inquiry into the Palais' past as time progressed. In the post revolution and current reunification phase of Germany, a renewed interest in the origins of elite architecture was assumed by the state authorities, allowing more than eager researchers to explore the wealth of information hidden in the walls that were since sworn to secrecy by the previous communist administration.

Provided the ensnaring ideological marshland of the GDR that architectural historians had to carefully traverse when researching elite architecture, investigations were often conducted in an asymmetric manner in which the architects were studied rather than only the works themselves. This was certainly the case for the Palais, as the two architects associated with its construction (Wolf Caspar von Klengel and Johann Georg Starcke) were both the subjects of highly detailed works by historians in the GDR such as Hermann Heckmann [11] and Eberhard Hempel [9]. These studies provide a wealth of information regarding the social and professional networks of the aforementioned architects and, consequently, critical information regarding the background of the various construction projects without providing a detailed construction analysis of the sites themselves. The construction research (or *Bauforschung*) of the Palais would remain outstanding until quite recently, though the groundwork for the architectural investigations has already been laid by researchers such as Stefan Hertzig [12], Walter May [13], Günter Passavant [4], Katrin Reeckmann [14].

With regard to the plaster and stucco work at the Palais, a 2015 paper explored the origins of the materials composing the interior decorations, shedding light on both the composition of the plaster as well as the construction method for applying it to the various surfaces [15]. The research was conducted upon the few remnants of the pre-war plaster and stucco decorations, including a single plaster column (Fig. 4). Due to the damage of the column, the components of its construction can be clearly seen, exhibiting a central wooden trunk, wrapped with a mesh-like layer of metal wire onto which the plaster was applied. Interestingly, Lenz discovered thermally stressed idiomorphic plaster crystals, indicating a low-temperature burning during the production phase of the plaster, likely from alabaster. Unfortunately, practically nothing remains of the plaster pilasters that once stood behind the various columns, though they had likely been constructed in the same manner [15].

Fig. 4. The single remaining plaster-covered column in the ballroom of the Palais. Note the wire mesh holding the plaster to the wooden interior. Image Source: Aaron Pattee.

The white plaster of the ceiling and walls consisted of coarsely ground gypsum as a binder, providing the intended effect of a very bright, yet matte surface. Only a few areas still exhibit the original plaster, mainly in the intrados of the arches composing the passages between rooms (Fig. 5). The ground floor, or vestibule, still displays a few original paintings surrounding by white plaster, though the upper floor, wherein the ball room is located, is currently unadorned by any paintings.

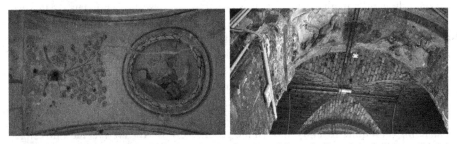

Fig. 5. Pre-war white plaster within intrados on the ground floor (left) and the ball room (right). Image Source: Aaron Pattee.

At least ten wooden spares for producing more columns still exist in the attic storage areas of the Palais (Fig. 6), demonstrating that perhaps more columns had been intended during construction or simply stored as spares. The storage area also consists of a multitude of molds for the patterned cornices that once formed the connection of the walls to the vaulted ceiling upon which the paintings had been completed.

Fig. 6. Spare columns discovered in the storage of the Palais. Image Source: Aaron Pattee.

In addition to the spare materials in the attic space, a number of fascinating construction materials can still be seen in the ballroom *in situ*, such as the iron anchors that once held the columns in place (Fig. 7). These were hammered in the wooden trunks of the columns and then installed into their proper positions in front of the pilasters that populated the vertical supports of the arcades.

Fig. 7. Iron anchors intended for holding the plaster-covered wooden columns in place. Image Source: Aaron Pattee.

2   Recording the Palace

As stated earlier, the key to gaining a holistic understanding of a building's history is dependent upon the available data. Given the emergence of 3D models within the field of cultural heritage over the past 20 years, generating such models provides researchers the opportunity to examine architectural objects and elements *ex situ*. It must be stressed that this does not negate the necessity of an *in situ* examination, but it certainly alleviates procedural constraints by eliminating the time-intensive manual illustrations typically associated with construction and archaeological research.

The combination of surveying with art-historical or building research-based interpretation has been routinely used before by this interdisciplinary group. The campaign to digitally record the site occurred from 4 to 8 October 2021, and was led by a team

Fig. 8. The 3D laser scan visualized of the interior of the palace, featuring the vaulted ground floor and ballroom in the first floor. Outside walls not shown. Image Source: Prof. Mona Hess and Dr. John Hindmarch.

consisting of architects, architectural art historians, and remote sensing experts from the Ludwig-Maximilians-University of Munich and the Otto-Friedrich-University of Bamberg. An integrated, multi-modal approach was used in the scanning campaign combining both *Structure from motion* (SfM) photogrammetry and 3D laser scanning. The entire Palais, interior and exterior, was additionally 3D recorded with a mobile laser scanner (Geoslam ZEB Horizon). Detailed photogrammetric recordings were made of two surviving stucco ceilings on the ground floor previously shown in Fig. 5, and a structured light scanner (Artec Eva) was used to scan several areas of surviving stucco in the ballroom and the damaged column shown in Fig. 4. The meshed and textured mesh of the column's plinth are show in Fig. 9. The ground and first floor interiors (Fig. 8) were also scanned using a Leica Geosystems BLK360 terrestrial laser scanner with a 3D point accuracy of approximately 4 mm at 10-m range [16], and a Faro Focus 350S TLS with 2 mm accuracy at 10m [17].

The entire first floor (including the ballroom) was also modelled with SfM, using four Nikon D3400 cameras with 18 mm lenses, mounted on a modified trolley (Fig. 10). The four camera set-up allowed the simultaneous capture of multiple angles, drastically reducing the time required for imaging. A total of 967 photos were captured, followed by raw image processing and color correction in *Adobe Lightroom* before being exported as 16-bit Tif files. The photogrammetric processing was carried out in *Agisoft Metashape Pro*, resulting in a dense point cloud of approximately 1.5 billion points. The TLS data was combined with the photogrammetric model, capitalizing upon the photo-realism of photogrammetry and the measurable geometric precision of TLS to capture an accurate 3D representation of the inner rooms of the palace, with an emphasis upon the ornate ballroom and its remaining traces of plaster.

Fig. 9. Structured Light Scan of the plinth of the only remaining pre-war in situ column. Image Source: Eliane Christ.

Fig. 10. The modified trolley for the SfM recording featuring four Nikon D3400. Image Source: Prof. Mona Hess and Dr. John Hindmarch.

3   Documenting the Ballroom

The high resolution 3D recording of the Palais im Grossen Garten resulted in image textures that revealed the outlines of nearly all of the materials in the construction of the site over time. Due to the use of the ballroom as a modern venue, some walls are covered with metal heating radiators and the upper cornice is enveloped with a braid of wires extending to the various electric recipients located throughout the room. Due to their proximity to the wall, much of the textured image data cannot be recorded at these positions, requiring an *in situ* examination of detailed photos in addition to the 3D model. Although shortcomings are to be expected in any digital recording campaign, the results were still highly favorable for the documentation of the walls of the ballroom.

The process consisted of producing textured and meshed orthophotos of each of the four walls in *CloudCompare*, after which each stone visible in the orthophotos was manually outlined in *Inkscape*—a typical process for as-built drawing and research of historic buildings [18].

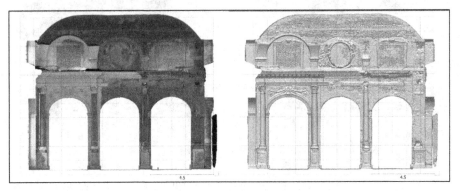

Fig. 11. The textured orthophotos, extracted from multi-modal digital recording, of the northern inside wall of the ballroom, featuring the outlines of stones and stucco work, using Inkscape. Image Source: Aaron Pattee.

Manually outlining the stones is more advantageous than relying upon an automatic segmentation, as a myriad of items and architectural elements could otherwise go unnoticed (Fig. 11). Such examples include the small pieces of wood, roof tiles, and nails that populated the larger mortar seams of the wall. Additionally, many of the iron anchors that once held the battalion of columns guarding the windows throughout the room can still be seen. Of particular note, is the arbitrary selection of building materials consisting of stone ashlars mixed with baked bricks (Fig. 12). This placement of stones and bricks is made even more intriguing by the modifications of the arched windows consisting of various sizes of bricks, though not uniformly among each arch. The result is a wide selection of materials of the pre-war masonry. The ceiling and roof were replaced with yellow bricks typical of the 1950s, as well as reinforced concrete to emulate the curvatures of the former ceiling. Still, portions of the stucco surrounding the lost paintings exist in batches irregularly distributed along the cornice.

4   Interpreting the Documentations

During the annotation process of outlining all of the stones and bricks, it became evident that seven of the ten arches forming the northwestern and southeastern side of the ball room had been adjusted during construction to become narrower. However, the two main arches forming the entrances into the ball room from the outside staircases do not exhibit any adaptations to their width. These adjustments are especially poignant on the northwestern side towards the northern corner in which the original design of the arches had been presumably altered (Fig. 13).

Fig. 12. Variety of stone and brick building materials in the walls forming the ball room. Image Source: Aaron Pattee.

Fig. 13. Modified arches along the northwestern interior wall of the ball room. Note the arch on the right with the double layer of bricks altering its width, using Inkscape. Image Source: Aaron Pattee.

Provided that the northern arch has the most extreme modification and that the others also feature additional bricks, it is likely that it had been the first arch to have been modified. Although this corner had been altered, it does not mean that the other arches had originally required modified, as it could well have been implemented into the overall plan to feature an inner lining of the intrados. The lengths of the bricks could have provided a smoother surface for applying plaster than the proximal ends of the bricks forming the arch. Provided the matte composition of the white plaster, any bumps would produce shadows disrupting the intended smooth surface. The obvious counter-argument is that the entrance arches do not feature this extra lining of bricks and were more likely to be seen than the other arches. Furthermore, the six arches of the ball room on the northeastern and southwestern sides do not exhibit the same modifications at all. In fact, they are more similar to the entrance arches on the other sides. For this reason, it is most likely that the eight narrow arches along the northwestern and southeastern sides flanking the entrance arches had been designed as too wide and had to be adjusted while construction progressed. The assumption that the structure had already been standing by 1683 is supported by these findings as it suggests a rather hurried progression. Additionally, the multitude of materials including bricks of various sizes, as well as limestone and sandstone ashlars (also of various sizes) confirms that the walls were quickly built using the soonest available material. Considering that everything was destined to be covered with plaster anyways, not much attention was paid to the aesthetics of the placement of the ashlars and bricks. In turn, this means that the emphasis of the construction was upon the plaster decorations and paintings that consumed the remaining time until 1692.

It must also be stated that the construction of the interior of the Palais was likely conducted by a different workforce than the outside that features finely crafted ashlars into a host of shapes indicative of the *style classique*. The conclusion is that the inner, skeletal structure was quickly built, followed by a more detail-oriented decoration of the outside using beige sandstone that presumably progressed concurrently with the plaster decorations of the interior. The post-war interventions regarding the structure of the site mainly consisted of patchwork done with bricks and reinforced concrete, though it is not immediately clear from photos where the pre-war materials end and the post-war material begins. Provided the results of the stone-by-stone architectural analysis, it is clear that post-war construction efforts begin precisely above the plaster niches wherein paintings and windows once stood (Fig. 14).

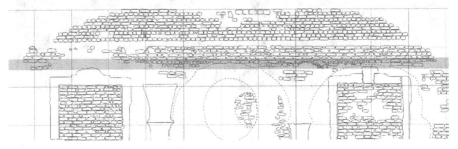

Fig. 14. Outlines of the bricks and plaster on the southeastern side of the ballroom. Note the red area highlighting where the pre-war (below) and post-war (above) brickwork commences and ends, using Inkscape. Image Source: Aaron Pattee.

5 Conclusions

The high-resolution 3D scan of the ballroom of the palace, paired with the detailed outlines of the materials using digital tools, allows researchers to conduct reproducible and accurate examinations of construction based upon quantitative measurements. More importantly, the interdisciplinary delegation of experts to record the site and then document its visible features provides a model to be replicated. Particularly in the case of a partially ruined building, the combination of digital methods and techniques presents a unique opportunity to examine the construction of elite historic architecture, while maintaining access to a larger network of researchers.

Acknowledgements. The project received funds by the *Deutsche Forschungsgemeinschaft* (DFG) in the context of the project plafond-3D, co-financed by the DFG and the French *Agence National de Recherche* (ANR), and conducted in close collaboration with the *Corpus of Baroque Ceiling Paintings in Germany* (CbDD) of the *Bavarian Academy of Sciences and Humanities.* We would like to thank the *Sächsische Schlösser Gmbh*, the *Staatsbetrieb Sächsisches Immobilien- und Baumanagement* as well as Stefan Herzig (Independent Art Historian, Dresden) for providing key, previously unpublished information.

References

1. Grossmann, G.U.: Einführung in die historische und kunsthistorische Bauforschung. Wissenschaftliche Buchgesellschaft, Darmstadt (2010)
2. Blanke, H.: Der Große Garten in Dresden. Die Entwicklungsgeschichte des Großen Gartens zu Dresden. In: Sächsische Schlösserverwaltung (ed.) Der Grosse Garten zu Dresden: Gartenkunst in vier Jahrhunderten, pp. 21–33. Sandstein, Dresden (2001)
3. Kremeier, J.: Die Reisen des Wolf Casper von Klengel, die Bauten des Johann Georg Starcke und das Palais im Großen Garten: Bemerkungen zur Architektur Dresdens in der zweiten Hälfte des 17. Jahrhunderts. Frühneuz.-Info. **14**, 103–129 (2003)
4. Passavant, G., von Klengel, W.C.: Wolf Caspar von Klengel: Dresden 1630–1691: Reisen, Skizzen, baukünstlerische Tätigkeiten. Deutscher Kunstverlag, München (2001)
5. Magirius, H.: Das Residenzschloss zu Dresden. Michael Imhof Verlag, Petersberg (2020)
6. Hertzig, S.: Das barocke Dresden: Architektur einer Metropole des 18. Jahrhunderts. Michael Imhof Verlag GmbH & Co. KG, Petersberg (2013)
7. Marx, H.: Staatspropaganda und Liebeswerben. Die Gemälde im Thronsaal Augusts des Starken im Dresdner Residenzschloß. In: Lupfer, G., Rudert, K. (eds.) Bau + Kunst - Kunst + Bau : Festschrift zum 65. Geburtstag von Professor Jürgen Paul, pp. 192–211. Dresden (2000)
8. Schuller, M., ICOMOS: Building Archaeology. Paris (2002)
9. Hempel, E.: Unbekannte Skizzen von Wolf Caspar von Klengel. Akademie-Verlag, Berlin (1958)
10. Arnold, P.: Die Münzentwürfe Wolf Caspar von Klengels und Samuel Bottschilds für Kurfürst Johann Georg III. von Sachsen. Jahrb. Staatl. Kunstsammlungen Dresd. 27, 25–29 (2000)
11. Baumeister des Barock und Rokoko in Sachsen. Verlag für Bauwesen, Berlin (1979)
12. Hertzig, S.: Das barocke Dresden: Architektur einer Metropole des 18. Jahrhunderts. Michael Imhof Verlag, Petersberg (2013)
13. May, W.: Das kürsächsische Oberbauamt: eine Ausbildungsstätte für Baumeister? In: Professur für Geschichte der Landschaftsarchitektur und Gartendenkmalpflege der Technischen Universität Dresden (ed.) AHA! Miszellen zur Gartengeschichte und Gartendenkmalpflege, pp. 6–13. Professur für Geschichte der Landschaftsarchitektur und Gartendenkmalpflege der Technischen Universität Dresden, Dresden (2016)
14. Reeckmann, K.: Anfänge der Barockarchitektur in Sachsen: Johann Georg Starcke und sein Zeit. Böhlau, Köln (2000)
15. Lenz, R.: Die kriegsbeschädigte Stuckausstattung im Festsaal des Palais im Großen Garten in Dresden – Material und Werktechnik: Zur ursprünglichen Gestaltung der Stuckoberflächen (2015). https://doi.org/10.11588/IH.2010.0.20449
16. Artec3D: Artec EVA handheld scanner Data Sheet (2020)
17. Faro: Faro Focus S350 Data Sheet (2023)
18. Hess, M., Luhmann, T., Götze, B.: 3D-Erfassung in der Denkmalpflege : Anforderungen und Perspektiven. In: Meydenbauer, Busch : Pioniere der Photogrammetrie, pp. 58–65. Bamberg : Otto-Friedrich-Universität, Bamberg (2021)

Potentials for Research in Urban History–Online Research Tool 4D Community Browser

Heike Messemer[✉]

Center for Open Digital Innovation and Participation, Technische Universität Dresden,
Strehlener Street 22/24, 01069 Dresden, Germany
heike.messemer@tu-dresden.de

Abstract. The online research tool 4D Browser was developed in the junior
research group Urban History 4D in 2016–2021 at Technische Universität Dresden
and the Universität Würzburg. It offers a spatio-temporal access to digital repositories of historical photographs within a 3D city model. The research tool can also
be used to quantitatively analyze photographs. This makes it possible to work on
even complex research questions in an innovative way. To open this research tool
to the community of experts in the fields of cultural heritage, digital humanities,
urban history, art and architectural history, history, photography, and the public,
it has to be developed further. As a basis a user study was recently evaluated. The
results presented here offer potentials for the implementation of new features and
the future development of the tool. They show who the community is and what
their needs of an innovative research tool in the field of cultural heritage are.

Keywords: 4D-Browser · Digital Research Tool · Digital 3D City Model ·
Urban History · Historical Photographs · Digital Humanities

1 Introduction

1.1 The 4D Browser

The 4D Browser is an online free accessible research tool, which was developed by the
interdisciplinary junior research group UrbanHistory4D (HistStadt4D) as a cooperation
between the Technische Universität Dresden and the Universität Würzburg [1]. Doctoral
students and postdocs of art history, photogrammetry, media informatics, computer science, information science, educational technology, psychology were jointly developing
the research tool from 2016 to 2021, funded by the BMBF (Bundesministerium für Bildung und Forschung) [2]. It offers the possibility to virtually browse through a 3D city
model of Dresden – as a case study – in which historical photographs are located where
the photographers potentially stood (Fig. 1). The photographs are implemented from the
Deutsche Fotothek. The metadata was taken from there and supplemented in part, for
example with keywords and the location.

An integrated timeline opens up the fourth dimension by allowing the user to select
any period or point in time. The display of historical photographs and 3D models changes
according to the selection.

S. Münster et al. (Eds.): UHDL 2023, CCIS 1853, pp. 32–42, 2023.
https://doi.org/10.1007/978-3-031-38871-2_3

Fig. 1. Graphical user interface of the 4D Browser with 3D viewport and interactive timeline.

This is possible on three different levels: The orange-colored brackets indicate the period within which the photographs were taken. In this way, the display of the photographs can be expanded or limited individually, which has a direct effect on the display in the viewport (Fig. 2).

Fig. 2. Graphical user interface of the 4D Browser with selected time period 1820–1920.

The blue indicator marks the point in time that the 3D model represents. For example, users can visualize the structural urban condition of the city in a specific year. It should be noted that the 3D city model of Dresden currently shows the structural urban condition in the 2010s and that earlier construction stages were also created in the 3D model for selected buildings as an example (Fig. 3).

Fig. 3. Graphical user interface of the 4D Browser with selected time slots of the 3D models, indicating the architectural history of the Sophienkirche: in 1930 with openwork spires (top), 1945 as a ruin (middle) and 2013 as memorial, Gedenkstätte Busmannkapelle (bottom).

With the help of the green indicator, historical maps from four different times can be selected, which are then shown instead of the default terrain model. In this way, users get a further visual impression of the city's appearance in the form of the street network, built-up areas and open spaces at a certain point in time (Fig. 4).

Fig. 4. Graphical user interface of the 4D Browser with selected historical maps: 1911 (top) and 1994 (bottom).

Via all these innovative features it is possible to get an impression of the historical development of the city [3]. The interplay of photographs, historical maps and 3D city models offers an innovative way of approaching the history of the city through different approaches.

Moreover, a selection of different visualization options enables the photographs to be examined quantitatively. For example, a heat map is used to colour the areas in the 3D model in which more (reddish) or fewer (bluish) photographs are located. The direction from which the photographs were potentially taken can also be examined with a so-called Vector Field (directed arrows) or Radial Fan (clusters). When evaluating, however, it should be noted that only the photo stock that was loaded into the 4D Browser is analysed here.

The tool is aimed at experts in the fields of cultural heritage, digital humanities, urban history, art and architectural history, history, photography and also the general public. With the help of the functions described, complex research questions can be worked on: In what period of time was a specific building photographed from which perspectives? Has this photographical behaviour changed over time? Which buildings were photographed more or less often in a certain period of time?

These kind of questions would be difficult to answer with the database and functionality of a standard image repository. On the other hand, the 4D Browser with the spatial localization of the photographs in connection with the timeline and the visualization displays provides innovative possibilities to work on such complex research questions in the field of cultural heritage.

1.2   The User Study

In order to find out what kind of research questions researchers would like to work on with the 4D Browser and how they assess the features of the tool, the junior research group conducted an online survey among the Digital Humanities Community in 2020. For this purpose, views were posted on relevant websites and blogs and sent via relevant mailing lists. A total of 50 survey forms were returned over a period of four weeks.

The core of the survey was a five-minute video in which the most important functions of the 4D Browser were explained using a screen capture with voice-over. In addition to general questions (technical/professional background, age, gender), questions were also asked about technical background knowledge or professional interest, whether, for example, historical photographs were used. With reference to the video, the participants were then asked to what extent the features of the 4D Browser were "important", "goal-oriented", "relevant for their work" and "exciting" from their point of view. This was followed by a request for an assessment as to whether certain functions are still missing or which existing functions are not understandable. Other questions were devoted to the potential use of the 4D Browser by the survey participants and the open question about research questions that they would like to answer with the tool. Finally, the participants had space to leave suggestions and comments on the 4D Browser.

The survey was evaluated as part of the 4D Community Browser project, funded by the National Research Data Infrastructure 4Culture (NFDI4Culture) in the period June to December 2022. This was carried out at the TU Dresden in close consultation with the former head of the junior research group Sander Münster at Friedrich-Schiller-Universität Jena and the computer scientist Jonas Bruschke at Julius-Maximilians-Universität Würzburg, who is largely responsible for the technical implementation of the 4D Browser.

2   Evaluation of the User Study

2.1   The Needs of the Community

The focus of the further development of the 4D Browser is the community and their wishes and needs for the research tool. The evaluation of the survey can thus make a significant contribution to adapting and expanding the features of the 4D Browser even better to their needs.

The Community. But who is the community? The 50 survey participants (18 female, 24 male, 1 diverse, 7 no answer) were distributed relatively evenly across the age groups 26–35 years (10), 36–45 (13), 46–55 (11) and 56- 65 (10), only three people said they were younger or older, three abstained. The professional/technical background of 24 people, i.e. almost half of the participants, was related to art history, five each to computer science or history, and two each to archaeology, digital humanities or architectural history. Other areas included museology, library science, interaction design, information science, and hobby photography. However, there were also entries that included two or more areas, so that it is not possible to make a clear distinction between the technical/professional background. In this respect, the survey participants represent exactly the intended target group of the 4D Browser, which was described in Sect. 1.1.

The majority of the participants work professionally with historical photographs and the subject of urban history (35 each), eight and ten respectively work with them privately. Online (research) tools such as the 4D Browser (or digital image databases, online platforms for viewing 3D models, etc.) are mostly of professional/technical and private interest to the majority of those surveyed and are generally known. Online image databases such as prometheus, europeana, Foto Marburg are professionally/technically very relevant and also very well known for half of the respondents, only for very few (3 each) they are hardly relevant or hardly known.

This feedback suggests that the target group has a high affinity for historical photographs and online repositories for 3D models and photographs. In this respect, it can be assumed that using the 4D Browser should not pose any major problems. Specific feedback on this is reflected in the Applicability section.

The Features. In the survey, the assessments of five essential innovative features of the 4D Browser were queried, which standard image repositories usually do not have, especially not in this combination. In each case, the question was whether the function was rated as "important", "target-oriented", "relevant to my work" and "exciting". Here one answer was possible on a scale from "6-very much" to "1-hardly" or "no answer". First of all, the 3D view, i.e. the digital 3D city model, through which you can navigate independently, was the focus of the question: the majority of the participants rated this feature as very important, goal-oriented and exciting (27, 27 and 25), for 13 people it was very relevant to their work.

A similar distribution of the assessments can also be observed with the other features: timeline (bar on the edge of the 4D Browser to independently select time periods, historical maps and construction states of the buildings), image comparison (possibility to select any two images to analyse them in a direct comparison), spatial search (independent virtual navigation through the 3D city model, which enables to search for and find buildings, photographs or perspectives of photographers without entering keywords in a search mask). More than half of the responses are distributed over the highest selectable values for the categories "important", "goal-oriented" and "exciting", only in the case of "relevance for my work" are the answers distributed over the entire spectrum (Fig. 5).

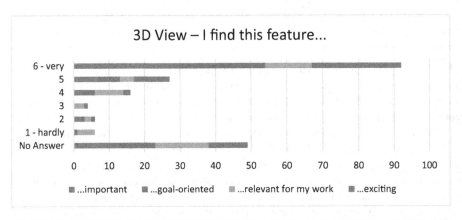

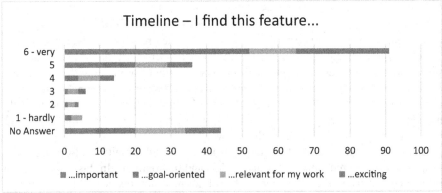

Fig. 5. Evaluation results of the questions to assess the five essential innovative features of the 4D Browser (n = 50).

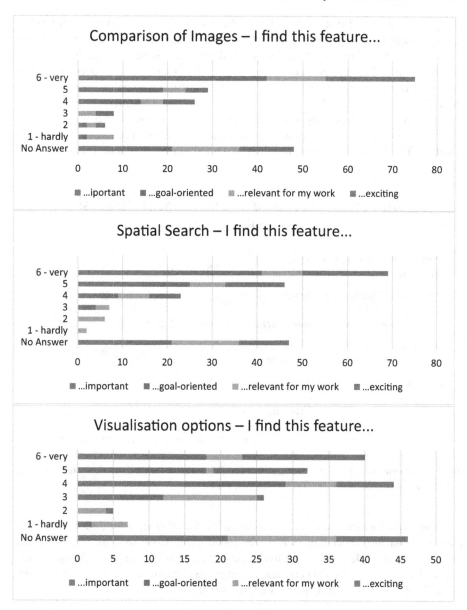

Fig. 5. (*continued*)

A deviation in the assessment of the functions can be observed in the feature of visualization options (possibility to analyse the location and direction of the photographs, taken by the photographer, with the help of visualizations such as heat map, vector field): A large number of the 50 participants found this function "exciting" (30), but only 17 or 19 people found this to be "important" and "goal-oriented", and the "relevance for work" was rated in the middle of the scale.

It should be noted that the features of the 4D Browser received a predominantly positive assessment. Regardless of the professional/technical relevance, they were very well received. In this respect, it can be assumed that the more relevant the feature is for the actual work, the more important, targeted and exciting the features become. This is also reflected in the answers to the question of which features an online image database should generally include. Here, out of a total of 43 people, 32 participants stated that a spatial search without entering keywords should be a basic function. So far, however, no standard image database such as europeana, prometheus, or Foto Marburg has such a feature. The 4D Browser can certainly be regarded as a pioneer here (Fig. 6).

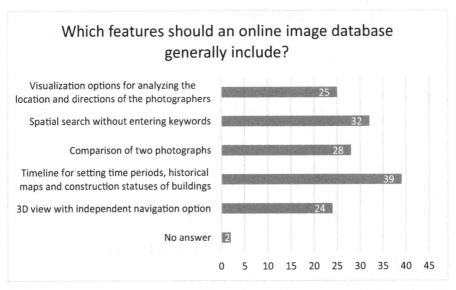

Fig. 6. Evaluation result on the question which features an online image database should generally include (n = 43).

When asked which features they missed in the 4D Browser, a third said they didn't miss any, and just under half (49%) mentioned at least one missing feature. These included, for example, links to archives/wikis/image sources/buildings, changes to the city model based on historical photographs, querying of coordinates via geo-referencing, visual display that the search query is being carried out.

The Applicability. The comprehensibility of the features can be regarded as consistently very high, so there was no ambiguity for 74% of the 43 people. The answer to the question of whether the participants could imagine using the 4D Browser to search for and find historical photographs was also unequivocal: 72% of the 43 people surveyed answered yes, only one person chose the answer No and six people maybe. The reasons for the positive feedback included: "One no longer has the feeling that important photographs are missing when searching, as is sometimes the case with classic search engines.", "Navigation in the cityscape is very useful", "I like the service appears very simple", "Alternative search option to language-determined search slots", "Good addition to the classic image database, especially in the case of a high density of available image sources for specific objects, ensembles, locations". Some of the responses indicate that people compare the 4D Browser to other image databases they know and appreciate its innovative features. This mood picture represents a good basis for the further development of the tool.

Community Research Questions. In order to be able to assess more precisely how the 4D Browser is used in the community and would continue to be used in the future, an open question was addressed to the research questions that the users would like to be able to answer or approach with the 4D Browser: "Tracking the change of the city, individual buildings or components over time", "Interrelationships between buildings in the cityscape", "When reconstructing historical events from written sources, the 4D Browser would be a good addition to the state of the city at the time in question", "Change in the perception of historical buildings/places/monuments over time (about 19th century, Weimar period, 30s/40s, GDR, post-reunification/90s in comparison: which motifs remained popular, which changed)", "reconstruction of lost states or entire objects", "growth of the historic townscape", "For municipal urban planning of the future the Browser would certainly be a generally understandable and plausible medium to explain and understand history and to apply it to new construction projects."

Based on the answers, it becomes clear that such complex research questions could not be answered with the help of conventional online image databases alone. Because the targeted research questions go far beyond pure image analysis and often include the urban space – and thus the 3D environment.

The comments that could be left at the end of the survey also provide information on how the 4D Browser and its possible uses are assessed by the community: "I could well imagine using the 4D Browser in teaching, e.g. in exercises/seminars on city history or digital humanities", "Very suitable for the virtual inspection of city models.", "The further development into a platform that can be used for different cities would be great. Citizen Science should be included in the concept.". In particular with regard to the last comment, it can be noted that it is now technically possible to explore other cities or any location via the 4D Browser. In addition, one result of earlier studies by the research group was that the target group of the 4D Browser wanted to be able to add and edit their own content [4]. This need is reflected in the user-centred approach to open up the 4D Browser to the community on the basis of the results of the survey presented here.

3 More Community Feedback

Another important building block for the further development of the 4D Community Browser is the direct feedback from the community when the tool is presented. In July 2022, the research tool was presented in a slot at the "Barcamp 3D and Cultural Heritage" of the NFDI4Culture (National Research Data Infrastructure). The participants showed great interest in the features and had various ideas for possible future fields of application.

At the international conference Cultural Heritage and New Technologies (CHNT) in November 2022, the 4D community browser was also presented to a heterogeneous audience [5]. In the session "Planning history and urban heritage. Historical towns atlases as a tool for research, heritage management and participation", the tool took on a special position, as it was the only project presented to include a 3D or 4D representation. In addition, a previously unconsidered focus on historical cadastral plans could be identified for the 4D Community Browser.

This feedback on the current status of the 4D Community Browser provides important impulses and indications in which directions the tool could be further developed. In this way, the potential for future cooperation with institutions with a specific specialist orientation that would like to use the tool for their own research can also be explored.

4 Summary and Future Steps

Overall, the survey was able to show that the 4D Browser is of high relevance for the community in the field of urban history, cultural heritage and digital humanities and is used in everyday research. Especially in comparison to conventional image databases, the survey was able to show that it will be important in the future to provide experts with a digital research tool with innovative features in order to work on complex questions.

Based on the answers, the existing features of the 4D Browser can be further improved and adjusted. The feedback from the participants also provides many starting points for further development of the tool and ideas for new functions. The aim is to make it technically possible to implement your own 3D models and data (photos, texts, metadata, etc.). In this way it will be possible to edit your own research questions on any location with the 4D Browser, thus opening it up completely to research in the field of cultural heritage.

References

1. 4D Browser Homepage. https://4dbrowser.urbanhistory4d.org. Accessed 15 Dec 2022
2. Urban History 4D Homepage. http://www.urbanhistory4d.org/wordpress/index.php/research-group-urban-history-4d/. Accessed 15 Dec 2022
3. Dewitz, L., et al.: Historical photos and visualizations: potential for research. In: Int. Arch. Photogramm. Remote Sens. Spatial Inf. Sci., XLII-2/W15, pp. 405–412. Copernicus Publications (2019). https://doi.org/10.5194/isprs-archives-XLII-2-W15-405-2019
4. Kröber, C.: German art history students' use of digital repositories: an insight. In: Toeppe, K., Yan, H., Chu, S.K.W. (eds.) iConference 2021. LNCS, vol. 12646, pp. 176–192. Springer, Cham (2021). https://doi.org/10.1007/978-3-030-71305-8_14
5. Messemer, H., Bruschke, J., Münster, S.: Exploring historical cities with the 4D community browser. requirements of a spatio-temporal research tool. In: CHNT Editorial board. Proceedings of the 27th International Cenference on Cultural Heritage and New Technologies, November 2022. Propylaeum, Heidelberg 2022 (to be published in 2023)

Data Handling and Data Schemes

Metadata for 3D Digital Heritage Models. In the Search of a Common Ground

Igor Bajena[1,2]([⊠]) [iD] and Piotr Kuroczyński[1] [iD]

[1] Institute of Architecture, Hochschule Mainz–University of Applied Sciences, Mainz, Germany
igorpiotr.bajena@unibo.it
[2] Department of Architecture, University of Bologna, Bologna, Italy

Abstract. The publication of 3D models has been an unregulated issue for many years. Recently, it has been possible to identify barriers that have prevented the proper preparation of 3D data for web-based publication, related to uncleared copyright issues, access to 3D files, targeted audiences, or distinction of requirements related to different stages of the digital asset lifecycle. In response to these challenges, numerous scientific infrastructures with diverse backgrounds and purposes have emerged, presenting different approaches to metadata documentation schemes. This publication aims to present an analysis of existing metadata schemas carried out in a workshop with selected initiatives and digital data repositories on metadata for digital heritage to find the common grounds between the various metadata schemas. The compilation of multiple documentation schemas is used to develop an approach for the creation of a universal documentation metadata patterns that could guide the work on the standardisation of 3D models of cultural heritage.

Keywords: 3d models · digital heritage · metadata schema · documentation · data repositories · data interoperability

1 Introduction

Recent years have seen a sharp increase in the production of 3D models in the various disciplines of digital humanities. They can be observed in heritage studies (human culture and behaviour related to heritage), museology (heritage presentation and education on public), archaeology (visualization of the past, site documentation) or the history of art and architecture (visualization and research tool) [1]. Diverse approaches to the creation and use of digital models have led to the development of numerous individual solutions for the documentation and preservation of produced assets. As a result, there is currently a lack of shared standards for the publication and exchange of digital heritage 3D assets, what limit access and use of published resources. Published content is not subject to any restrictions that would prepare the models for future reuse. Additionally, the metadata accompanying the models often does not allow a full assessment of the relevance of the model for further possible use scenarios [2]. Moreover, a huge amount of digital assets is not made available to the scientific community, as it is only stored in archives on private computers.

Coming up with an appropriate solution addressing these issues is a challenging and complex process, requiring the involvement of the whole, very diverse community, which is coming with various requirements and applications of 3D models [3]. It is therefore possible to observe the formation of smaller groups among scientific digital heritage developers, who will emphasise quite different aspects regarding the publication of 3D models. As a result, newer and newer platforms for sharing 3D data are emerging, which raises a new problem concerning the findability of data on the web. The most popular 3D data repositories are still commercially owned while the visibility of scientific platforms is negligible [4]. The great solution seems to be data aggregation, which results in rich libraries of digital resources by collecting data from other repositories. The example of Europeana[1] platform, which collects digital heritage resources from all over the Europe, already successfully aggregates over 5,900 3D models from 36 institutions [5]. However, compared to the entire repository collection (over 55 million digital objects), the numbers indicate how recent the topic of 3D data aggregation is.

With such low visibility of 3D assets, a collective effort by the entire community in developing standards can go a long way in fostering efforts to bring 3D models beyond the scientific community and closer to the public audience. And according to the rules of the "FAIR Guiding Principles for scientific data management and stewardship" [6], one of the first steps towards this goal is to provide appropriate metadata set that will enable the findability, accessibility, reusability and interoperability of published content. In this matter, there are already many general standards for digital media in broad sense, that do not consider the specific characteristics of 3D models. At the same time, individual repositories present their own proposals for documenting 3D models based on very diverse assumptions. Thus, this publication aims to analyse existing of metadata schemas for 3D models of digital heritage to seek common ground and develop a universal metadata schema for web-based publication of 3D models.

2   Documentation Factors

The first step towards the common grounds between the various 3D model documentation schemas is to understand the factors influencing such a wide variety of approaches to metadata. The most important of these is to identify for what purpose 3D models are published, how they can be used and to which audience the data is directed [7]. The answers to these questions are often not so obvious and require a deeper understanding of the 3D model medium itself and its full capabilities. A study of the lifecycle of a digital asset (see Fig. 1) can help with outlining the goals associated with publishing digital assets at five different stages:

1. Creation (about designing, capturing, and tagging)
2. Management (about reviewing, annotating and approving)
3. Distribution (about sharing and delivering)
4. Retrieval (about searching, finding and reusing)
5. Achieving (about preserving and expiring).

---

[1] https://www.europeana.eu/en (last access: 22.05.2023).

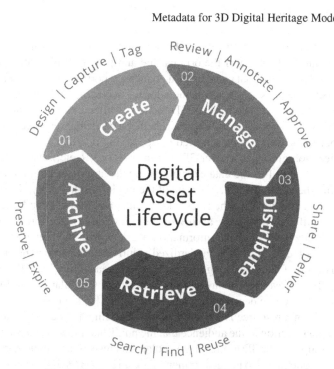

Fig. 1. Digital asset lifecycle chart (Filecamp 2020)

Each stage will be described in a slightly different way depending on the type of digital medium involved. Recommendations for metadata in the context of the life cycle of digital 3D models have already been developed by the Community Standards for 3D Data Preservation (CS3DP) [8]. The first two stages of the cycle are most often carried on local computers. Data is not shared externally, which often implies the lack of even basic documentation. Even if no further use of the models is planned, it is worth considering at **creation** phase (first stage of the cycle) a documentation of basic metadata set. It should contain information regarding the methods used to create the file, specifications in terms of geometry, materials and textures, source data used, as well as administrative data about the project and people involved in the creation of the model. For further **management** of the 3D file (the second stage of the cycle), the collected metadata should be further enriched with an explanation of legal information, the specifics of the file in terms of its size, format, version, or time of creation, as well as technical information in terms of the scale of representation of the object, the number of vertices and faces. The next stages of the cycle are linked to the release of data to the public, which requires appropriate structuring of information and enrichment of the set with additional information. **Distribution and publication** of the model (the third stage of the cycle) requires the inclusion of a lot of non-3D-oriented metadata, the role of which is to fulfill FAIR's principals to achieve a high level of findability for published content [6], as well as clarifying the legal policy on released asset. Often the publication of a digital model on the web is motivated by obtaining a quick and easily accessible visualization of the created content, keeping metadata at a minimum. Relevant metadata for this stage also includes the available formats of the 3D model, the purpose for which it is created, information about the location of the original file and provision of contact data to the creators, or text description that can convey a condensed portion of various information. Very similar metadata package should be included for **accessing and reusing** 3D models (fourth stage of the cycle). The reuse of 3D models is often extremely challenging, so the metadata included should clearly express whether a particular resource is suitable for a variety of purposes. This can be achieved by specifying possible derivatives based on presentation technologies (web-viewer, 3D printing, AR or VR, etc.), sharing the original native file format as well as the data exchange formats, and describing the methods of work, including the accuracy and resolution of the model. Additionally, the description of the copyrights should clarify the rules under which a 3D model can be reused. The final stage in the life of 3D models, **archiving**, requires additional effort in terms of the metadata record itself. Most of the information overlaps with the previous stages. The difference here is the need of use standardized solutions and permanent identifiers to ensure preservation of data over long time and the data readability by both humans and machines [7]. To achieve this, authority files, controlled vocabularies and linked open data tools such as resource description framework (RDF) [9] are used.

The life cycle of a resource is not sufficient to determine the necessary metadata. It also requires consideration of the audience that the published model is targeting. Among the audience groups for the 3D models are: scholars and researchers, educators, students, museums, public outreach and nongovernmental organizations (NGO), professionals and general users [7]. Each of these groups will need slightly different requirements, starting with students who need easily accessible data that they can quickly assess for use, and ending with researchers who need accurate technical specifications, methods used, terms of use and the possibility of citation of the resource in their own work.

Knowing and considering all these factors before the publication process will help with selection of the complexity level of metadata submission. CS3DP's published guidelines give general requirements for each case introducing three levels of requirements complexity described as good (for general users, educators, and students), better (for museums, professionals, NGOs, and public outreach) and best (for scholars, researchers, and preservation). However, in terms of documentation, there is only a distinction between basic metadata (good), more robust metadata (better) and robust metadata including technical information and paradata (best). A similar division in terms of recommendations is carried out for metadata at the different stages of the already described life cycle of a digital resource (good, better, and best). The combination of these recommendations for a particular case with the requirements of the creators' fields can allow to outline a general scheme for documentation.

3   Classification of Existing Schemas

The guidance prepared by CS3DP is a relatively new publication in comparison to the history of 3D models on the web. Data repositories have produced many documentation schemes based on experience with other digital resources and dedicated to the specific application cases. In result, it is easy to see a large difference in the metadata documented [10], based on the mentioned factors: the audience or the purpose of publication.

Although the publication aim often overlaps with the objectives of the different stages of the life cycle of a digital resource, some inconsistencies can be noted. Based on the results of the CS3DP study and the author's own analysis, six main objectives for 3D model publication (VORDAS) were distinguished on which online repositories are based:

V – Easily accessible **visualization** in a 3D environment;
O – Digital documentation of **object** embedded in the 3D model;
R – Presentation of scientific **research** results;
D – Sharing models for reuse by data **download**;
A – Data a**ggregation** and advanced analysis on entire digital collections;
S – **Storytelling** about object based on annotations and hotspots;

Digital repositories often fulfil several of these objectives. Some documentation schemas are quite elaborated to fit into every possible usage scenario, while in other cases they are heavily simplified requiring only some basic information. To fill the gap with poor metadata sets, repositories give the opportunity to provide more details in a text field containing a description of the published resource. The questions arise: which is the right solution and what may influence the choice of a particular approach. To answer it, representatives from a variety of 3D repositories were brought together to exchange experiences and seek common ground on metadata during series of workshops organized by authors[2].

Initially, activity included a group of six repositories. Five of them are new infrastructures related to digital heritage (DFG 3D-Viewer[3], IDOVIR[4], baureka.online[5], FID BAUdigital[6] and Semantic Kompakkt[7]) and 3D models from ongoing research projects. Last participant is an infrastructure maintained by university library (heidICON[8]). In further cooperation the group was extended by three institutions related to data aggregation (Europeana, Share3D[9], CARARE[10]) and one museum repository (Smithsonian3D[11]). 3D repositories whose representatives did not participate in previous activities yet are planned to be included in further work.

---

[2] Activity in the form of workshops on the topic of metadata for 3D models of digital heritage took place twice: in December 2022 in Mainz and in March 2023 in Munich. The joint work to develop common ground between the infrastructures is still ongoing, with publication of the first results planned for autumn 2023.
[3] https://3d-repository.hs-mainz.de/ (last access: 23.05.2023).
[4] https://idovir.com/ (last access: 23.05.2023).
[5] https://baureka.online/de (last access: 23.05.2023).
[6] https://www.fid-bau.de/en/ (last access: 23.05.2023).
[7] https://semantic-kompakkt.de/home (last access: 23.05.2023).
[8] https://heidicon.ub.uni-heidelberg.de (last access: 23.05.2023).
[9] https://share3d.eu/ (last access: 23.05.2023).
[10] https://www.carare.eu/en/ (last access: 23.05.2023).
[11] https://3d.si.edu/ (last access: 23.05.2023).

Table 1. Preliminary identification of the objectives, types of resources and data schemas used of the repositories participating in the metadata workshop.

Repository	3D model type	Scope	Data model
DFG 3D-Viewer	–Hand-made models, –3D scans;	Oriented on 3D models. Focus on visualization and reusability of 3D models.	CIDOC CRM, OntSciDoc3D
IDOVIR	–Hand-made models;	Oriented on projects – 3D models are not required but can be s supplementary material. Focus on documentation of digital 3D reconstruction projects.	CIDOC CRM (considered)
baureka. online	–3D scans, –Point clouds, –SfM-models, –BIM models;	Oriented on objects – 3D models are not the only collected medium, some entries can exist without it. Focus on documentation and provision of research data concerning architecture.	RADAR (DataCite)
heidICON	–3D scans, –Hand-made models;	Oriented on digital asset – 3D models are relatively new in the system. Most entries are about other type of media. Focus on archiving of digital cultural heritage object with multidisciplinary approach.	Object-oriented and event-based, like the XML schema LIDO.
FID BAUdigital	–Hand-made models, –3D scans, –point clouds, –BIM models;	Currently available workbench is oriented on 3D models. Focus on digital research data in the disciplines of civil engineering, architecture, and urbanism.	For 3D architectural models: DURAARK-Modell for Arch. Data (buildm, e57m, ifcm)
Semantic Komappkt	–Hand-made models, –3D scans;	Oriented on 3D models. Focus on visual representation of cultural objects with semantic description of annotations.	Wikibase Generic Model for Digital Objects
Europeana	–Hand-made models, –3D scans, –Point clouds;	Oriented on digital asset – 3D models are relatively small part of the whole collection. Focus on aggregation of digital heritage resources from the whole Europe.	Europeana Data Model (EDM)
Share3D	———	Oriented on 3D models. It is not repository itself, it is an infrastructure, which allows to publish models directly into Europeana with use of Sketchfab repository.	Not known
Smithsonian 3D	–3D scans;	Oriented on 3D models. Focus on digitization museum collections.	Not known
CARARE	–Hand-made models, –3D scans,	Oriented on digital asset including 3D models. Focus on guidance in creation, publication, and use of digital data, includ-	CARARE metadata schema

In the preparation of the workshop, identification of characteristics and purposes of all repositories were clarified, allowing creation of a comparison, and giving an overview for the discussion about the common ground (see Table 1). Some repositories document not only 3D models, but also other media (Europeana, heidICON, CARARE, baureka.online), and that one infrastructure treats the 3D model as additional material, which is not listed as a separate unit in the repository available for viewing from the resource overview level (IDOVIR). One of the platforms does not have its own repository, acting only as an intermediary for publication in other infrastructure, but using a proven documentation scheme and checking the substantive quality of the entry (Share3D).

In addition, the representatives from participating projects prepared a visualization of their metadata schema based on the template provided by the DFG 3D-Viewer project team[12]. In result, all metadata was presented by the participants in a split graphical layout prepared on the Miro Board. In this way, each platform was able to visualize the metadata structure, the fields required to create an entry and the types of data contained in the individual fields by color-code (see Fig. 2). Currently, 10 infrastructures prepared and shared their work giving a visual snapshot of their schemas in a comparative way.

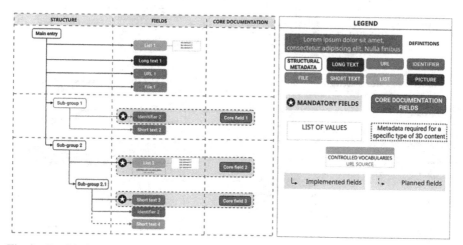

Fig. 2. Graphic layout for the presentation of the documentation schema during the metadata workshop with a legend on the meaning of colors (type of documentation field) and graphic symbols (AIMAINZ/Igor Bajena 2022).

During the workshop, each scheme was presented by its author, allowing representatives of other infrastructures to understand the meaning of the names of the different fields and their use in the context of a given repository. Subsequently, the search for common ground began from looking for similarities in the structure and mandatory fields. The core metadata schema of the repositories is summarized in a table to carry out an initial mapping. After the first edition of the workshop, the overview was prepared for the first six repositories (see Fig. 3).

---

[12] The progress of the work can be tracked through the Miro Board, which is publicly available for viewing at the following address:https://miro.com/app/board/uXjVPDUEGMY=/?share_link_id=777858896545(last access: 20.05.2023).

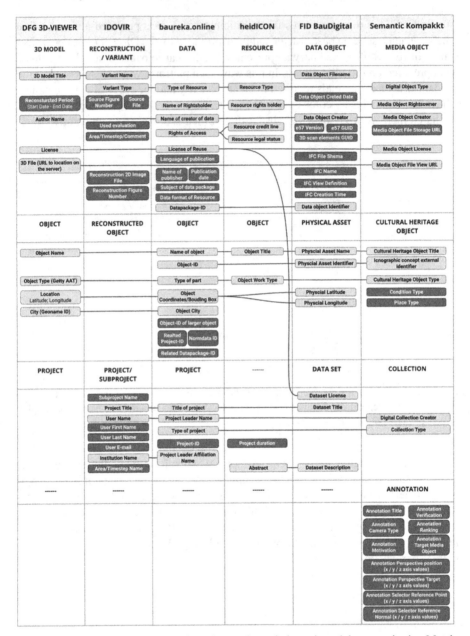

Fig. 3. Overview of core documentation schemas from six investigated data repositories. Matching fields were connected with lines and highlight in brighter color (AI MAINZ/ Igor Bajena 2022).

The overview reveals main structural elements regarding:

- digital resource,
- object presented by digital resource,
- grouping elements, which collects digital resources with some similarities (models from one research project, models presenting the same type of objects, models made by one author, etc.).

An additional fourth section is the annotation, which is a topic in only one of the repositories participated in this phase. It may also be noted that not fields from core meta-data schemas have their equivalents in other repositories, suggesting that the objectives of a particular platform may modify the set of necessary metadata. Two repositories, how-ever, showed the greatest versatility, finding equivalents for almost all mandatory fields in other repositories: heidICON (university library repository) and DFG 3D-Viewer (repository for 3D models of digital heritage). Their schemas can form the basis for establishing a universal documentation scheme in the basic scope.

The graphical representation of the metadata schemas in Miro Board allowed the participants to explore the mapping across the repositories. Similarities were sought between the structural elements of the documentation, as well as the individual fields. It was noted that even when some fields had counterparts in several repositories, they were not necessarily a mandatory field in each one. Structural representation of the schema was in the most cases based on the data form from data upload process. However, there were two exceptions. The Semantic Kompakkt schema was based on the overview of the classes hierarchy and their properties. The FID BAUdigital gives the user the ability to modify fields in the data form and add their own ontologies. Their contribution was based on two selected ontologies related to 3D models, but this does not reflect their full documentation capabilities. There were also disambiguates between fields with the same label, but a different data type which they supposed to store. Currently, five mappings between the DFG 3D-Viewer and the other repositories were prepared and there are under revision process. It is planned to complement the work with mapping between all workshops participants and invite other relevant repositories storing 3D digital models of cultural heritage to join the process. This attempt also showed problems with the readability of the complex graphical representation of data mapping in Miro Board, so it is planned for further graphical development to clearly divide the metadata according to groups of the functions they perform, distinguishing the following:

- descriptive metadata;
- administrative-preservation metadata;
- administrative-technical metadata;
- administrative-rights metadata;
- structural metadata.

Change of the fields order and data structure in metadata schemas is considered to increase the readability of the final output. It is also necessary to sort the metadata according to the context in which they are used, as not all metadata refers directly to the digital resource. Therefore, the following groups of contexts were distinguished based on gathered data:

1. **Digital resource:** 3D model;
2. **Object**: The object represented by the 3D model. It can refer to heritage objects that still exist, objects that have been partially or completely destroyed, as well as those that have never been realized and information about them is only kept in drawings and historical plans.
3. **Project**: The creation activity of the 3D model, usually (but not always) carried out in a scientific context;
4. **Dataset**: the digital data set to which the 3D model belongs. It can be found in repositories collecting various types of digital data about a specific cultural heritage resource;
5. **Annotation**: An additional note about a part or the whole 3D model, most often permanently fixed in the 3D space of the model itself, which can take the form of both text and any multimedia;
6. **Repository**: A data repository that has a 3D model in its collections and provides a digital resource for further data aggregation.

As part of the expansion of the study, a search was initiated for well-established 3D repositories that can provide information in terms of documentation. Using existing scientific publications on 3D repositories [4, 11, 12], online materials prepared by 3D hobbyists [13–15], and own practical experience [16], a compilation of existing repositories was created. Although the total analysis covered nearly 50 repositories, only the top 15 repositories each from commercial and institutional offerings are presented below (see Table 2). Their ranking was based on the number of available models, the quantities of which were taken from information published by the repositories themselves, external sources providing an approximate number, or through the author's analysis of available resources in repository. In addition to the number of models, three other aspects were examined.

The first was the type of models available in the repository, distinguishing between four different types: the models of digitization of reality-based of a mesh (M) and in the form of a reality-based point cloud (P), HBIM information models (I) and 3D models made by hand (H).

Consideration was also given to the complexity of the metadata schema in the repository. As in the CS3DP study, three levels of complexity were considered, based on the target groups:

- **basic** group covering documentation prepared for general users, educators, and students, where the available metadata contain only the necessary information (provided by publisher) and technical specification of 3D model (which could be automatically acquired). It requires low effort from the user uploading the data;
- **professional** group including groups like museums, professionals, NGOs, and public outreach, where metadata are based on existing standards and persistent identifiers;

- **advanced** group covering group of scholars and researchers, where metadata is supported by paradata and specification of methods, techniques, and source materials.

The last criteria considered was the purpose for which the repositories exist. The classifications in this regard were based on the possible purposes of the model's publication on the web, VORDAS, outlined at the beginning of the chapter: V – visualization, O – object record, R – research documentation, D – data reuse, A – data aggregation, S – storytelling.

Table 2. Summary of specifics of selected repositories from the institutional offer.

Repository	Num. of models	Content type				Complexity	Aims					
		M	P	I	H		V	O	R	D	A	S
Institutional												
Morphosource	71 400+	■				advanced	■					
Shape Net Core	51 200+			■		basic		■		■		
NIH 3D	12 600+				■	advanced	■					
Europeana	5 900+	■				professional					■	
3D-ICONS	4 200+			■		basic	■	■				
Smithsonian3D	2 600+				■	basic	■					■
Conservatoire National des Données 3D	1 200+				■	professional		■				
STARC	700+				■	advanced			■			
UMORF	600+			■		professional	■					
OpenHeritage3D	390+		■			professional			■			
NASA 3D Resources Site	380+	■				basic	■					
Kompakkt	240+				■	basic	■					■
tDAR	160+				■	professional			■			
Three D Scans	120+	■				basic	■					
3D Repository	110+			■		advanced	■					
CyArk	100+	■				basic	■					
Commercial												
GrabCAD	5 690 000+				■	basic	■					
Sketchfab	5 000 000+				■	basic	■					■
Thingiverse	2 500 000+				■	basic	■					
CG Trader	1 640 000+				■	basic					■	
Turbosquid	1 215 000+				■	basic						
Free3D	1 162 000+	■				basic						
Cults 3D	998 000+	■				basic						
3D Export	418 000+	■			■	basic						
Printables	394 000+	■				basic	■					
3D Warehouse	190 000+				■	basic	■					
MyMiniFactory	154 000+	■				basic	■					
Unity Asset Store	47 000+				■	basic						
Hum3D	25 000+				■	basic						
BlendSwap	25 000+				■	basic						
Pinshape	13 000+				■	basic						

The classification of repositories by specification shows the relationship between metadata, their complexity, and the purpose the repository serves. It also shows focus of commercial repositories mostly on data reusability. Their metadata schema can be useful in terms of developing the necessary set of technical specifications for a file with a focus on reuse for a specific purpose. These repositories emphasize distinguishing possible uses of a 3D file, differentiating between 3D printing (sometimes with a description of specific printers and techniques to which the file may correspond), AR/VR applications (distinguishing low-complexity files called "low poly"), use in art (ready-made components for use in commercial programs) or game development (ready-made assets for use in game engines). This issue that is not recognized by many institutional repositories. Even after making a 3D model available for download and describing its specifications, institutional repositories do not provide information on how the model can be used. In turn, the wide variety of repositories of institutional offerings gives the opportunity to consider description of the model from other perspectives. They provide some contributions regarding heritage records in museum collections, scientific documentation related to architectural, historical, and archeological research, storytelling about object guided by hotspots and annotation or data aggregation to established digital resources collections.

4   Universal Metadata Patterns for 3D Digital Heritage

The above-mentioned review of the 3D repository, showing state of the art, may lead to the conclusion that a universal documentation scheme for 3D models may not exist. Each of the VORDAS objectives requires a different approach and the development of different fields that would form part of the core metadata schema. Determined factors for the classification of repositories, documentation schemes and metadata itself showed that covering all aspects would require the creation of very extensive and complex documentation. Therefore, it was decided to create documentation patterns corresponding to the purposes of publishing the model on the web. To this end, a life diagram of the digital cultural heritage resource has been developed, considering the elements and activities that require documentation (see Fig. 4). Although the diagram resembles the life cycle of a digital resource, setting it in the context of scholarly activity and cultural heritage has changed its appearance The schema created is based on five phases, during which different types of information must be captured: planning, creation, publication, reuse, and aggregation phases.

The **planning phase** is the part before modelling begins, during which administrative guidelines, funding, the duration of the work, the subject of the model is agreed, and research is carried out to acquire the source material on which the model will be created (field work, scanning the site, carrying out measurements or working in archives and searching for historical sources). The **creation phase** is based on modelling or processing the collected data. In this phase the purposes for which the model is to be used should already have been clarified. Based on this, the requirements, and constraints that the model should meet should be developed. The methods of modelling (or 3D data acquisition) should also be documented along with the hardware and software used.

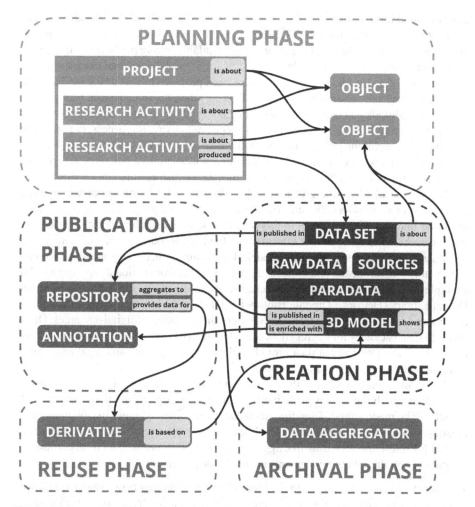

Fig. 4. Diagram of the life cycle of a 3D digital cultural heritage model highlighting the instances relevant for documentation (Igor Bajena 2023)

The **publication phase** is based on making the 3D model available online. This involves choosing a platform for publication, which will determine the findability and accessibility of our model and whether it reaches the audience we are addressing. The phase also requires analysing legal issues, as the 3D model is subject to copyright and may not be published in every case. The publication itself can also be done in several ways, from publishing the project documentation itself, through renderings or animations, making the model available in the web-viewer, and finally making the 3D files available in raw or final form, in the software's native format (BLEND[13], PLN[14], C4D[15], etc.) or using 3D data exchange formats (GLB/GLTF[16], OBJ[17], DAE[18], etc.). The **reuse phase** applies only to cases where 3D files were made available during publication. It requires in addition to the file itself, its technical specifications, and the original use for which it was prepared. If any additional elements have been prepared as part of the model (such as textures/materials, animations, or scene lighting) then the intended file use requires all files and components included in the shared package. If, on the other hand, the file is to be made available for the possibility of further development, it is necessary to provide working files, including native formats. In the case when the file supposed to be used in a broader context (e.g., putting a finished church model into a city model) then data exchange formats should be used to use the file. Reuse also requires that conditions of use be made available to the user before downloading. The **archiving phase** requires publication in a repository that ensures the longevity of files over the long term, such as digital libraries. The metadata in this regard should be as rich as possible to ensure that the archive has all available information about the resource. A certain solution in this regard may be to submit one's model along with the necessary metadata to data aggregator like Europeana that collects digital resources from national repositories. An example of a national repository aggregating its resources to Europeana is German Digital Library (Deutsche Digitale Biblithek – DDB), which aims to provide access to cultural and scientific heritage from all over Germany captured in digital resources. DDB prepares data packages for aggregation, including data quality check, enriching data set by adding information about data provider, clarifying copyrights and legal issues and mapping metadata to aggregator data model.

The most crucial moment of the cycle in terms of metadata is publication, as this is the point at which the person publishing decides how much information about the 3D model will be made public. Therefore, metadata from previous stages like planning and creation should be considered during publication, as well as considering the metadata needed for future use scenarios like aggregation or reuse. This means that according to the publication the following elements should be documented:

1. **Project** - the activity highest in the hierarchy of the whole process, under which we can assign all activities related to the creation of a 3D model. It most often lasts several months, requires acquisition of funds, is carried out by several institutions covered by the partnership for a specific purpose with a foreseen result. Project may involve multiple **research activities** and may covered multiple **3D models**.
2. **Research activity** - The activity of carrying out scientific research on a single object. It may consist of archival research to find historical sources, taking measurements and

---

[13] Native file format of Blender by Blender Foundation.

[14] Native file format of Archicad by Graphisoft.

[15] Native file format of Cinema4D by MAXON COMPUTER GMBH.

[16] GL Transmission Format (GLTF) is a standard 3D file for three-dimensional scenes and models. It is open-source solution developed by Khronos Group.

[17] Wavefront is a geometry definition file format first developed by Wavefront Technologies for its Advanced Visualizer animation package.

[18] COLLADA is an interchange file format for interactive 3D applications, developed by the Khronos Group.

collecting information in the field, or digitising an existing site. The scientific activity should end with clear guidelines for modelling in terms of scope, quality, accuracy, or reliability of the study based on the source material collected and the administrative requirements of the **project**. A single research activity may produce multiple **3D models**, considering different variations of a single solution, or the progression of work overtime.

3. **Object** - an object that is the subject of a **project, research activity**, about which a **data set** is collected, and which is represented on **a 3D model**. It can be equally a physical existing object, a destroyed object or a concept represented by plans that have never been realised.

4. **Data Set** - a set of all collected material about the object, including historical sources, scientific publications, raw data, paradata, final files and **3D models** in a single **scientific activity** or **project**.

5. **3D Model** - A digital resource showing a specific **object**, providing a visual representation of the results of a **research activity** in three-dimensional space, created as part of the **project** and forming part of the **data set**.

6. **Publication** - Activity of publishing a **data set** or **3D model** on the web in a selected **repository**. It may (but need not) be carried out independently of the **project** and **research activity**, as part of a completely different activity

The elaboration of listed elements in terms of metadata is presented by Table 3. Three levels of complexity are distinguished to classify the repositories based on the target audience (basic, professional, advanced). Fields described in the table are based on a survey of metadata frameworks and schemas and research projects related to the topic [17–20]. Metadata fields for each level of complexity are described by the **name** (marked as bold text), which indicates field meaning, and datatype it represents (in blue color). Fields that do not directly describe any of the six listed elements above, requires assignation of a class attribute (in green color) instead of a datatype. The used classes and datatypes values are taken from the described schemas for structured data on the Internet by schema.org [21]. Fields with class attribute were given an additional attribute: "complexity" (in red color), to express the level of comprehensiveness of the field description in context. Four levels of complexity attribute were distinguished:

- **Identification:** A class shall be described in a minimal way allowing its identification by a single field of the text type;
- **Context:** a class description allows it to be identified in a more sophisticated way through the use of external identifiers, as well as containing additional information that defines its use in a given context, e.g. through described roles, types or relationships to other elements documented in the repository;
- **Reference:** while class is referred to the use of particular resource in context, the description should be prepared accord to the rules of bibliographic reference;
- **Record:** The class is described in a precise way, with metadata that not only allows the element to be identified in the context used, but also provides additional background information focusing on the broader view of the element.

Table 3. Definition of the metadata for the different categories related to the publication of a 3D digital heritage model in a three-level scale of comprehensiveness: basic, professional, and advanced.

	Basic	Professional[19]	Advanced[20]
Project	**-Title**, datatype:Text **-Description**, datatype:Text **-Start**, datatype:Date **-End**, datatype:Date **-Funds** class:Organization complexity:Identification **-Partners** class:Organization complexity:Identification	Increase of complexity level for **Funds** and **Partners** to "Context". **-Aims**, datatype:Text **-Website**, datatype:URL **-Participants** class:Person complexity:Context **-Contact** class:ContacPoint complexity:Identification	**-Final results** class:MediaObject complexity:Identification **-Object** class:Thing complexity:Context **-Data set (output)** class:DataSet complexity:Identification **-3D Model** class:3DModel complexity:Identification **-Research publications** class:CreativeWork complexity:Reference
Research Activity	**- Type**, datatype:Text **- Topic**, datatype:Text **-Participants** class:Person complexity:Identification **-Object** class:Thing complexity:Identification	Increase of complexity level for **Participants** and **Object** to "Context". **-Methods**, datatype:Text **-Project** class:Activity complexity:Context	**-Accuracy**, datatype:Text **-Uncertainty**, datatype:Text **-Data set (sources)** class:DataSet complexity:Context **-Data set (input)** class:DataSet complexity:Identification **-Data set (output)** class:DataSet complexity:Identification **-3D Models** class:3DModel complexity:Identification **-Research publications** class:CreativeWork complexity:Reference
Object	**-Title**, datatype:Text **-External Identifier**, datatype:URL **-Classification**, class:Class complexity:Identification **-Location** class:Place complexity:Identification	Increase of complexity level for **Classification** and **Location** to "Context". **-Description**, datatype:Text **-External Records**, class:WebPage complexity:Reference	complexity:Record *Full object record should additionally include the creators of the object, its history, and physical attributes such as current condition, dimensions, materials, etc.*
Data set	**-Title**, datatype:Text **-ID**, datatype:Text **-Publication** class: PublicationEvent complexity:Context **-Files** class:Mediaobject complexity:Identification	Increase of complexity level for **Files** to "Context" **-Description**, datatype:Text **-Holder** class:Agent complexity:Context **-Research activity** class:3Dmodel complexity:Identification	complexity:Record *Full data set record should describe the methods of obtaining the data set, the context in which it was obtained and the precise conditions of its possible use.*

(continued)

Table 3. (*continued*)

3D Model	-**Title**, datatype:Text -**Description**, datatype:Text	Increase of complexity level for **Creators** and **Object** to "Context".	-**Project** class:Activity complexity:Context
	-**Publication** class: PublicationEvent complexity:Context -**Specification** class:Property complexity:Record -**Creators** class:Creator complexity: Identification -**Object** class:Thing complexi- ty:Identification -**Visualization** class:Mediaobject complexity: Identification	-**Used Software**, datatype:text -**Used Device**, datatype:text -**Creation Date**, datatype:date	-**Data set (sources)** class:DataSet complexity:Context -**Data set (input)** class:DataSet complexity:Identification
		-**Participants** class:Participant complexity:Context -**Research activity** class:3DModel complexity:Context -**Data set (output)** class:DataSet complexity: Identification	
Publication	-**Publication Date** datatype:Date -**License**, datatype:Text	Increase of complexity level for **Publisher** and **3D Model** to "Context".	Increase of complexity level for and **3D Model** and **Data Set** to "Record".
	-**3D Model** class:3Dmodel complexity: Identification -**Publisher** class:Agent complexity: Identification	- **Terms of use**, datatype:Text -**Data Set** class:DataSet complexity:Identification	-**Data Record Reference:** datatype:URL -**Repository** class:WebPage complexity:Context

The resulting three-stage elaboration of metadata against the various elements associated with the publication of 3D models on the web gives an overview of the expansion of the various sections in relation to a diverse audience. This, however, does not catch the topic of matching metadata to the purpose of publishing on the web. For this reason, an additional study was developed in which the comprehensiveness of the documentation of individual elements was matched to the purpose of publication (visualization, reuse, monument record, documentation of scientific research, data aggregation) (see Table 4). In this way, documentation patterns were obtained that take into account both the purpose of the model's publication and the audience to which it is directed.

Table 4. Documentation patterns that determine the level of complexity of documentation of individual elements related to the publication of 3D models on the web in relation to the purpose of publication.

	Visualization	Reuse	Heritage Record	Scientific research	Data aggregation
Project	Not required	Not required	Basic	Advanced	Not required
Research Activity	Basic	Professional	Basic	Advanced	Basic
Object	Basic	Basic	Advanced	Professional	Professional
Data set	Not required	Basic	Professional	Advanced	Not required
3D Model	Basic	Advanced	Basic	Professional	Professional
Publication	Basic	Professional	Basic	Professional	Advanced

5   Conclusion

The surveys carried out made it possible to analyse the issues related to the documentation and publication of 3D models, demonstrating the barriers that hold the community back from developing standards in this area. Factors influencing the diversity of approaches to 3D model documentation on the web were identified, and an analysis of existing repositories from commercial and institutional offerings was conducted based on these factors. In parallel, a cooperative effort was launched with representatives of individual repositories.

The workshops and the research activity of the authors reveal promising findings for further development of standardization of the process of documentation and publication of digital 3D models of cultural heritage. The developed documentation patterns are intended to provide guidance for those entering the world of 3D repositories in terms of the complexity of documentation versus the goals of publication and the targeted audience. However, they do not constitute an exact study, which can be realized only after the completion of the joint efforts of the entire community on the issue of mapping the patterns and the open discussion about results.

Acknowledgements. The workshops on metadata for digital 3D heritage models were prepared as part of the project "DFG Viewer 3D – Infrastructure for digital 3D reconstructions" (2021–2023) funded by German Research Foundation (DFG), Funding code: MU 4040/5–1. Research on metadata and 3D repositories and infrastructures was conducted as a part of scholarship for 37th cycle for PhD students of Department of Architecture of University of Bologna. Administrative and organizational work on both workshops was supported DFG 3D-Viewer project team especially project manager Sander Münster and project coordinator Clemens Beck. Special thanks go to hosting institutions of first and second workshop: Hochschule Mainz – University of Applied Sciences and Ludwig Maximilian University of Munich together with organizers of the UHDL Workshop 2023.

I'd like to also acknowledge all presenters for their work on preparation of the workshop materials and fruitful discussions, representatives of the following projects:

1) IDOVIR: Jonas Bruschke, Marc Grellert, Markus Wacke, Daniel Beck;

2) baureka.online: Tobias Glitschke, Sophie Helas;

3) heidICON: Nicole Sobriel, Leonhard Maylein, ;

4) FID BAUdigital: Andreas Noback, Roger Winkler; Stephan Tittel;

5) NFDI4 Culture/Semantic Komapkkt: Lozana Rossenova, Zoe Schubert, Lucia Sohmen;

6) IIIF: Ronald Haynes;

6) CARAE: Kate Fernie;

8) Europeana: Henk Alkemade, Liana Heslinga.

References

1. Muenster, S.: Digital 3D technologies for humanities research and education: an overview. Appl. Sci. **12**, 2426 (2022). https://doi.org/10.3390/app12052426

2. Kuroczynski, P.: Virtual research environment for digital 3D reconstructions – Standards, thresholds and prospects. Stud. Digit. Herit. **1**, 456–476 (2017). https://doi.org/10.14434/sdh.v1i2.23330

3. Moore, J., Rountrey, A., Kettler, H.S.: 3D Data Creation to Curation: Community Standards for 3D Data Preservation. ACRL, Chicago, Illinois (2022)

4. Champion, E., Rahaman, H.: Survey of 3D digital heritage repositories and platforms. Virtual Archaeol. Rev. **11**, 1–15 (2020)

5. Fernie, K.: 3D Content in Europeana Task Force. Europeana Network Association Members Council, The Hague (2020)

6. Wilkinson, M.D., et al.: The fair guiding principles for scientific data management and stewardship. Sci. Data. **3**, 160018 (2016). https://doi.org/10.1038/sdata.2016.18

7. Golubiewski-Davis, K., et al.: Best practices for 3D data preservation. P In: 3D Data Creation to Curation: Community Standards for 3D Data Preservation, pp. 15–88. Association of College and Research Libraries, Chicago, Illinois (2021)

8. Blundell, J., Clark, J.L., Devet, K.E., Hardesty, J.L.: Metadata requirements for 3D data. In: 3D Data Creation to Curation: Community Standards for 3D Data Preservation, pp. 164–211. Association of College and Research Libraries, Chicago, Illinois (2021)

9. RDF - Semantic Web Standards. https://www.w3.org/RDF/. Accessed 27 May 2023

10. Bajena, I., Kuroczyński, P., Münster, S.: Metadata scheme for 3D reconstructions. How to capture the source–based 3D reconstruction of Cultural Heritage? In: CHNT 26, 2021-ABSTRACTS, CHNT Committee, Vienna (2021)

11. Hardesty, J., et al.: 3D Data Repository Features, Best Practices, and Implications for Preservation Models: Findings from a National Forum. (2020). https://doi.org/10.5860/crl.81.5.789

12. Community Standards for 3D Data Preservation (CS3DP): Selected Repositories. https://cs3dp.org/repositories/. Accessed 23 May 2023

13. The best sites to download free STL files, 3D models and 3D printable files for 3D printing, https://www.aniwaa.com/guide/3d-printers/best-sites-download-free-stl-files-3d-models-and-3d-printable-files-3d-printing/. Acessed 25 May 2023

14. Top 10 3D model databases. https://i.materialise.com/blog/en/3d-model-databases/. Accessed 25 May 2023

15. Best Websites for 3D Printing Models – 2022. https://www.obico.io/blog/best-3d-model-web sites-for-3d-printing/. Accessed 25 May 2023

16. Bajena, I., Dworak, D., Kuroczyński, P., Smolarski, R., Münster, S.: DFG 3D-viewer – development of an infrastructure for digital 3D reconstructions. In: DH2022 Conference Abstracts, DH2022 Local Organizing Committee, Tokyo (2022)

17. LIDO Schema v1.1. http://www.lido-schema.org/. Accessed 26 May 2023
18. SARI Documentation, https://docs.swissartresearch.net/. Accessed 26 May 2023
19. Dublin Core Metadata Terms. https://www.dublincore.org/specifications/dublin-core/dcmi-terms/. Accessed 26 May 2023
20. Basic data set 1: mandatory data for analogue output objects. https://www.dfg.de/formulare/12_155/index.jsp. Accessed 26 May 2023
21. Schema.org, https://schema.org/. Accessed 26 May 2023

Towards Querying Multimodal Annotations Using Graphs

Jonas Bruschke[1]([⊠]) [iD], Cindy Kröber[2] [iD], Ronja Utescher[2],
and Florian Niebling[1,3] [iD]

[1] University of Würzburg, Würzburg, Germany
{jonas.bruschke,florian.niebling}@uni-wuerzburg.de
[2] Friedrich-Schiller-Universität Jena, Jena, Germany
{cindy.kroeber,ronja.utescher}@uni-jena.de
[3] Hochschule Fulda, Fulda, Germany
florian.niebling@informatik.hs-fulda.de

Abstract. Photographs and 3D reconstructions of buildings as well as textual information and documents play an important role in art history and architectural studies when it comes to investigating architecture, the construction history of buildings, and the impact these constructions had on a city. Advanced tools have the potential to enhance and support research workflows and source criticism by linking corresponding materials and annotations, such that relevant data can be quickly queried and identified. Images are a primary source in the 3D reconstruction process, with the possibility to create spatializations of additional photographs of buildings which were not part of the initial SfM process, enabling the linking of annotations between these photographs and the respective 3D model. In contrast, identifying and locating respective annotations in text sources requires a different approach due to their more abstract nature. This paper presents concepts for automatic linking of texts and their respective annotations to corresponding images, as well as to 3D models and their annotations. Controlled vocabularies for architectural elements and a graph representation are utilized to reduce ambiguity when querying related instances.

Keywords: Digital Humanities · Annotations · Vocabularies · Knowledge Graph

1 Introduction

Photographs and other images as well as textual information and documents serve as important source materials and provide a foundation for many subject-orientated and theory-based investigations within historical studies, e.g., architectural studies, art history, and cultural studies. Among other scenarios, the sources may be used for (digital) reconstruction or to investigate different buildings, their construction history, and the impact they had on a city. A lot of

---

The original version of this chapter was revised: The error in Fig. 5 has been corrected. The correction to this chapter is available at
https://doi.org/10.1007/978-3-031-38871-2_16

S. Münster et al. (Eds.): UHDL 2023, CCIS 1853, pp. 65–87, 2023.
https://doi.org/10.1007/978-3-031-38871-2_5

sources are needed to get a thorough understanding of a building. Searching for images and texts but also the contextualization and the evaluation of these heterogenous data types can prove challenging.

The 4D Browser is already an innovative and unique research tool with the ability to search for such relevant data [17]. With the city of Dresden as use case, about 2,300 historical photos are spatialized within a digital 3D city model (Fig. 1). This allows users to search for images spatio-temporally, i.e., they do not need to rely on the images' metadata only as in common image repositories. Due to the spatial relation between the images and the 3D models as representatives of the buildings, it can be determined which buildings are visible on which image. Additional annotations present in the images and in the 3D models, e.g. 2D image segmentation or 3D architectural components, can be projected from image to 3D model, and vice versa [41] (cf. Fig. 2). Hence, there are explicit links between instances of 2D images and 3D models leading to implicit links between images depicting either the same building, or even only parts of the same building.

Next to photographs, textual information and documents are another important source for art and architectural historical research. To further enhance and support the source criticism of the researchers, our aim is to find and show images that depict content that is described in sections of the texts. Due to their abstract nature however, texts cannot be represented and oriented in a three-dimensional space. Hence, any annotation cannot be spatially projected directly onto images or 3D models, i.e., automatically linking instances of texts, images, and 3D models remain challenging. Simply querying common metadata may remain insufficient, while considering the spatial and semantic contexts and looking for their similarity can enhance the search results [9].

Fig. 1. Interface of the 4D Browser showing spatio-temporal photographs in a 3D city model.

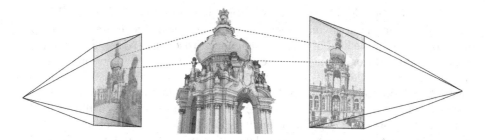

Fig. 2. Annotations of spatialized images can be projected to 3D models and vice versa.

This paper presents concepts on how texts and their annotations can be linked automatically to corresponding images and 3D models and their respective annotations utilizing controlled vocabularies and graphs.

2   Related Work

The Urban History 4D research project is developing a 3D web environment to enable researchers to search and access historical photographic images in spatial contexts [11,17]. During automated Structure-from-Motion (SfM) workflows, photographs of historical buildings are spatialized with respect to 3D models of buildings [40], linking keypoints in images to 3D objects, allowing images to be used as textures for models [39,47] and enabling spatial browsing of the photographic source material [48].

Annotations in general have various application scenarios. Within textual documents, it is common to track changes to the text, and also apply semantic annotation. Some annotations merely provide further information on the content, where speech tagging consists of annotating each word in a sentence to distinguish whether a word is a noun, a verb, an adjective, and so on [29]. Annotations for images often classify parts of an image for image retrieval, or apply visual metadata like circles etc. to emphasize a certain point. Previous projects have focused on annotation within image archives to support scientific research [3].

Usually, annotations are enhanced with metadata relating to existing content and also clarifying properties and semantics of the annotated content. This is also the way we view annotations necessary to match different types of data. Existing data like text understandable only to people is complemented with semantic metadata which computers can process in order to allow for automation, integration, and reuse of data across various applications [26]. Therefore, annotations have to conform to certain specifications which define the structure, the semantics, the syntax, and even the values of the annotations [2]. They deal with a subject and an object and provide the connecting relation and context [49]. The annotations and annotated objects need to be uniquely identified and linked [2]. There is also a temporal aspect to annotations, especially when they can change adding new insights and data.

Text annotation is, in our case, the semantic enrichment of texts. Widely used in digital humanities, most methods of automatically generated text annotation originate in the field of Natural Language Processing (NLP). For example, Named Enitity Recognition (NER) can be used to retrieve mentions of people and institutions and has been evaluated or fine-tuned on historical documents [20]. More generally, large language models and their ability to extract abstract semantic representation of text lend themselves to custom-defined text classification [8,46,60]. Traditionally, classification of text elements using machine learning approaches requires labeled training data, but this is increasingly bypassed using abstract semantic information provided by general language models [5].

Thesauri and controlled vocabularies in general are used to classify entities in various domains. These vocabularies are generally organized as hierarchies, from generic to specific concepts. They use identifiers agnostic to language, and often provide multilingual labels [4]. In digital cultural heritage research, the Getty Art & Architecture Thesaurus (AAT) is a major domain-specific resource. The AAT is a faceted thesaurus, meaning that it contains a small number of facets such as physical attributes or objects which contain separate hierarchies [27]. It is also particularly notable due to its exhaustiveness in its domain. In comparison, Wikidata is a huge knowledge base not only implementing a hierarchical classification scheme, but also an ontology storing semantic relationships between the entities [58]. It is increasingly used in the cultural heritage domain [54] and is in many instances linked with domain-specific vocabularies such as the AAT. The class identifiers that are attached to entities can be used to match a pair or a whole set of entities [33]. López et al. [38] annotates 3D models in a HBIM context with identifiers of the AAT for a more efficient retrieval of information.

In NLP, different approaches exist to semantically enrich text. Mirza et al. [44] extract counting quantifiers to further enrich relations between identifiable entities. The semantics of spatial relations can also be captured and encoded to reconstruct the positioning of objects in 2D/3D space [34,51].

Recommendation systems play an important role not only in e-commerce and social networks, but also in many other application fields [30]. Their key task is to filter information to "provide suggestions for items that are most likely of interest to a particular user" [53] and, thus, to support the decision making of the user. Basically, any data and knowledge can be used as source for recommendation. This can be metadata about the item or user including the contents such as images, and the interaction, i.e., the relationships between users and items (e.g., rating a product). There are two major categories of recommendation systems: *Content-based filtering* tries to find items that are similar to those that the user interacted with in the past. *Collaborative filtering* tries to recommend items that other users with similar interests and behavior interacted with. In literature, there are also mentioned community-based, knowledge-based, as well as hybrid systems [53], which are special variants of the first two categories. The key is how the features of interest are compared against each other to compute a similarity measure to eventually recommend those items with a high similarity value. The toolbox to achieve this objective is extensive: from similarity functions like the Euclidean distance as well as Jaccard and Pearson coefficients to approaches like k-Nearest Neighbors (kNN) [18], clustering, and matrix factorization (i.e., evaluate item features and store them as vectors, usually referred to as embeddings) [31] to neural networks [30].

Graph matching is a fundamental problem in computer science and has many application fields [61]. Finding exact graphs or subgraphs (graph isomorphism) is a rather small topic. In most real-world use cases, inexact weighted graph matching plays a bigger role. The challenge is to match non-identical graphs by "finding an optimal correspondence between the vertices [...] to minimize [...] their node and edge disagreements (affinities)" [61]. Graph embeddings are one (but not only) important method to create a baseline for further algorithms, such as similarity functions, machine learning approaches, and others [36]. Multiple attributes including node properties and relationships can be encoded in low-dimensional vectors that represent the node in the graph [15,25,50]. Based on these embeddings, similar nodes can be found with similarity functions (e.g., cosine, Euclidean, Pearson) and kNN. Chatzakis et al. [14] creates embeddings on RDF triples from a Linked Open Data database combined with cosine similarity function to browse similar entries.

3 Relevance and User Scenarios for Research in Art History

3.1 Research and Source Criticism in Art History

Source research and source criticism are essential and time-consuming when conducting research in art history. Annotations for sources have the capabilities to support these complex steps. Incorporating the approach might even strengthen source criticism and argumentation and enhance reliability, trustworthiness and accuracy of interpretations and analysis through offering a tool to verify initial ideas, apply numeric analysis, eliminate bias, and ensure a reproducibility.

Annotations can provide and link information on a source's external aspects like naming, dating, localizing and attributing a document as well as internal aspects related to the content, conventions, internal coherence and intention of the document [52] functioning as a kind of metadata. AI has the potential of assigning and even adding annotations dynamically once new findings or data come into play continuously filling in missing information and growing the data sets. Most online search and filtering algorithms rely on possible flawed metadata [6,37]. Hence, organizing and categorizing with the help of annotations instead of metadata is immensely beneficial for retrieval and search of sources especially within large collections and repositories.

When dealing with sources, understanding the context is of particular importance and a central point of consideration. Connected to this contextualization is the need to recognize an importance related to the initial creation and dissemination of an object or source [52]. This is especially useful in assessing reliability and intentions. Also, the credibility and reliability of the author of a source needs to be considered to evaluate the author's knowledge on the subject as well as his attitude and potential biases. Computer linguistics offers many approaches for analyzing text which can provide annotations on language, tone, and rhetoric to identify potential biases, agendas, or underlying motivations of the authors as well as omissions, contradictions, or exaggerations that may influence the interpretation. However, adding a subsequent structure to a continuous text will not do, since the researcher will usually consider the whole source. But it might be helpful to incorporate keywords for topics covered by the text. This can indicate if a source comprises the desired information on, e.g., architecture, or if further search is necessary to satisfy the need.

Interpretation of sources can be aided by intertextualizing them with other sources and multimodal data. Besides the broader environment that surrounds a source, it is also a goal to investigate its "traces in a web of intertextual meanings" [28]. Therefore, the methodology of contextual analysis asks the researcher to verify his interpretations by showing that it can be found in other sources. Through annotation researchers can be assisted in developing a comprehensive understanding of the data considering significant details and mention of stylistic elements as well as cultural and historical contexts that are explained. Multimodal data often consists of different types of information, such as images, text, audio, video and even 3D models. Annotations can provide links or associations between these different modalities, allowing researchers to establish connections and explore relationships between them. By assigning annotations to sources, related information can be directly connected making the search for relevant information much faster. Furthermore, annotations and labels can be visualized alongside multimodal data to enhance the presentation and interpretation and speed up comprehension. This can be achieved by highlighting relevant passages of text or adding tags at certain positions as well as emphasizing specific areas in images and 3D models.

Usually, comparison in art history is used to date an object with the help of similar ones or to identify a style, creator or even just the period of creation. In a comparative study multiple sources related to a subject of investigation are also analyzed and compared in order to identify any discrepancies, inconsistencies, inaccuracies, manipulations or biases [1]. Annotations can support researchers in comparing and analyzing multiple instances of data to identify common characteristics, themes, patterns, or attributes across different data sources. This approach can help to gain insights that might not be apparent from analyzing each modality in isolation. Additionally, access to a variety of sources can facilitate discovery of changes like building restorations or alterations.

Not only the creator of an art piece is relevant when reconstructing its history. Provenance research investigates the origin and ownership history of the artwork or primary source, including its previous owners, exhibition history, and documentation [22]. The connection of multimodal data through annotations makes it easier to trace or track an object or document. Especially for images it is relevant to certify the qualities of a reproduction and link between the original and the copy as well as understand the path taken from the author or sponsor of a photograph to its inclusion on a repository or site.

Data and knowledge sharing among scholars is ubiquitous and annotations can further promote collaboration for researchers working with multimodal data. By sharing annotated data sets, scholars can contribute to a collective pool of knowledge adding their peer-reviewed relevant publications and data, exchanging insights, and building upon each other's research. Annotations also enable others to understand the researcher's thought process and engage in constructive dialogue.

3.2   Specific User Scenarios for the 4D Browser

User scenarios are narrative descriptions of a user interacting with a system to achieve a specific goal. It usually elaborates on motivation, behavior, and context of the user. The aim is to better understand user needs, requirements, and expectations, inform design decisions and validate the usability. It helps to identify potential issues as well as necessary features and improvements.

The 4D Browser offers several features to investigate sources and approach research questions. Three specific scenarios will highlight the potential of linking multimodal data through annotations for art historical research. For the purpose of the project and the sake of efficiency, we selected a monumental palatial building from which we own a detailed 3D model and have access to several scholarly publications and texts as well as a large collection of (historical) photographs from the Saxon State and University Library Dresden (SLUB) with some images already geo-referenced within the 3D city model of the 4D Browser. The site is the Zwinger and its associated buildings located near the royal residence in Dresden, Germany. Besides its visual appeal, the Zwinger is also one of the most iconic Baroque buildings in the world, featuring a complex history of destruction and reconstruction. The scenarios focus on simple but realistic research questions concerning the Zwinger.

Investigating a Certain Architectural Element. A potential goal is to investigate a specific architectural element: a sculpture right by the Kronentor of the Zwinger in Dresden. Related research questions might be: Where can you find the sculpture? Who created it and when? What or who is depicted? Why were the motif and position chosen? How was or is the sculpture perceived and how does it work in the context of the building and area? Are there similar or other sculptures worth researching, maybe within the building, of a similar motif, or by the same creator? Is the current sculpture the original or a copy? Has it always been at this location, or has it been moved?

The starting point is the architectural element – the sculpture – within the 3D model. After locating the element in the virtual model, it is possible to use a filtering feature of the 4D Browser to display geo-referenced images that correspond to the selected object. This can be achieved through a projection of the images onto the 3D model. Once a sufficient image was found, it can be used

len beugen sich mit dem vollen Volumen ihrer Körper unter dem Balkon vor. Sie lösen sich von der Architektur und bleiben dennoch an sie gefesselt. Diese Betonung der angespannten Körper übernahm Permoser bei seinen Hermen um so mehr, als sie seinen Vorstellungen entsprach. Hat man das erkannt, dann spürt man auch die Verwandtschaft mit dem schweren, schattenreichen Dekor der Schäfte: Die flächig gelegten, tieffaltigen Lendentücher und die Muschel als Abschluß sind in Toulon wie in Dresden vorhanden und auch in Berlin taucht schon das Muschelmotiv auf. Die Kenntnis von Toulon muß also früher, doch wohl nach Rom, dennoch in der italienischen Zeit erfolgt sein.

Aber Permoser ist der jüngere Meister. Bei aller Körperschwere gibt der aufwärts strömende Bewegungszug der Dresdner Hermen eine neue Leichtigkeit, ein Schwingen und Schweben, das dem älteren Puget in seiner spannungsstarken Dramatik noch versagt blieb.

Unter den zahlreichen *Faunskonsolen*, die sehr wahrscheinlich erst beim Bau des Wallpavillons unter die Galeriefenster eingefügt wurden, fällt ein Faun, der an der westlichen Ecke zum Wallpavillon, beson-

mit seinen Meistern zu zeigen, wie er's meinte. Der späteren Einfügung der Konsolen in den Verband der Galerien zur Zeit der Errichtung des Wallpavillons um 1716/1718 entspricht auch der enge stilistische Zusammenhang der Faunskonsole mit der Skulptur des Wallpavillons. Man kann die Entstehung der Faunskonsole um 1716/1718 ansetzen.

Anders als die Satyrhermen, als der Herkules und der Faun sind die *Götter am Kronentor* mit der Architektur verbunden *(W, 79).* Sie trägt, die ihren Reichtum schon durch vervielfachte Pilaster, durch Simse und Säulen entfaltet hat, noch einen Schleier voller Ornamentik: Blütenbüsche, Fruchtgehänge, Konsolen. Insoweit fügen sich die Statuen dem dekorativen Gesamtbild ein. Mag auch *Ceres (W. 79, Abb. 232-234)* dem allen sich zuordnen in schmückendem Reichtum, mit Diadem und Spangen, vielgefaltetem Gewand mit ausgebogtem Saum, dazu noch mit der betont ziselierenden Art der Meißelführung, die die Ähren als kostbare Perlenschnüre erscheinen läßt – sie ist mehr noch: Sie erscheint als vollgültige Statue, als Monument und dafür gab ihr die Architektur, wie auch den zu ihr gehörenden anderen Göttern den ausgegrenzten Raum der Nische.

Fig. 3. Example for multimodal research based on annotations: image of the Kronentor with a variety of annotated architectural elements together with a descriptive text on the design. Image: © SLUB/Deutsche Fotothek/Wolff, Paul (1876). Text: Asche, S.: Balthasar Permoser. Leben und Werk (1978)

to look for identical images with TinEye search or Google's image search which allows the internet user to find sites with an identical image. External websites can help to clarify what the sculpture depicts and will probably provide more information on the sculpture by itself. To retrieve usually more important textual resources relevant for the research on the sculpture, it is currently necessary to annotate the texts within the 4D Browser beforehand. Any sources with annotations corresponding to the word "sculpture" or other identified keywords will be relevant as well as texts connected to the retrieved images (Fig. 3). A more specific annotation will help to reduce search results. Text-image connections are based on, e.g., annotations of textual descriptions related to the images and specific terms indicating the location of the element. The textual information usually reveals more on the object like a description of what is depicted and can provide more search terms. The additional keywords can help to identify other relevant sources. The search for the sculpture can go on and lead to creators, clients, architectural styles, city history etc. It can also uncover that a sculpture has been moved to the current place from a different building and therefore is not original to the Zwinger. The whole setup is dynamic, so that new data can be included anytime. It is important to emphasize that this approach does not dependent on metadata or image captions.

An exhaustive list of all sculptures of the Zwinger was created for a dissertation [19]. This straightforward process of identifying sculptures in the 3D model can help to complement the inventory and provide a spatialized overview which can gradually be filled and updated with more information. This has potential to become a very valuable research contribution presenting new finding and linking information.

Detecting a Structural Change. Very often, older buildings have been subjects to renovations or reconstructions with different degrees of modification.

Fig. 4. Kronentor of the Zwinger in Dresden before (1937) and after (1946) destruction during the war. © SLUB/Deutsche Fotothek/Möbius, Walter, © SLUB/Deutsche Fotothek/Heinrich, Gertrud

Investigating when and what has been changed is tedious. Reasons for a reconstruction as well as who planned and executed it are also important. The Zwinger in Dresden had to undergo greater reconstruction efforts after the destruction during the war (Fig. 4). At present, the Zwinger is again under reconstruction with a focus on the fountains and green spaces. The 4D Browser with the large number of geo-referenced images and a timeline functionality offers a great tool to examine structural changes of buildings. Currently, a feature is in development that automatically detects changes in images. The structure is of course annotated in the corresponding images and can therefore be a starting point for retrieval of textual information either through the annotations within the 4D Browser or with the help of identified keywords and external search engines.

This approach also offers a method to investigate if statues and sculptures have been replaced for only a short time due to reconstruction efforts or if the changes are long-term because a structure was destroyed. Any textual resources will of course provide more information on the whereabouts and fate of an element.

Researching Stylistically Similar Objects. Comparison is an incredibly important method in art history research. A goal can be to study the development of an artist through his works or to discover the inspiration behind a certain building. Matthäus Daniel Pöppelmann, the architect of the Zwinger, undertook many trips for the purpose of architectural studies and to absorb project-related stimuli and comparative impressions. A trip to Apeldoorn in the Netherlands lead him to Het Loo Palace, which has long wings and pavilion-like corner buildings similar to the Zwinger. In many cases, the biography or list of work of an artist or architect will provide necessary names and places. Therefore, at the beginning, a retrieval of relevant texts on the person is required. Either only places and objects are named calling for further search with the new keywords or the texts include descriptions linked to images via annotations which can be compared visually.

4   Storing Multimodal Annotations

The main content consists of text sources, images, and 3D models representing the buildings. These instances and their metadata can be stored conform to the CIDOC CRM [7], an ontology in the field of cultural heritage and museum applications. An ontology consists of entities, i.e., nodes, and semantic relationships between them. Applying the CIDOC CRM for describing images and buildings quickly becomes complex, because every metadata can form a chain of multiple nodes. For example, an image and all its metadata can be described by up to 18 nodes. The photographer, the place and the date taken, as well as the used camera are linked to the image (*E36 Visual Item*) by a *E65 Creation Event* counting already eight nodes. Texts (*E33 Linguistic Object*) are structured very similar, since both entities are immaterial, conceptual objects. In contrast, buildings are considered as *E22 Human-Made Object* having construction and destruction dates and a reference to a digital 3D model (*D1 Digital Object*).

In our paper, we refer to the term *annotation* as segmentation of a media associated with additional information, i.e., specifying what is outlined by the segmentation. Annotations are defined differently in each type of source: Text sources are one-dimensional, hence, annotations only need a start and end point to encircle a phrase. Sections of 2D images are defined by polygons. A 3D model can be segmented by splitting it up into sub-objects or defining additional geometry that comprises the volume of interest. Despite of different definitions of the sections, the semantic link is always the same: any annotation is a part of the whole media item. In terms of the CIDOC CRM, this can be described by a *P148 has component* relationship between the text, image, or 3D model instance and the annotation. The annotation node defining the segmentation would be an intermediate node referring to the associated information (cf. Fig. 5).

Structuring thousands of entities this way creates a complex network of information making it predestined to be stored in a graph database enabling fast querying across multiple relationships [12]. Basically, this can be mapped to a Linked Open Data format for publicly accessing the enhanced metadata.

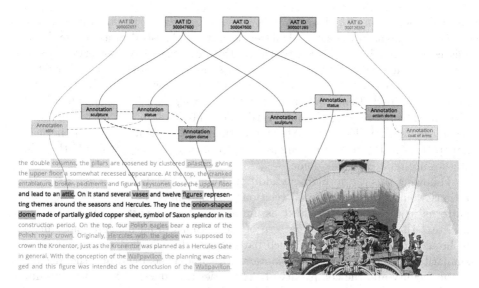

Fig. 5. Concept of linking annotations and identifiers beyond different types of sources. In this example, the statues, sculptures, and the dome spatially relate to each other as represented by the dashed lines.

5   Contextualizing and Querying Annotations

To find a related text to an image or vice versa, only a simple link between the instances is sufficient. However, if a more in-depth analysis of the text and corresponding images is required, these source materials need to be annotated and those annotations need to be linked that refer to each other. Since architecture is central to our text and image collections, our approach is to first identify instances of architectural elements and map them to controlled vocabularies and their identifiers [57], namely the Getty Art & Architecture Thesaurus (AAT) and Wikidata. These vocabularies define a hierarchy of concepts from general to specific elements, using language-agnostic identifiers [4]. The identification of the architectural elements and thus the annotation of the different types of media can be achieved by utilizing, e.g., NLP methods for texts [21,32] and computer vision and machine learning for images [23,43] as well as 3D models (via point clouds) [16,24,45]. However, this challenge is not subject of this paper. Especially the segmentation of architectural elements using AI-based methods requires extensive training datasets that also include more domain-specific elements and support various architectural styles. Instead, it is preconditioned that the media items are already equipped with annotations pointing to respective identifiers of architectural elements. To this end, a test dataset has been set up to include automatically annotated texts and manually annotated images and 3D models [10].

In the example of Fig. 5, multiple architectural elements including various statues, sculptures, and the dome of the Kronentor of the Zwinger in Dresden,

Germany were annotated in different types of sources. The statues identified in the text point to the same identifier as statues identified in an image. From this connection, it can be inferred that this text may have something to do with the image. But this connection is very ambiguous: there may be a lot of statues being part of the whole building, it is not clear which specific statues are meant in the text. Hence, a match of single annotations will not be sufficient to retrieve valuable results. In this regard, the context of an annotation needs to be considered, i.e., looking at the annotations in the vicinity. One of the next annotations in the text is an onion-shaped dome. It is more probable that the statues are related to this dome.

Following this assumption, an additional analysis of the media and its annotations would create additional relationships and information forming specific patterns in the graph. The next assumption is that a pattern of annotations in a text that is similar to a pattern of annotations in an image is more likely to be about the same objects. Such patterns can be matched utilizing a set of similarity algorithms in a graph context. Multiple levels regarding the analysis of the vicinity and the complexity of the queries are conceivable in order to find relevant data.

5.1   Unweighted

If a media has multiple annotations, these annotations are initially not yet connected to each other explicitly. Instead, they are only linked implicitly via the media. A first approach to query similar annotations while also considering the other annotations in a media is to take all annotations attached to a media into account equally. The similarity between two media items could be computed with the Jaccard index, i.e., the ratio of intersection over union, by comparing the quality and quantity of the different identifiers corresponding with the annotations (Fig. 6). For this purpose, the corresponding identifiers, which are stored as separate nodes (cf. Fig. 5), are set as a property of the annotation nodes reducing the complexity of the graph and making these nodes easier to compare.

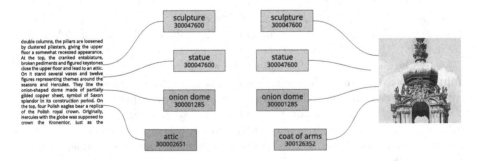

Fig. 6. Media items may be closer related to each other, the greater the overlap is between the type and quantity of the corresponding annotations.

Of course, this approach has some disadvantages. Only a subset of annotations in a text, image, or 3D model may occur in the search media. Especially texts, but also 3D models can be quite extensive and images may reference only a small part of them. If there are a lot identifiers that are missing in one of the comparing media items or the number of same identifiers diverges, it will have a negative impact on the similarity index. Hence, this approach would only get valid results when the media items roughly comprises the same content.

5.2 Spatial Distance Weight

Not all parts of a text, an image, or a 3D model are equally relevant for a section of interest. In fact, texts for example can be very long, many paragraphs may be about a completely different topic. The assumption is that only the annotations nearby are relevant or somehow related to each other. Therefore, the media also needs to be analyzed spatially at least once. In images and 3D models, neighboring annotations relate more to each other than annotations further away. This can be determined by simply measuring the distance between the annotations, either pixel-wise in images or within the corresponding coordinate space of the 3D model. This distance can be either the closest distance between the boundaries of two annotations or the distance between the centers of both annotations.

Similarly, this can be also applied to texts. Without taking into account any semantics of the words in between, there could be different approaches: a) determining the number of words in between (cf. Fig. 7), b) considering only annotations within the same phrase or paragraph, or c) a combination of a) and b) (e.g., the number of in-between words, but if the annotations are in different sentences, it would be considered as a greater distance).

The distance were measured in different units, because the types of media are very different. Hence, the distance values need to be normalized to make them comparable. Theoretically, the distances of annotations of spatialized images could be aligned to the coordinate space of the corresponding 3D model by projection. In general, this normalization needs to be empirically determined to find the right balance.

For this approach, the annotations of a media would be linked explicitly to each other, i.e., an additional relationship in the graph. The respective distance would be attached to this relationship as a weight value (Fig. 7). The relationship is bidirectional, because the distance is the same regardless from where to start measuring. However, the relationship will only be created if a maximum distance threshold is not exceeded. The query for similar annotation nodes can now be accomplished by looking for nodes with equivalent properties (i.e., identifier) and similar neighboring nodes considering the weights at the same time. This can be accomplished by creating embeddings for each node based on their attributes and relationship to neighboring nodes and executing kNN algorithm on these embeddings.

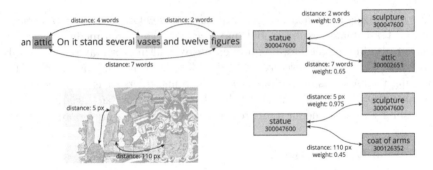

Fig. 7. Concept of measuring the distance between annotations: For texts, the number of words in between the annotations is taken. For images, the closest distance between two annotations is measured in pixels. In this example, the distances are normalized to weights by using a maximum distance threshold of 20 words for texts and 200 pixels for images.

5.3 Indication of Quantity

Occasionally, there are accumulations of the same type of architectural elements. In an image or 3D model, each instance would optimally be a single annotation in the media. In contrast, there might be only one occurrence in a text resulting in only one annotation. Instead, this occurrence is prefixed by a quantifier semantically inferring multiple instances. This can be an explicit number (e.g., *four, 12*) or an ambiguous indication like *some, several, multiple*. Those quantifiers need to be identified [44] and transformed into additional annotation nodes (Fig. 8). Since elements were mentioned in the text as a compound, the assumption is that they are spatially close to each other. Hence, the additional nodes are linked to each other with a relative high weight indicating a close distance (cf. Sec. 5.2).

Fig. 8. Text annotations prefixed with quantifiers result in additional annotation nodes. In this example, the prefix *twelve* leads to eleven additional nodes of type *statue*. The ambiguous *several* prefix adds three *sculpture* nodes. All these nodes are linked to each other with a spatial distance weight. However for simplicity, the relations are shown for only one annotation node.

For ambiguous quantifiers, it is not clear how many additional nodes should be added. So, this can only be an estimation. Nevertheless, adding a few more nodes should be more accurate than only one single annotation node, which should increase node similarity. Whereas the number of instances may be identified well in texts and 3D models, images that show only a certain perspective of the architecture will possibly depict only a subset of them. This would decrease node similarity.

5.4   Encoding Spatial Relations

The spatial distance weight already takes greater account of annotations within the vicinity. The results can be further narrowed down by analyzing the orientation of these annotations to each other. Spatial relations are conveyed in a wide range of natural language expressions. Terms such as *left, right, above, beneath, in front, behind, east, south*, etc. can be used to identify spatial proximity. On the NLP side, approaches like Shin et al. [55] can be used to extract spatial information from text. In combination with the classification of architectural elements in the text, this can yield information about the relative physical positions and orientations of said elements. Similarly in the image and the 3D model, it can be determined which annotations spatially relate to each other taking into account where the contents are located within the image and 3D model with respect to their position and orientation. These spatial relations between the annotations need to be encoded and stored so that they are comparable.

One approach to encode these relations is using vectors indicating the direction and distance from one to the other annotation. For geo-referenced 3D models, these vectors can be three-dimensional Cartesian coordinates. Terms like *above, beneath, east*, or *south* are universal, i.e., they are independent of any perspective. They can also be expressed in 3D vectors, however with uncertain distance. Annotations of spatialized images can be mapped to the corresponding 3D model and, thus, their spatial relations can also be transferred to 3D vectors.

The spatial relations between annotations of images that have not been spatialized and terms like *left, right, in front*, or *behind* heavily depend on the perspective, which would be only hard to infer within a computational analysis step. Hence, they cannot be expressed as 3D vectors. Due to these multiple obstacles, only two dimensions can be inferred for all types of media: a vertical dimension with the range $-1..1$ indicating if an annotation is above or below, and a horizontal dimension with the range $0..1$ only indicating if the annotations are within a common horizontal plane.

Since the resulting vectors can have different directions, a vector is only valid for one annotation. For the corresponding annotation, the opposite direction is inferred by negating the vertical component of the vector and is stored as separate relationship. Consequently, only outgoing relationships need to be considered for querying similar nodes. This time, multiple weights exist for a relationship: a distance weight and a direction weight. Both weights need to be considered when creating node embeddings in order to find similar nodes.

representing themes around the seasons and Hercules. They line the onion-shaped dome made of partially gilded copper sheet, symbol of Saxon splendor in its construction period. On the top, four Polish eagles bear a replica of the Polish royal crown. Originally, Hercules with the globe was

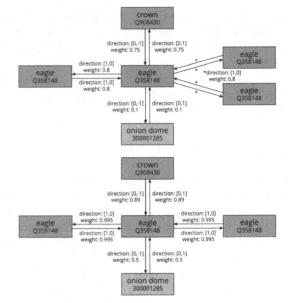

Fig. 9. Horizontal and vertical relations can be determined well in images. In texts, these relations are expressed by words: The eagles are *on the top* of the dome. The term *bear* also implies a vertical relation between the eagles and the crown. The quantifier *four* implies multiple instances of *eagle* that are considered as horizontally related, whereas in the image, only three of them are visible. These relations are stored as vector property on unidirectional edges between the corresponding annotation nodes.

The example in Fig. 9 shows that spatial relations are not only described by terms like *left*, *above*, etc., but also by less usual verbs like *bear* implying a vertical relation. Those texts about architecture are no technical instructions, but well expressed articles usually written by humanities scholars. A deeper understanding of the text is needed to fully locate all annotations in a 3D (or at least 2D) space. Due to the variety of how spatial relations can be expressed in words, only a small subset of them will probably be identified in the text. This raises the question how annotations should be compared by means of similarity if no spatial relations could be detected.

5.5   Semantic Similarity

Until now, only annotations with the same identifiers as the query annotation and its neighbors were considered. However, some elements might have been identified differently, although they represent the same. For example, an annotation representing a *statue* in one media could have been annotated by the similar term *figure* in another media. The identifiers are completely different, because they are categorical. But semantically, they are related to each other.

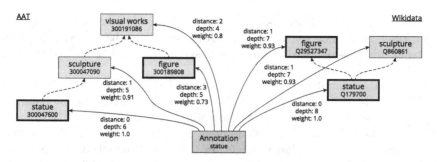

Fig. 10. The Getty Art & Architecture Thesaurus (AAT) is structured differently than Wikidata: the hierarchical distance between the classes *statue* and *figure* is 3 for the AAT, whereas in Wikidata, *figure* is one of the parent classes of *statue* resulting in a distance of 1. The weight is computed using Eq. 2 considering the depth of the elements in the respective hierarchy.

This relation is also expressed in the hierarchy of the vocabularies, resp. ontologies (Fig. 10). If two annotations share the same identifier for an architectural element, the distance is 0. If one annotation is identified by a broader term (i.e., parent class) than another annotation, the distance is 1. With each additional step, the distance increases and thus the semantic similarity decreases. Similar to the spatial distance (Sec. 5.2), the distance needs to be normalized to a weight value.

Knowledge bases in general can be utilized to determine the semantic similarity between two terms [13]. The similarity measure can be used as weight value for the relation between annotation and vocabulary entry. Taking two terms in a vocabulary, the similarity can be simply calculated by measuring the hierarchical distance, i.e., shortest path length, and using its inverse (Eq. 1) [13]. In this case, the similarity is proportional to the distance. However, two entries deeper down the hierarchy have in general a more specific meaning and, hence, being presumably more similar to each other, whereas two entries representing a more generic concept can have the same distance to each other [13]. Wu et al. [59] proposes a similarity measure that considers the depth of the entries including the depth of the least common ancestor in the hierarchy of the knowledge base (Eq. 2). This results in a higher similarity between two concepts with same path distance if they are deeper down in the hierarchy. Li et al. [35] proposes another formula taking the shortest path length and the depth into account and claiming that the measure is close to individual human judgment.

$$sim_1(t_1, t_2) = \frac{1}{1 + min\_len(t_1, t_2)} \tag{1}$$

$$sim_2(t_1, t_2) = \frac{2 * depth(t_{lca})}{depth(t_1) + depth(t_2)} \tag{2}$$

The AAT and Wikidata are structured differently, which may lead to different similarity measures for same pairs of terms (Fig. 10). At best, an annotation is referenced with the identifiers of both vocabularies. In case of diverging similarity, the higher value would be used. Other knowledge bases, resp. linguistic ontologies, where semantic relations such as synonyms could be queried from are WordNet [42] and ConceptNet [56].

Next to the spatial distance, this analysis of the semantic similarity adds another dimension to the graph and the resulting query. On the one hand, an annotation node is connected to other annotation nodes with a spatial distance weight. On the other hand, the same node is connected to multiple identifier nodes with a semantic similarity weight. In this case, two embeddings per node can be computed, each encoding its specific neighborhood. Both can then be used to determine the node similarity between two annotations.

6   Conclusion

The most important benefit for art historical research is the possibility to link multimodal data and therefore support a thorough and prompt retrieval of relevant information which provide an overview of connected topics and available information. Any visualizations through simple highlighting and emphasizing via links helps with quickly scanning a source and assessing the relevance. However, annotations within scholarly texts have to consider the needs of the researchers in art history to be helpful. If a source seems to be relevant, the art historian will read the whole source. Hence, a table of content is more instrumental in evaluating if a source needs further investigation.

In order to enhance source criticism and further support the workflows of researchers in historical studies, quickly finding corresponding images, 3D models, and texts would be very beneficial. To perform such queries, it is a prerequisite that these instances and their annotations are linked to each other database-wise. Spatialized photographs have strong relationship to corresponding 3D models as representatives of the buildings, since their contents can be projected almost unambiguously to each other. In contrast, textual sources are more abstract and cannot be directly related to other instances. This requires the analysis of the context of the annotations, i.e., considering annotations in the vicinity, identifying specific keywords, and determining spatial relations. That information is stored in a graph-based structure forming patterns which can then be queried. Similar patterns may relate to each other with a higher probability. Multiple levels for implementation with rising complexity have been discussed.

Next, it needs to be validated which quality and quantity of parameters is required to retrieve valid results that is offered to the user when searching for related media and annotations. Since automatically identifying architectural elements and creating qualitative annotations is still an issue, a test dataset [10] will be used to implement and evaluate these different approaches. The result would ideally be a recommendation system for architectural research able to find relevant segments in texts, images, and 3D models starting from an annotation of interest.

Acknowledgments. The work presented in this paper has been funded by the German Federal Ministry of Education and Research (BMBF) as part of the research project "HistKI", grant identifier 01UG2120.

References

1. Abe, S., Elsner, J.: Introduction: some stakes of comparison. In: Comparativism in Art History, pp. 1–15. Routledge (2017). https://doi.org/10.1109/BigData47090.2019.9005633
2. Agosti, M., Ferro, N.: A formal model of annotations of digital content. ACM Trans. Inf. Syst. **26**(1), 3-es (2007). https://doi.org/10.1145/1292591.1292594
3. Agosti, M., Ferro, N., Orio, N.: Annotating illuminated manuscripts: an effective tool for research and education. In: Proceedings of the 5th ACM/IEEE-CS Joint Conference on Digital Libraries, JCDL 2005, pp. 121–130. ACM, New York, NY, USA (2005). https://doi.org/10.1145/1065385.1065412
4. Baca, M., Gill, M.: Encoding multilingual knowledge systems in the digital age: the Getty vocabularies. In: Smiraglia, R.P. (ed.) Proceedings from North American Symposium on Knowledge Organization, vol. 5, pp. 41–63 (2015). https://doi.org/10.7152/nasko.v5i1.15179
5. Baker, S., Kiela, D., Korhonen, A.: Robust text classification for sparsely labelled data using multi-level embeddings. In: Proceedings of COLING 2016, the 26th International Conference on Computational Linguistics: Technical Papers, pp. 2333–2343. The COLING 2016 Organizing Committee, Osaka, Japan, December 2016
6. Beaudoin, J.E.: An investigation of image users across professions: a framework of their image needs, Retrieval and Use. Ph.D. thesis, Drexel University Philadelphia (2009)
7. Bekiari, C., et al.: Definition of the CIDOC conceptual reference model v7.1.1. In: The CIDOC Conceptual Reference Model Special Interest Group (2021). https://doi.org/10.26225/FDZH-X261
8. Beltagy, I., Lo, K., Cohan, A.: SciBERT: a pretrained language model for scientific text. In: Proceedings of the 2019 Conference on Empirical Methods in Natural Language Processing and the 9th International Joint Conference on Natural Language Processing (EMNLP-IJCNLP), pp. 3615–3620. Association for Computational Linguistics, Hong Kong, China, November 2019. https://doi.org/10.18653/v1/D19-1371
9. Bernhauer, D., Nečaský, M., Škoda, P., Klímek, J., Skopal, T.: Open dataset discovery using context-enhanced similarity search. Knowl. Inf. Syst. **64**(12), 3265–3291 (2022). https://doi.org/10.1007/s10115-022-01751-z
10. Bruschke, J., Kröber, C., Maiwald, F., Utescher, R., Pattee, A.: Introducing a multimodal dataset for the research of architectural elements. Int. Arch. Photogramm. Remote Sens. Spatial Inf. Sci. **XLVIII-M-2-2023**, 325–331 (2023). https://doi.org/10.5194/isprs-archives-XLVIII-M-2-2023-325-2023
11. Bruschke, J., Niebling, F., Maiwald, F., Friedrichs, K., Wacker, M., Latoschik, M.E.: Towards browsing repositories of spatially oriented historic photographic images in 3d web environments. In: Proceedings of the 22nd International Conference on 3D Web Technology. Web3D 2017, ACM, New York, NY, USA (2017). https://doi.org/10.1145/3055624.3075947

12. Bruschke, J., Wacker, M.: Application of a graph database and graphical user interface for the CIDOC CRM. In: Access and Understanding-Networking in the Digital Era. Session J1. The 2014 Annual Conference of CIDOC, the International Committee for Documentation of ICOM (2014)

13. Chandrasekaran, D., Mago, V.: Evolution of semantic similarity-a survey. ACM Comput. Surv. **54**(2), Article 41 (2021). https://doi.org/10.1145/3440755

14. Chatzakis, M., Mountantonakis, M., Tzitzikas, Y.: RDFsim: similarity-based browsing over dbpedia using embeddings. Information **12**(11), 440 (2021). https://doi.org/10.3390/info12110440

15. Chen, H., Sultan, S.F., Tian, Y., Chen, M., Skiena, S.: Fast and accurate network embeddings via very sparse random projection. In: Proceedings of the 28th ACM International Conference on Information and Knowledge Management, pp. 399–408. ACM (2019). https://doi.org/10.1145/3357384.3357879

16. Croce, V., Caroti, G., De Luca, L., Jacquot, K., Piemonte, A., Véron, P.: From the semantic point cloud to heritage-building information modeling: a semiautomatic approach exploiting machine learning. Remote Sens. **13**(3), 461 (2021). https://doi.org/10.3390/rs13030461

17. Dewitz, L., et al.: Historical photos and visualizations: potential for research. Int. Arch. Photogramm. Remote Sens. Spatial Inf. Sci. **XLII-2/W15**, 405–412 (2019). https://doi.org/10.5194/isprs-archives-XLII-2-W15-405-2019

18. Dong, W., Moses, C., Li, K.: Efficient k-nearest neighbor graph construction for generic similarity measures. In: Proceedings of the 20th International Conference on World Wide Web, pp. 577–586. ACM (2011). https://doi.org/10.1145/1963405.1963487

19. Dürre, S.: Die Skulpturen des Dresdner Zwingers : Untersuchung zur Aufstellung, Ikonographie, zum Stil und zu den Veränderungen 1712–2002. Ph.D. thesis, Technische Universität Dresden (2003)

20. Ehrmann, M., Hamdi, A., Pontes, E.L., Romanello, M., Doucet, A.: Named entity recognition and classification on historical documents: a survey. arXiv preprint arXiv:2109.11406 (2021). https://doi.org/10.48550/arXiv.2109.11406

21. Erdmann, M., Maedche, A., Schnurr, H.P., Staab, S.: From manual to semiautomatic semantic annotation: about ontology-based text annotation tools. In: Proceedings of the COLING-2000 Workshop on Semantic Annotation and Intelligent Content, pp. 79–85. International Committee on Computational Linguistics, Centre Universitaire, Luxembourg, August 2000

22. von Fellenberg, V., Schoen, H.: Externe impulse und interne imperative: Zur bedeutung von provenienzforschung und kulturgutschutz in deutschland für die kunstgeschichte. Kunstchronik. Monatsschrift für Kunstwissenschaft, Museumswesen und Denkmalpflege **69**(7), 322–327 (2016)

23. Fiorucci, M., Khoroshiltseva, M., Pontil, M., Traviglia, A., Del Bue, A., James, S.: Machine learning for cultural heritage: a survey. Pattern Recogn. Lett. **133**, 102–108 (2020). https://doi.org/10.1016/j.patrec.2020.02.017

24. Grilli, E., Farella, E.M., Torresani, A., Remondino, F.: Geometric features analysis for the classification of cultural heritage point clouds. Int. Arch. Photogramm. Remote Sens. Spatial Inf. Sci. **XLII-2/W15**, 541–548 (2019). https://doi.org/10.5194/isprs-archives-XLII-2-W15-541-2019

25. Grover, A., Leskovec, J.: node2vec: scalable feature learning for networks. In: Proceedings of the 22nd ACM SIGKDD International Conference on Knowledge Discovery and Data Mining, KDD 2016, pp. 855–864. ACM, New York, NY, USA (2016). https://doi.org/10.1145/2939672.2939754

26. Handschuh, S., Staab, S.: Annotation for the Semantic Web. IOS Press, Amsterdam (2003)
27. Harpring, P.: Development of the getty vocabularies: AAT, TGN, ULAN, and CONA. Art Documentation J. Art Libr. Soc. North Am. **29**(1), 67–72 (2010). https://doi.org/10.1086/adx.29.1.27949541
28. Heller, M.: Rethinking historical methods in organization studies: organizational source criticism. Organ. Stud. **44**(6), 987–1002 (2023). https://doi.org/10.1177/01708406231156978
29. Jurafsky, D., Martin, J.H.: Speech and Language Processing: An Introduction to Natural Language Processing, Computational Linguistics, and Speech Recognition. NJ, 2nd edn, Pearson/Prentice Hall, Upper Saddle River (2009)
30. Ko, H., Lee, S., Park, Y., Choi, A.: A survey of recommendation systems: recommendation models, techniques, and application fields. Electronics **11**(1) (2022). https://doi.org/10.3390/electronics11010141
31. Koren, Y., Bell, R., Volinsky, C.: Matrix factorization techniques for recommender systems. Computer **42**(8), 30–37 (2009). https://doi.org/10.1109/MC.2009.263
32. Koroteev, M.V.: BERT: a review of applications in natural language processing and understanding. arXiv preprint arXiv:2103.11943 (2021). https://doi.org/10.48550/arXiv.2103.11943
33. Leme, L.A.P., Brauner, D.F., Breitman, K.K., Casanova, M.A., Gazola, A.: Matching object catalogues. Innov. Syst. Softw. Eng. **4**, 315–328 (2008). https://doi.org/10.1007/s11334-008-0070-3
34. Li, S., Cai, H., Kamat, V.R.: Integrating natural language processing and spatial reasoning for utility compliance checking. J. Constr. Eng. Manage. **142**(12), 04016074 (2016). https://doi.org/10.1061/(ASCE)CO.1943-7862.0001199
35. Li, Y., Bandar, Z.A., McLean, D.: An approach for measuring semantic similarity between words using multiple information sources. IEEE Trans. Knowl. Data Eng. **15**(4), 871–882 (2003). https://doi.org/10.1109/TKDE.2003.1209005
36. Livi, L., Rizzi, A.: The graph matching problem. Pattern Anal. Appl. **16**(3), 253–283 (2013). https://doi.org/10.1007/s10044-012-0284-8
37. Lopatin, L.: Library digitization projects, issues and guidelines: a survey of the literature. Library Hi Tech **24**(2), 273–289 (2006). https://doi.org/10.1108/07378830610669637
38. López, F.J., Lerones, P.M., Llamas, J.M., Gómez-García-Bermejo, J., Zalama, E.: Linking HBIM graphical and semantic information through the Getty AAT: practical application to the castle of Torrelobatn. IOP Conf. Ser. Mater. Sci. Eng. **364**, 012100 (2018). https://doi.org/10.1088/1757-899X/364/1/012100
39. Maiwald, F., Henze, F., Bruschke, J., Niebling, F.: Geo-information technologies for a multimodal access on historical photographs and maps for research and communication in urban history. Int. Arch. Photogramm. Remote Sens. Spatial Inf. Sci. **XLII-2/W11**, 763–769 (2019). https://doi.org/10.5194/isprs-archives-XLII-2-W11-763-2019
40. Maiwald, F., Bruschke, J., Schneider, D., Wacker, M., Niebling, F.: Giving historical photographs a new perspective: introducing camera orientation parameters as new metadata in a large-scale 4d application. Remote Sens. **15**(7), 1879 (2023). https://doi.org/10.3390/rs15071879
41. Manuel, A., Gattet, E., De Luca, L., Véron, P.: An approach for precise 2D/3D semantic annotation of spacially-oriented images for in-situ visualization applications. In: Digtal Heritage International Congress (2013)
42. Miller, G.A.: WordNet: a lexical database for English. Commun. ACM **38**(11), 39–41 (1995). https://doi.org/10.1145/219717.219748

43. Minaee, S., Boykov, Y.Y., Porikli, F., Plaza, A.J., Kehtarnavaz, N., Terzopoulos, D.: Image segmentation using deep learning: a survey. IEEE Trans. Pattern Anal. Mach. Intell. **44**(7), 3523–3542 (2022). https://doi.org/10.1109/TPAMI.2021.3059968

44. Mirza, P., Razniewski, S., Darari, F., Weikum, G.: Enriching knowledge bases with counting quantifiers. In: Vrandečić, D., et al. (eds.) ISWC 2018. LNCS, vol. 11136, pp. 179–197. Springer, Cham (2018). https://doi.org/10.1007/978-3-030-00671-6_11

45. Morbidoni, C., Pierdicca, R., Paolanti, M., Quattrini, R., Mammoli, R.: Learning from synthetic point cloud data for historical buildings semantic segmentation. J. Comput. Cult. Herit. **13**(4), Article 34 (2020). https://doi.org/10.1145/3409262

46. Mozafari, M., Farahbakhsh, R., Crespi, N.: A BERT-based transfer learning approach for hate speech detection in online social media. In: Cherifi, H., Gaito, S., Mendes, J.F., Moro, E., Rocha, L.M. (eds.) COMPLEX NETWORKS 2019. SCI, vol. 881, pp. 928–940. Springer, Cham (2020). https://doi.org/10.1007/978-3-030-36687-2_77

47. Münster, S., Maiwald, F., Lehmann, C., Lazariv, T., Hofmann, M., Niebling, F.: An automated pipeline for a browser-based, city-scale mobile 4d VR application based on historical images. In: Proceedings of the 2nd Workshop on Structuring and Understanding of Multimedia HeritAge Contents, SUMAC 2020, pp. 33–40. ACM, New York, NY, USA (2020). https://doi.org/10.1145/3423323.3425748

48. Niebling, F., Maiwald, F., Barthel, K., Latoschik, M.E.: 4D augmented city models, photogrammetric creation and dissemination. In: Münster, S., Friedrichs, K., Niebling, F., Seidel-Grzesinska, A. (eds.) UHDL/DECH -2017. CCIS, vol. 817, pp. 196–212. Springer, Cham (2018). https://doi.org/10.1007/978-3-319-76992-9_12

49. Oren, E., Möller, K.H., Scerri, S., Handschuh, S., Sintek, M.: What are semantic annotations? Relatório técnico. DERI Galway **9**, 62 (2006)

50. Pande, A., Ni, K., Kini, V.: SWAG: item recommendations using convolutions on weighted graphs. In: International Conference on Big Data, pp. 2903–2912. IEEE (2019). https://doi.org/10.1109/BigData47090.2019.9005633

51. Ramalho, T., et al.: Encoding spatial relations from natural language. arXiv preprint arXiv:1807.01670 (2018). 10.48550/arXiv. 1807.01670

52. Régimbeau, G.: Image source criticism in the age of the digital humanities. In: Saou-Dufrêne, B. (ed.) Heritage and Digital humanities, pp. 179–194. Lit Verlag (2014)

53. Ricci, F., Rokach, L., Shapira, B.: Recommender systems: techniques, applications, and challenges. In: Ricci, F., Rokach, L., Shapira, B. (eds.) Recommender Systems Handbook. pp. 1–35. Springer, US, New York, NY, USA (2022). https://doi.org/10.1007/978-1-0716-2197-4_1

54. Schmidt, S.C., Thiery, F., Trognitz, M.: Practices of linked open data in archaeology and their realisation in Wikidata. Digital **2**(3), 333–364 (2022)

55. Shin, H.J., Park, J.Y., Yuk, D.B., Lee, J.S.: BERT-based spatial information extraction. In: Proceedings of the Third International Workshop on Spatial Language Understanding, pp. 10–17. Association for Computational Linguistics, November 2020. https://doi.org/10.18653/v1/2020.splu-1.2

56. Speer, R., Chin, J., Havasi, C.: ConceptNet 5.5: an open multilingual graph of general knowledge. In: Proceedings of the AAAI Conference on Artificial Intelligence, vol. 31, no. 1, February 2017. https://doi.org/10.1609/aaai.v31i1.11164

57. Utescher, R., Patee, A., Maiwald, F., Bruschke, J., Hoppe, S., Münster, S., Niebling, F., Zarrieß, S.: Exploring naming inventories for architectural elements

for use in multi-modal machine learning applications. In: Workshop on Computational Methods in the Humanities (2022)

58. Vrandečić, D., Krötzsch, M.: Wikidata: a free collaborative knowledgebase. Commun. ACM **57**(10), 78–85 (2014). https://doi.org/10.1145/2629489

59. Wu, Z., Palmer, M.: Verb semantics and lexical selection. In: 32nd Annual Meeting of the Association for Computational Linguistics, pp. 133–138. Association for Computational Linguistics, Las Cruces, New Mexico, USA, June 1994. https://doi.org/10.3115/981732.981751

60. Xu, H., Liu, B., Shu, L., Yu, P.S.: BERT post-training for review reading comprehension and aspect-based sentiment analysis. In: Proceedings of the 2019 Conference of the North American Chapter of the Association for Computational Linguistics: Human Language Technologies, Volume 1 (Long and Short Papers), pp. 2324–2335. Association for Computational Linguistics, Minneapolis, Minnesota, June 2019. https://doi.org/10.18653/v1/N19-1242

61. Yan, J., Yin, X.C., Lin, W., Deng, C., Zha, H., Yang, X.: A short survey of recent advances in graph matching. In: Proceedings of the 2016 ACM on International Conference on Multimedia Retrieval, ICMR 2016, pp. 167–174. ACM, New York, NY, USA (2016). https://doi.org/10.1145/2911996.2912035

The *Accademia de lo Studio de l'Architettura*—A Database Project

Bernd Kulawik[(✉)] [ID]

Indipendent Architectural Historian and Musicologist,
Münstergasse 24 (c/o Strauss), CH-3011 Bern, Switzerland
`be_kul@me.com`

Abstract. Between 1531 and 1555, the forgotten Roman *Accademia de lo Studio de l'Architettura* (original 16th-century spelling) developed and executed the first and presumably largest project in the history of architecture and urbanism. Its aim was to reconstruct all theoretical and practical knowledge on architecture from Roman antiquity to make it available to any future architecture. While the program for this project is known, its execution has not been noticed by modern research—mostly, because the rather informal *Accademia* split the immense amount of work into portions suitable for smaller groups and individuals which have not been identified as parts of the project by modern research. In addition, large groups of documents generated by the *Accademia* have even been ignored so far. The paper presents an overview of the *Accademia*'s project and its results, an already started database project to make them available for further investigation, the identification of other, still unknown sources, and future research. The *Accademia*'s project is not only important because of the wealth of still understudied or unknown documents about all kinds of ancient material objects related to architecture and urbanism, but also because of the first known development of an interdisciplinary scientific methodology which seems to have influenced even the beginnings of the natural sciences a few decades later.

Keywords: Early Academies · Study of Antiquity · Scientific method

1 Introduction

This paper presents recent and ongoing research about the Roman «*Accademia de lo Studio de l'Architettura*» which was operating in Rome between c. 1530 and—at least—unto 1555. (I will keep the contemporary spelling of the name here to distinguish it from the otherwise very general sounding denomination.) Modern research has usually identified this group erroneously with the «*Accademia della Virtù*» and other, contemporary groups (see part 2). The group developed a vast program to study ancient Roman architecture in theory and practice and extend this research from architecture itself to all aspects or contexts related to architecture and its interpretation and understanding—and to publish the results in a 24-volume series of books (part 3). One of these

S. Münster et al. (Eds.): UHDL 2023, CCIS 1853, pp. 88–103, 2023.
https://doi.org/10.1007/978-3-031-38871-2_6

parts was dedicated to the urban history of the *Urbs Roma* in antiquity—and it resulted in some of the first and most remarkable early examples of such studies in general. The *Accademia*'s project may, therefore, be seen as the first and most important foundation stone of *urbanistics* as well as several other disciplines which may acknowledge their roots in the 16th century but did not realize the connections of these roots to those of other modern disciplines all based in the *same* research and publishing project developed methodologically and executed systematically by the more than 200 persons which can be counted among the members and external collaborators of the *Accademia de lo Studio de l'Architettura*. Contrary to a still widespread common belief, this program was not unrealizable, but instead produced large amounts of materials—mostly drawings, manuscripts, but also printed books—which had a deep impact on later developments in severals disciplines, but usually have not been identified yet as stemming from the same original contexts or published and studied at all (part 4). From the description of the *Accademia*'s work and its results as well as from experience with database projects in the *Digital Humanities* in the last 25 years, consequences can be drawn regarding the requirements for a database supporting the ongoing research project on this *Accademia* which needs to be extended to a larger community of interdisciplinary researchers (part 5). The working database actually used for my research will be presented though it is—also technically—an ongoing project itself (part 6). Finally a reasoning is presented why the rediscovering project on the *Accademia* has to be regarded as an important desideratum for all fields of research in the *Digital Humanities*, i.e. not only the history and archaeology of ancient Rome or historical disciplines in general, but also other humanities and even social and natural sciences (part 7).

2   The *Accademia*

The *Accademia de lo Studio de l'Architettura* is one of several academies, i.e. rather informal groups pursuing common interests of their members and working in Rome during the reign of Pope Paul III Farnese (1534–1549). They are listed in a commentary by the Italian humanist, philologist and poet Dionigi Atanagi to a poem published in his collection «*De le rime di diversi nobili poeti toscani*» (i.e.: «From the poems of diverse noble Tuscan poets») in two volumes in Venice with Lodovico Avanzo in 1565 [9]. There, on pages LI2 *verso*–LI3 *recto* Atanagi lists seven academies, given here in his original spelling:

> «[...] [academia] de la Virtu, de la Poesia nuoua, de lo Studio de l'Architettura, de l'Amicitia, del Liceo, l'Amasea, & piu altre. Tra le quali non inferiore ad alcuna fu l'Academia de lo SDEGNO, [...]»
> «[...] [the academy] of the Virtue, of the new Poetry, of the Studium of Architecture, of the *Liceum*, [the one called] *Amasea*, and others. Among those non inferior to some was the academy of the Outrage, [...]»

His last formulation suggests that there must have been even more academies, but which he regarded as not worth mentioning here. Atanagi himself claims

to have been a member of the *Accademia dello Sdegno* or *degli Sdegnati*, i.e.
«Outraged». The reason for their outrage was the plundering of ancient Roman
remains by—mostly foreign—cardinals and merchants divesting the already
ruined Eternal City of its most valuable objects.

Because the Siennese humanist Claudio Tolomei is regarded as the (sole)
founder of the *Accademia della Virtù,* and the letter describing the program was
written—but surely not conceived alone—by him, the *Accademia della Virtù*
has usually been regarded as the one not clearly mentioned in his letter and
pursuing the described program. But this academy mostly focused on a reform
of the Italian language and on (neo)Latin as well as Italian poetry. In addition,
the only interest of the *della Virtù* supposed by modern research was a better
understanding of the *De architectura libri decem,* the Ten Books on Architecture
by the Roman author Vitruvius. But, as the program described by Tolomei
clearly shows, this was only the smaller part of the entire program (see part 3).
The mistake may go back to Giorgio Vasari who attended at least some of the
meetings of the *Accademia de lo Studio de l'Architettura* and surely knew several
of its leading members. Vasari writes in his short biography of Jacopo Barozzi
da Vignola in the *Vita* of Taddeo Zuccari, that Vignola had been «measuring all
the antiquities in Rome» in the 1530s for an academy dedicated to the «lecture»
of Vitruvius:

> «Ma dopo, essendo allhora in Roma un'Accademia di nobilissimi gentil-
> huomini, e signori, che *attendevano alla letione di Vitruuio* ... si diede
> il Vignuola per seruitio loro a misurare interamente tutte l'anticaglie di
> Roma [...]» [10, p. 700]

It is obvious, that this academy cannot have limited its work to the «lecture»
of Vitruvius alone, i.e. a rather theoretical work, when it ordered Vignola to
measure all the antiquities in Rome. That Vignola did so is confirmed by his
biographer Egnatio Danti, who posthumously published Vignolas treatise on
perspectives, in the *Vita* put in front of the book: Vignola measured and depicted

> «[...] misurò, & ritrasse per seruitio di quei Signori [i.e. the same academi-
> cians already mentioned by Vasari] tutte l'antichità di Roma: [...]» [11,
> unnumbered sedond page of the «vita»]

The *Accademia de lo Studio de l'Architettura* must have traced its origins to
the first *Accademia Romana* founded by Pomponio Leto already in 1464 and
perished in the *Sack of Rome,* the *Sacco di Roma* in 1527. This academy had
the first printed edition of Vitruvius published by Giovanni Sulpizio (Sulpitius)
in around 1486. This edition is characterized by wide margins intentionally left
explicitly to allow for annotations to the still often unintelligible Latin text.

Marcello Cervini, who died in 1555 after only three weeks as Pope Mar-
cellus II, and others like—presumably—the architect Antonio da Sangallo the
Younger, who had been members of the *Accademia Romana* before 1527 seem to
have (tried to) re-established it in the 1530s. This would explain why the brothers Luigi and Valerio Dorico, printers in Rome, name themselves «*acacemiae*

romanae impressorum» = the printers of the Roman academy, in their edition of Bartolomeo Marliano's third (but first illustrated) edition of his *Topographia Urbis Romae*, the topographic description of ancient Rome. Only the other Roman academies emerging in the late 1530 s or 1540 s may have caused the 'original' academy to address itself as the «Academy of the Study of Architecture». With Cervini's untimely death in 1555 and the severe change of the intellectual climate usually known as the 'counter-reformation' it did not seem appropriate anymore that intellectuals in Rome, many of them clerics, went on dealing with the pagan culture of ancient Rome and investigating it with a very unprejudiced attitude. Instead, the so-called Christian archeology was propagated, often using methodological tools developed by the older *Accademia*, but substituting its 'scientific' approach in cases where religious dogma may have (been) interfered.

Due to its fragile existence as a voluntary circle of learned men and artists, the *Accademia* did not have a fixed program defining, e.g., the duties of its members or the meeting places and schedules. (Other academies like the *Accademia degli Intronati* in Siena did so already in 1525.) Therefore, these places shifted from the private houses of members like Tolomei or Antonio Agustìn to the (then still unfinished) *Palazzo Farnese*, residence of cardinal Alessandro Farnese, who was a leading supporter of the *Accademia*'s project and collector of items of interest for its work: books and manuscripts, ancient statues and inscriptions, and other objects like coins. (It was during one of the regular evening meetings with some academicians at Farnese's dining table that the idea to Vasari's *Vite* was developed, as the author himself reports [10, p. 996].)

The long timespan covered by the *Accademia*'s activities and the fluctuation of its members due to professional, familiar, religious or health reasons understandably also led to a large number of members who were not active, participating members for the entire period. But Tolomei's claim that the very ambitious program would be realized by a very large number of collaborators sharing the large amount of work like a heavy weight would be divided into smaller parts to move it, and dedicating their special abilities and proficiencies to the appropriate parts of the project dividing it, too, into separate 'working groups' which would join their results regularly in what may be called the first example of systematically planned inter- or trans-disciplinary work, is supported by the fact that—by now, but still counting—some 220–250 persons can be related to the *Accademia*. Many of them worked in Rome only for several years, others joined later and picked up the work, and many also participated in the project over time from their home in other parts of Italy and Europe from where they, e.g., sent drawings and descriptions of coins and inscriptions. While it cannot be established by now how many of the c. 35–50 anonymous draftsmen have to be identified with persons known by name as supporters or members of the *Accademia*, it is clearly deducable from the drawings that they, too, shared their work according to special interests: E.g., the persons who measured the ancient buildings usually formed groups of 3–6 working on one specific building, but exchanged their position in other cases. And they all did hardly ever record sculptural parts aside from the typical architectural decoration like capitals or bases or inscriptions. Though they *measured* the size of the letters in large inscriptions, they did not recort their entire texts—because this was the duty of another group centered around the French humanist Jean Matal (Ioannes Metellus), secretary and close friend of Atonio Agustìn, a collector of medals and coins who later published an important book about the interpretation of Latin inscriptions and Roman coins [13]. And even among these groups of draftsmen and collaborators, a somewhat 'hierarchical' structure between leaders or organizers and others, between surveyors and preparators of printable drawings etc. may be distinguished.

3   The *Accademia*'s Program

In 1547 the Siennese humanist Claudio Tolomei (1492–1556) published a letter written to Agostino de'Landi in 1542 [1] in which he describes the large *publishing* project regarding the theoretical and practical knowledge on ancient Roman architecture and its architectural, urbanistic, cultural, political and social contexts. The program represents an extended version of one proposed already in 1531 (with minor changes from 1539) by the Florentine architect Antonio da Sangallo the Younger (1484–1546) [2], then one of the leading architects working in Rome and, with Baldassarre Peruzzi, the head of the construction of Saint-Peter's in the Vatican, the largest European building project after antiquity. While Sangallo's manuscript has been regarded by modern research as an 'introduction' to a lost or unrealized edition and/or translation of Vitruvius' *De architectura libri decem* — the *Ten Books on Architecture* —and, accordingly, named «*Proemio*», i.e. foreword, Sangallo instead sketches the shortages of earlier editions of the only surviving ancient *tractatus* on architecture and a program to overcome those problems in a new edition [12].

Besides a philological reconstruction of the «original» ancient text and its lost illustrations, the main point in Sangallo's program is a measured survey of ancient Roman buildings allowing to compare them with the rules given by Vitruvius. Tolomei extends this project by a more philological approach in the first part (numbers 1–11 in the list below) including translations and lexica as well as practice-oriented derivations from the *Ten Books*, and by adding several books (numbers 12–24) representing and describing the measured buildings and all other ancient material objects which could be helpful to understand those buildings, their history, design, and decoration as well as their execution—starting this practice-oriented section with a book (n° 12) reconstructing the urban history of the *Urbs Roma* in antiquity, i.e. the development of the three known major stages of its history. While Tolomei does not give a numbered list of the 24 books—leading modern interpreters to numbers between 8 and 20 [6]—he and his large circle of collaborators planned to realize, the following list can be derived from his letter:

[Theory]

1. explanation of difficult passages in Vitruvius' *Ten Books on Architecture*
2. philological comparison of all manuscripts and editions
3. new Latin edition of Vitruvius' *Ten Books on Architecture*

4. annotated Latin lexicon of Vitruvius' Latin technical terms
5. annotated Latin lexicon of Vitruvius' Greek technical terms
6. commentary on Vitruvius' Latin and its comparison with other authors
7. new translation of the *Ten Books* into a better, «more classical» Latin
8. new translation of the *Ten Books* into modern [i.e. Tuscan] Italian
9. annotated Italian lexicon of Vitruvius' technical terms
10. annotated Italian lexicon of all tools and architectural details
11. practice-oriented overview of the rules given by Vitruvius

[Practice]

12. illustrated chronology of Rome's urban development in antiquity
13. annotated and illustrated documentation of all surviving buildings
14. *dito* of tombs and sarcophagi
15. *dito* of statues extended by stylistic & historical comments
16. *dito* for reliefs and friezes and other sculptured objects
17. *dito* for single surviving architectural elements like bases etc.
18. *dito* for vases and similar decorative objects used in architecture
19. *dito* for tools and instruments
20. *dito* for inscriptions
21. *dito* for all known paintings
22. *dito* for coins and medals
23. *dito* for building and other machines
24. reconstruction of the aqueducts leading to Rome

It should be obvious that this program is not focusing on but—rather logically—just starting with Vitruvius, the establishment of a trustworthy text of his *Ten Books* and the derivation of anything usable for theoreticians as well as craftsmen from the text which should, of course, also be translated. (Only books 6 and 7 seem to be of a rather curious character and, accordingly, never seem to have led even to first attempts of preparation.) It should be noted that the first part, somewhat paradoxically, does not start with the full text but with a book of annotations explaining difficult passages and, therefore, helpful e.g. to owners of one of the earlier full editions or even of manuscripts. It is surely not by accident that this book is set on the first position—and that it is the first to have been realized by the academician Guillaume Philandrier and printed in 1544 by Antonio Bladio in Rome [13] who became the printer/publisher of many more works generated by the *Accademia*.

But the—not only by numbers—significantly *larger* part of the program is the second one, dedicated to all practical aspects and a wide range of contexts related to architecture and/or helpful for its understanding. This part, too, starts with a book published in 1544 (i.e., two years after the letter was written, but three years before its publication) and—again—surely not by accident, the afore-mentioned *Topographia Urbis Romae* by Bartolomeo Marliano [3]. While two different editions of the book had already appeared in Rome and Lyon in 1534, this one from 1544 contains illustrations and, among them, three topographical maps of the three stages of early Rome: the mythological *Roma quadrata* founded by Romulus, the Republican Rome defined by the Servian Walls, and the imperial Rome inside the Aurelian Walls. The latter one should be seen as the forerunner to Leonardo Bufalini's famous topographical map, the first of its kind, printed in 1551 by Blado.

The other books in the second part somehow (would) use Rome's topographic description and depiction as a framework layed out in the first volume of the group, i.e. n.° 12, to situate not only the buildings, places (*fora*), roads, bridges, and gates but also other artifacts. Therefore, it makes sense to situate this book at the opening of the second part even before the full measured description of all known (!) surviving ancient buildings in and—some—outside the walls.

4   The Results

Large amounts of preparatory materials in the form of manuscripts and/or drawings exist for almost all of the planned books. Several books fulfilling Tolomei's descriptions almost literally have been printed between 1544 and 1555, while books published later slightly deviate from the program. In addition, students and heirs of the academicians or the *Accademia*'s materials published books until the early 1600 s. And there are also books complementing the program with additional information not strictly related to architecture but, e.g., helpful to understand the documented objects like: books on the interpretation of inscriptions or coins, descriptions of ancient theology or prosopographic and calendrical works on ancient Rome's civilization. Altogether, some 100 books published between 1544 and 1625 can be connected to the *Accademia*'s program, some of them foundation stones in (the histories of) urbanistics like Marliano's [3], architectural theory [4], and architecture [5], numismatics [14], epigraphy [15], etc. Those books not related directly to the program cover fields like Roman prosopography, history, mythology etc. In relation to the program it is obvious that it is not by accidents, that member of the *Accademia* and the friends or heirs published such books. E.g., the difficult iconographic interpretation of statues, reliefs or coins could only be done based on a fundamental knowledge of ancient mythology— which was provided by the first edition and translation of [Pseudo-] Apollodorus of Athens' *Bibliothèke* [16], published by Benedetto Egio with, again, Antonio Blado in Rome, and dedicated to Jean Matal. The still growing list of books from the *Accademia* and its personal environment contains 129 books by now—mostly not including reprints or translations.

But the by far largest part of materials relatable to the *Accademia*'s program survived as manuscript and drawings only. Usually, these very rich materials have not been studied yet sufficiently, let alone published, were not associated with the program or only—very rarely—used as secondary sources of information without recognizing their importance. Because most of this material is passed down as «anonymous», i. e. not related to any «big» name in the history of architecture, the arts or other disciplines, these materials did not find the attention they deserve. By now, the following materials can be related to the *Accademia*'s program—but more may wait to be discovered by future research:

Architectural Drawings. Some 4,150 single drawings on more than 1,450 sheets in over 25 collections are already known; an unknown number of drawings after building decorations like *stucco* ceilings may have to be added since some sheets presumably belonging to a larger collection of such drawings have been discovered [17]. There are very many single sheets of such drawings which have not been compared and set into relation to each other, but may also form elements of this part of the *Accademia*'s project.

Sculptural Drawings. There are several volumes and many single drawings after ancient sculpture—statues, reliefs, ornamental friezes, tombstones etc.— that have been or can/could be attributed to members of the *Accademia*. Among them are drawings called «the first systematic archeaological book» [13], the *Codex Coburgensis* at the collections of the *Veste Coburg* in Germany and its parallel *Codex Pighianus* in Berlin, together with several drawings in manuscripts like the *Codex Ursinianus* in the Biblioteca Apostolica Vaticana. To these, drawings from the workshop of Jacopo Strada in the Österreichische Nationalbibliothek at Vienna may be added, as well as hundreds of similar anonymous drawings or some dozens sheets attributable, e.g., to the painter Battista Franco and today in private collections. Three parchment sheets in Vienna showing parts of the long relief covering Trajan's Column in Rome seem to be the remains of an important full documentation of these reliefs that seem to have been made independently—like many of the other drawings—of earlier drawings. This seems to be a general characteristic of the *Accademia*'s production: Older sources documenting ancient artefacts like buildings, sculptures, coins or inscriptions may have been used for orientation about these objects, but their accuracy has been checked again and, usually because of necessity, updated in a more precise representation of the same artefact if available. Altogether, there are at least 3,000 single drawings of sculptures already identified as belonging to the circle of the *Accademia* or deriving from its production. To these, some 200 drawings and prints after ancient vases and similar objects may have to be added—many of them believed to be fantasy, but these should be checked because this never has been done systematically.

Inscriptions. Besides the six volumes containing 10-15,000 thousand inscriptions collected and coordinated by Jean Matal there are c. 20 other volumes by his friends and students, many of them including pieces of paper with inscriptions written by other persons. Matal established the standard to register not only the text of an inscription but adding also the name of the person who transcribed it, and the place and date. When these were not known, he records the source like an older manuscript or print. Most importantly, he tried to preserve the original appearance of the piece of stone or metal with all damages, and separated the original text from comments and reconstructions of lost words. This is the standard used 300 years later by Theodor Mommsen for the *Corpus Inscriptionum Latinarum*, the still (but not for very long anymore) ongoing documentation project at the *Berlin-Brandenburgische Akademie der Wissenschaften*, the former *Preußische Akademie*. Mommsen had studied Matal's collection of inscriptions in Rome before starting his project. But the source for this method seems to be a *sylloge* of ancient Roman inscriptions collected by Andrea Alciato and kept at the *Sächsische Landes- und Universitätsbibliothek Dresden* [18]. Matal and Agustìn studied with Alciato, as well as some leading members or supporters of the *Accademia* like Alessandro Farnese, Hans Jakob Fugger or Antoine Perrenot de Granvelle. Alciato's *sylloge* in Dresden should be seen as the first (?) application of his historical-critical method outside the realm of classical—mostly legal—texts. More volumes of inscriptions like the one by Maximilian van Waelscapple [19], who lived with Matal in Rome, or the *Codex Pighianus* [20] can be found in other collections, archives, or libraries.

Maps and Plans. Other sources stemming from the *Accademia*'s project may exist, like, e.g., the notes taken by the Vatican librarian and friend of Marcello Cervini, Agostino Steuco, during his search for the original course of the Roman aqueducts, only a very small part of which has been published in 1547. They prepared the reconstruction of the *Aqua Virgo* or *Acqua Vergine* still feeding the famous *Fontana di Trevi* in Rome as well as—after a later prolongation—Bernini's famous fountains including the *Fountain of the Four Rivers* in the *Piazza Navona*.

Another set of maps which now can be attributed to the *Accademia*'s project and its environment, are those of Rome, including the first topographical map (not only) of Rome by Leonardo Bufalini. Bufalini was a military engineer and architect who worked for Antonio da Sangallo the Younger, one of the leading members of the *Accademia* and inventors of its project, in the reconstruction of the Roman defense system and was also himself interested in archeological research: He even dived into the *Nemi* lake for the wrecks of the ships built for emperor Caligula which were then visible from the surface. The third map in Marliano's *Topographia* drawn by Giovanni Battista Palatino, who later gained fame as inventor of one of the first 'classical' serif scripts, may be seen as the first forerunner of Bufalini's. Many other plans (mostly not in the orthogonal projection used by Bufalini) for the first time in a printed map were designed and/or cut by members or collaborators of the *Accademia* like Pirro Ligorio, Etienne Dupérac, Nicolas Beatrizet or Francesco Paciotto.

Collections (of Drawings) of Roman Coins. Several of the promoters of the *Accademia* like cardinal Alessandro Farnese or its—during the 1550s—leading member Antonio Agustìn owned large collections of ancient Roman coins still preserved today. According to the *Accademia*'s program (book 22) they were to be used as historical sources about persons, but also buildings and political events. Several thousands (15–20,000!) of these coins were drawn by Jacopo Strada and his workshop for Strada's 30-volume *Magnum ac Novum Opus* at Gotha [21], Germany, and a dozen of similar volumes kept in Vienna, Prague, Paris, and London. Strada also wrote an 11-volume description of some 1-2,000 coins. Because his drawings show much more details than the coins they have not been taken seriously by modern research. But a short investigation into the coins showing ancient buildings could reveal that at least some of them do not consist of fantastic additions but that these additions must be based on additional information about the buildings available in the circle of the *Accademia* from the mentioned architectural drawings documenting precise surveys of the ruins [21].

Machines. The penultimate volume in the *Accademia*'s program was to be dedicated to the reconstruction of ancient machines after descriptions and depictions. It is known that there are at least three unpublished privately owned volumes containing some 500 drawings by Jacopo Strada showing machines. His grandson Ottavio Strada published prints after 50 of these drawings (extended in a second edition to 100), but these only show hydraulic machines for pumps, fountains etc. presumably useful in his times. It is not known yet if some of the other drawings show reconstructions of machines from antiquity.

Music. *Musica* as part of the classical canon of higher education, the *quadrivium*, from antiquity to the late Renaissance was the mathematical theory of proportion. Its application to the *musica humana* (music made by humans, i.e. singing) and *musica instrumentalis* (music made with instruments) was just only the 'lowest' level of its realization, while the *musica mundana*, the 'music of the cosmic spheres' was regarded as the highest. Music as the theory of proportion does not appear in the *Accademia*'s program even though its terms like harmony or proportion and their derivates have been used by architects and critics since antiquity to describe (good) architecture. It did not have to be reconstructed from ancient sources as part of the program because it was 'alive and well' in the Renaissance: The theoretical writings, e.g., by Glarean or Zarlino were easily available and contained all the information useful for the development of a general overview or even theory of 'good' architecture. Therefore, no book about *musica* can be found among those planned by the *Accademia*, but at least Daniele Barbaro—who already had extended Vitruvius' remarks on music largely in his commentaries—planned to publish such a volume of which two manuscript versions survived.

Letters. The c. 250 persons—and maybe more—involved in the *Accademia*'s project wrote thousands of letters, many of which were published in the first collections since the middle of the 16th century: It even seems that Claudio Tolomei's collection containing the letter describing the program, was the first of its kind regarding the correspondence of a living person. (Only the letters by Aretino, containing the 'gossip' of his time, were published in a personal collection before those of Tolomei.) Tolomei's collection was very popular and has been reprinted almost 25 times until the early 17th century. It may be, therefore, reasonable to regard the *Accademia* as the real beginning of the *Republic of Letters*.

Copies. Last but not least it should be mentioned that Pirro Ligorio was closely related to the leading academicians for most of his lifetime, but also separated from the Roman circles because of disagreements. Therefore, it would be no surprise to find traces of the project pursued by the *Accademia* in Ligorio's more than 40 volumes of writings on antiquity—and vice versa. Also, the collections used and re-arranged by Cassiano dal Pozzo for his *paper museum* surely may contain drawings or copies of drawings that originated in the academic project in Rome several decades before.

All of these materials, printed as well as manuscript sources and drawings, seem to form the largest known corpus of interrelated documents, objects and persons in the history of the *humanities*, if not even the sciences (understood in the more general sense of the German term «Wissenschaften»): It seems and could be an interesting sub-project of investigation, that the physicists and other early modern scholars who 'invented' the modern, experiment-based natural sciences stood in contact with several of the academicians and may, therefore, have been influenced in their methlogy by the ideas and norms developed by the *Accademia*.

5 Requirements for a Research Database

It should be obvious that this large amount of materials cannot be overseen, let alone fully investigated by one person alone, not even by a comparably small group of 10–20 persons like one, e. g. financiated by a grant from the *European Research Council* in a maximum timespan of 10 years. Instead, an open web-database has to be created where institutions and scholars alike could contribute their materials, observations and information as registered users in a *wiki*-like way.

This database has to handle all material artefacts, i. e. drawings, manuscripts, included notes, books and prints, but also persons and all relations between them and any information about them as single *data objects* which can be extended and annotated by other collaborators. E. g., the relations between persons, persons and drawings or drawings and real-world artefacts like a building, sculpture, a vase, inscription or coin should appear in the database as links which themselves are data objects that can be annotated, extended or linked with other objects. All data objects should be represented by simple web pages to which scholars can easily contribute information.

The database software should automatically make links reciprocal, i. e., if a link is set from a person to a drawing, it should also show up in the drawing's entry as a backlink to the person.

These objects, and most of all the link-objects, should reflect temporary changes: E. g., it is known that the relations between persons changed from an employment to friendship or from close collaboration to hostility. It would not be helpful to represent all such connections between persons or any other 'class' of objects as obects of the same kind like it seems to be the case in most graph databases, because the relations did not only change over time but have been even at the same time very different: It is not enough or even misleading to represent a relation between two persons working closely together as of the same level (of intensity) as the relation between two persons who wrote each other only very few (but even important) letters over long distances.

It should also be obvious by now that these artefacts and persons form large and evolving networks comprising sub-networks of a higher denseness. These networks contain numbers of elements between 250 (persons) to thousands (architectural or sculptural drawings) or even tens of thousands (coin drawings, transcribed inscriptions). One may visualize them as two-dimensional horizontal layers in different colours with the sub-networks and the different and changing links between their elements. These layers would form a three-dimensional structure with countless 'vertical' links between the elements of different layers. At the moment, I do not see how usage and representation of all these information in a relational or graph database should be easier or more flexibel than in an object-oriented database: Relational databases seem to be to limited in their convertibility; graph databases do not (as far as I know) offer any more possibilities than object-oriented databases but rather limitations.

After almost 25 years of experience with database projects and their users in the *Digital Humanities* this author is convinced that the most important basic and fundamental requirement for such a database (project) is formulated in the «KISS» principle: «Keep It Short and Simple!» All of these data objects *and* their content information—like, e. g., dimension of a sheet, descriptions of a drawing or biographical data—have to be of a very simple structure and, therefore, easily to understand. It has to be easy to work with them for scholarly contributors, i. e. without long introductory courses (e. g. like in the original *WikiWiki* systems). The leading idea behind very complex database systems and the resulting interfaces has been to split up the information via high levels of granulation into elementary pieces that could be searched separately and in combined searches like: «show all objects created between 1536 and 1538 (by a certain group of persons not including others)». From my point of view, questions of this kind usually require that the research for their answers has already been done and somehow put into the system. But *this* requires a rather or very complex structure and handling of the database and its interface—a complexity which keeps normal users from asking such question or finding such answers accidently. And, as we all know, the complexity of an interface and the structure behind it *do not* encourage users to work with the software or contribute their own information gained in research. That is one reason why *Wikipedia*— even though limited by closed circles of administrators—has a larger and (in the meantime: slowly) growing group of contributors: Because it is/was *easy* to contribute information to articles or even new entire articles!

But another argument against a high complexity is the maintainability: I know of only *one* database project existing for more than 25 years. (Should our research not be important enough to make our results available for even much longer times?) Besides the limited time of funding for such projects—who would regard it as rational to fund a research library of 'real' books for only 5, 10, 15 years?—the maintainability is the crucial aspect—stable funding provided. The mentioned database has been entirely rewritten in different software—from a file-system-based datastructure to a (proprietary) object-oriented database to a now (also proprietary) relational structure—for lots of money, consuming lots

of (paid) time that could not be used for research and the insertion of new data...
Any database of a high clompexity like it would be designed, developed and used
for a project collecting all available information about the *Accademia* in the
typical way would not survive for more than c. 20 years—because the migration
to new versions of the database engine, the programming languages used, the
basic operating system and compilers and especially the hardware sooner or later
would require a re-building of the entire structure with new means, something
not even done by enthusiasts if the timespan is long enough...

Another important requiremens: The data objects and their components and
relations need to be findable and addressable over the internet and, therefore,
should have an stable http(s) address and be searchable for internet robots once
their content has been published. E. g., the objects themselves should contain
their original URL to make them findable even if they should be moved in- or
outside the database and receive a new URL. This could garantee that they
will be found, as long as the URL is part of a text string readable to search
engines. The addressability would also allow to connect and integrate information
(objects) from other sources on the internet via links—as long as these sources
may be findable. But the simple case of images which can be integrated into
an html-page via h-ref-links that break as soon as the original URL is not valid
anymore may demonstrate that this may not be a practicable idea—even though
such connectivity was the basic concept of the WWW developed in the early
1990s...

Last but not least: To facilitate research, clones of the database—maybe
without large, memory-consuming files like images or movies—should be easily
transferable to other computers with different operating systems like laptops for
archival work when no internet connection is available. Afterwards, the changes
should be merged (half) automatically with the main database. Therefore, the
database system has to be a Free and Open Source Software. It has to be available for any common operating system and should easily be adaptable to any
foreseeable future operating system.

To preserve the data and keep them interoperable for the longest foreseeable
future, the entire database as well as parts of it (e. g. hierarchical trees of data
objects) has to be exportable in XML format *and* has to be printable at any
time without further editorial work.

6   The Database

A prototype database fulfilling almost (!) all of these requirements is already
working for eight years: http://www.accademia-vitruviana.net. Including its forerunner, a private database on the history of Saint-Peter's basilica in the Vatican,
it is working now for even 22 years. But, of course, it still needs 'some' tuning
and, of course, insertion of more data. It is usable as the working 'notebook' for
the author and can be used in reader-mode, i.e. without data adding or editing,
by external users for those data already published—many data are still 'hidden' in a 'private' modus, mostly due to copyright restrictions. It is planned to

make it publicly available as soon as possible—some funding presupposed—and to invite all interested scholarly persons to contribute. By now, lacking functionality consists with regard to reciprocal back links, fine-tuned structures of different data object structures and incorporation of web-standards or more meta data into these structures. The software used is the free Content Management System PLONE, based on the free Web Application Server ZOPE and (both) written (mostly) in the free script language Python. ZOPE contains its own object-oriented database and handles every 'webpage' as a data object that can be reached via human-readible URL addresses and links avoiding the unspeakable long chains of numbers, characters, and commands usually found in URLs from such systems. Even HTTP links are objects and, therefore, can be addressed, extended, or commented like any other data object. The shift from PLONE 4 to 5 unfortunately changed some basic concepts and functionalities, therefore, the project website has not made this step by now. It should and will be done as soon as possible, because an important functionality—i. e. a modul providing additional functions—co-develloped by the author has by now been extended and is available only for PLONE 5. This modul can handle an entire sub-tree of the hierarchical database—a folder and its subfolders and included pages or other objects like links—as a 'book'. Using the many different styles provided by LaTeX for scientific publikations, this book can be exported at any time from the website into printable PostScript or PDF files which—of course—look much better and offer better structure and organization of the text than any document—let alone book—written with the usual (proprietary) text software or offered by, e. g., *Wikipedia* or similar CMS as printable version of single articles. For instance, any HTML link (object) ist automatically transformed into a footnote pointing to the correct page of the print displaying the linked object.

7 Reasoning

The main reason to rediscover the rich materials left by the *Accademia* is their wealth of lost or any information otherwise lost and not reconstructable by modern research on buildings and artefacts from ancient Rome—surely influential on (not only) European and Western culture: Many of the *Accademia*'s documents describe lost or damaged objects and provide information about their original place, provenance or their history in or since the Renaissance.

In addition, the *Accademia*'s project seems to be not only the first but also the—by far—largest *ever* undertaken in the history of European (scholarly) culture—at least up to the late 20th century. To facilitate their work, as Tolomei writes, its over 200 members and collaborators shared the work among themselves in several 'disciplinary working groups' being prototypes of the disciplines of historical and archaeological research *and* interdisciplinary collaboration invented decades or centuries later. (In fact, this split-up seems to have caused the *non*-recognition of the entire project by later research and, therefore, its disappearing from the memory of historical research!)

But the *Accademia*'s members also developed a methodology [6–8] which seems to have been the first that deserves to be called *scholarly* or *scientific*—or, in German: *wissenschaftlich* covering both 'scientific cultures': It consisted mainly in the *exact* documentation of the given object without interference from presupposed ideas or suppositions to facilitate impartial, open-minded interpretation. Several of the collaborators—like, e. g., Ulisse Aldrovandi—worked in Rome with the *Accademia* and applied its methodology later to objects from the natural world. And doing so in Padua may have influenced—among other ways of transmission from the same academic Roman background—the beginning natural sciences, i. e., e. g. Galilei.

To reconstruct the work and the results of the *Accademia de lo Studio de l'Architettura* may, therefore, not only change our understanding of the ancient Roman world—and especially its influential architecture—and its scholarly *and* artistic reception in and since the Renaissance, but also the history of the humanities and—presumably—even the sciences.

References

1. Tolomei, C.: De le lettere di M. Claudio Tolomei Libri sette. Gabriel Giolito de Ferrari, Venice (1547), fol. 81 recto-85 recto
2. Sangallo, A. da [il Giovane = the Younger]: [untitled manuscript, so-called] «Proemio». In: Barocchi, P. (ed.): Scritti d'arte del Cinquecento, Vol. III. - Einaudi, Milano, pp. 3028–3031 (1977)
3. Marliano, B.: Topographia Urbis Romae. (3rd ed.) Dorico, Rome (1544)
4. Barozzi da Vignola, J.: Regola delli cinque ordini d'architettura. [Labacco], Rome (1562)
5. Palladio, A.: I Quattro Libri dell'Architettura. Franceschi, Venice (1570)
6. Daly Davis, M.: Wissenschaftliche Bearbeitung und Entwicklung einer Systematik: Archäologische und antiquarische Studien antiker Reste in der Accademia Vitruviana in Rom. In: Daly Davis, M. (ed.) Archäologie der Antike, pp. 11–19. Harassowitz, Wiesbaden (1994)
7. Harprath, R., Wrede, H. (eds.): Der Codex Coburgensis: Das erste systematische Archäologiebuch. Kunstsammlungen der Veste Coburg, Coburg (1986)
8. Kulawik, B.: Wissenschaftliche Begriffsbildung im Humanistenkreis der interdisziplinären Accademia della Virtù in Rom. Berichte zur Wissenschaftsgeschichte **38**, 140–152 (2014). https://doi.org/10.1002/bewi.201501722
9. Atanagi, D.: De le rime di diversi nobili poeti toscani, raccolte da M. Dionigi Atanagi. Lodovico Avanzo, Venice (1565)
10. Vasari, G.: Le vite de' piu eccellenti pittori, scultori, e architettori. Secondo, et vltimo Volume della Terza Parte. Giunti, Florence (1568)
11. Barozzi da Vignola, J. [also: Iacomo]; Danti, Egnatio (ed.): Le Dve Regole della Prospettiva pratica. Francesco Zanetti, Rome (1583)
12. Kulawik, B.: Sangallo, Vignola, Palladio and the Roman «Accademia de lo Studio de l'Architettura». In: Temporanea. Revista de Historia de la Arquitectura, vol. 2, pp. 52–79 (2021)
13. Philandrier, G.: In decem libros M. Vitruvii Pollionis de Architectura Annotationes. A. Blado (for A. Dossena), Rome (1544)

14. Agustìn, A.: Dialogos de medallas, inscriciones y otras antiguedades. Felipe Mei, Madrid (1587) [The two different Italian translations published in 1592 have been reprinted several times in the 17th century.]

15. Smet, Martin; Lipsius, Justus (ed.): Inscriptionum antiquarum quae passim per Europam, liber. Plantin, Antwerpen (1588)

16. [Pseudo-] Apollodorus of Athens; Egio, B. (ed./transl.): Apollodori Atheniensis Bibliotheces. A. Blado, Rome (1555)

17. Brunetti, M.: Tre disegni della Domus Aurea agli Uffizi: disiecta membra di un taccuino di antichità? In: Memoirs of the American Academy in Rome 63/64, pp. 291–322 (2018/2019)

18. Alciato, A.: Monumentorum veterumque Inscriptionum quae cum Mediol. tum in eius agro adhuc extant collectanea libri II. Manuscript «Mscr.Dresd.F.82.b» at the SLUB Dresden, Germany. [online: https://digital.slub-dresden.de/werkansicht/dlf/53844/1]

19. Waelscapple, M.V.: Inschriftensammlung des Maximilian van Waelscapple. Staatsbibliothek zu Berlin SPK: Ms. lat. fol. 61s, 1554. http://resolver.staatsbibliothek-berlin.de/SBB0001AE0600000000

20. Pighius, St. W.: [so-called] Codex Pighianus. Staatsbibliothek zu Berlin SPK, Ms. lat. fol. 61

21. Heenes, V., Jansen, D.J.: Jacopo Strada's Magnum Ac Novum Opus: A Sixteenth-Century Numismatic Corpus. (= Cyriacus. Studien zur Rezeption der Antike; 14) [1st of 2 volumes] - Petersberg: Imhof Verlag (2022)

Machine Learning and Artificial Intelligence

Semi-automatic Generation of Historical Urban 3D Models at a Larger Scale Using Structure-from-Motion, Neural Rendering and Historical Maps

Ferdinand Maiwald[1,2]([✉]) [iD], Dávid Komorowicz[2,3] [iD], Iqra Munir[2] [iD],
Clemens Beck[2] [iD], and Sander Münster[2] [iD]

[1] Institute of Photogrammetry and Remote Sensing, TU Dresden,
01069 Dresden, Germany
`ferdinand.maiwald@uni-jena.de`
[2] Chair for Digital Humanities (Images/Objects), FSU Jena, 07743 Jena, Germany
[3] Computer Vision Group, Technical University of Munich, 85748 Garching, Germany

Abstract. This paper presents two different strategies for the exploitation of historical photographs and maps and their usage in a three-dimensional (3D) and four-dimensional (4D) space. In the first approach, over 4000 historical photographs of Jena are collected via a citizen competition. These images are filtered in a semi-automatic way and processed in an adapted Structure-from-Motion workflow leading to multiple historical 3D models. As an innovative approach, two of the resulting reconstructions are refined using two different Neural Rendering approaches. For the first time, this enables the detailed seamless 3D visualization of sparse historical datasets, including defunct buildings. In cases where no photographs of buildings are available, an alternative strategy is demonstrated using historical maps. With an increasing amount of digitized historical maps, it becomes possible to segment and vectorize the building footprints for different points in time. The approach uses a semi-automatic workflow where a part of a historical map of Jena in 1936 is labeled manually in order to derive the remaining footprints automatically. At the moment, this labor-intensive step still has to be transferred to other historical maps to generate varying simple building models for different points in time. A combination of both approaches will allow the generation of detailed urban 4D models at a larger scale.

Keywords: 4D · building models · historical photographs · Structure-from-Motion · Neural Rendering · historical maps · segmentation

1 Motivation

Virtual historic cityscapes are used in various scenarios [1,6,41,46], e.g. to teach history and heritage in informal settings like museum experiences, serious games, or television broadcasts [9,10,12,13,15,16,32,34,36,38]. As one example, interactive applications for city exploration [18,19,22] allow virtual visits and remote

S. Münster et al. (Eds.): UHDL 2023, CCIS 1853, pp. 107–127, 2023.
https://doi.org/10.1007/978-3-031-38871-2_7

spatial learning [11], guide visitors through the city [4,11,19], provide access to additional information, and enable users to gather a virtual view of temporal change and historic spaces, buildings, and monuments or covered parts [1,3,4,25,43,45]. In order to make urban historical information a more immersive experience, four-dimensional (4D) representations are advantageous (cf. [33,44]). The fourth dimension is created by merging three-dimensional (3D) information with a temporal component. While previous approaches mostly operate with different models of time slices, in our application this is done by time-varying texture projection of historical photographs onto three-dimensional geometry models [35]. It is aimed to generate these historical depictions automatically at a larger scale (e.g., for multiple cities) (Fig. 1).

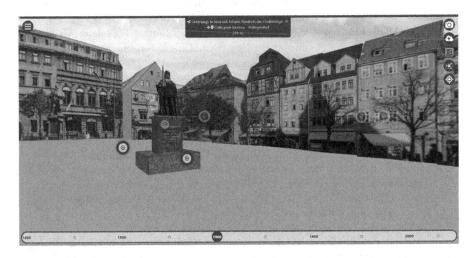

Fig. 1. 4D browser application in VR that uses historical photographs to texture three-dimensional building models (retrieved 11/21/2022 from https://4dcity.org).

However, this requires the determination of building footprints at different points in time or the automatic reconstruction of historical 3D models to match the date of the historical photograph. This contribution shows two different approaches on how to tackle both issues. The first method uses a modified Structure-from-Motion (SfM) workflow to retrieve the accurate camera orientation parameters of the historical photographs and a sparse point cloud. Subsequently, the resulting model is used in conjunction with two different Neural Rendering approaches [30] to obtain accurate geometric information from historical photographs. Therefore, the presented workflow is initially tested on a state-of-the-art benchmark dataset, adapted, and transferred to the historical datasets. To the knowledge of the authors, this is one of the first approaches that use Neural Rendering approaches on sparse historical image collections.

The second approach uses a historical map to generate building footprints in a semi-automatic way. Semantic segmentation in ArcGIS Pro is used to initially annotate several buildings by hand and consequently detect further footprints automatically. Depending on the historical sources of the respective city, it is intended to use one of both approaches or a combined strategy to semi-automatically retrieve urban 4D models at a larger scale.

2   Data

This section gives an overview of the contemporary benchmark dataset and the historical datasets used for the evaluation of methods. The historical data covers mainly the area of the city of Jena, Germany. The image data is provided by the Jena4D project (https://4dcity.org) and was collected via citizen participation. The historical maps are provided by the Thuringian University and State Library (ThULB) in high resolution to enable building footprint segmentation.

2.1   Contemporary Image Data

For the initial evaluation of the different NeRF approaches a contemporary benchmark dataset is used. This Phototourism dataset [17] consists of in-the-wild tourist photographs scraped from the internet and their corresponding 3D reconstruction created in COLMAP [40]. We use the Brandenburg Gate scene for evaluation purposes because ground truth data in the form of lidar scans are available [5]. Further, the transformation matrix referring to the COLMAP model is provided [42]. The dataset consists of 1336 images out of which 136 are reserved for validation.

2.2   Aggregating Historical Images via a Citizen Contest

To aggregate historical images of Jena, a citizen contest was held between 25th October 2022 and 4th December 2022. The citizens of Jena were asked to provide private historical photos, postcards, and further historical images from the period between 1900 and 2000. All tasks of the contest could be solved using the application 4DCity (https://4dcity.org/). Images could be submitted in three different ways:

1. If the photos were already digitized, they could be uploaded via an *upload* function in the app.
2. If the photos were still in an analog form, they could either be photographed directly with a camera function in the app or provided to us in analog form so that the digitization was handled within the project (especially for larger quantities).
3. To determine the position of the photos, citizens were also asked to *rephotograph* images already in the database. To do this, participants had to identify where the respective historical photo was taken and position themselves in

such a way that the modern photo corresponded to the original in terms of viewpoint and angle. The corresponding geo-information was then automatically transferred from the mobile phone to the database.

To motivate the citizens, prizes were awarded in a total of six categories shown on the official website (Fig. 2) created for the competition by advertising agency C4[1].

Fig. 2. Screenshot of the website for the contest (https://das-schoenste-jena.de/)

4–5 public stands were held every week in the Jena City Museum, the University Library, or the Jena Market Square to address citizens directly. Here, people could also hand in analog pictures directly. To ensure maximum accessibility, we kept the participation process low-threshold. Therefore, participants were only required to provide their name, email address, and telephone number (for two-factor authentication) in the application. This also allowed the transfer of the rights of the photographs, if the participants accepted.

In total, over 4000 historical photos and rephotographs were submitted of which a selection is used to evaluate the following 3D reconstruction methods.

2.3   Historical Maps and City Plans of Jena

Jena is a German city in the federal state of Thuringia and is first mentioned between 830 and 850 AD. Therefore, historical maps are already available for several centuries. The presented research focuses on a map of 1936 to get an idea of Jena's early urban development. The historical map has a scale of 1:10000 spanning a region between 50° 56' 16 N, 11° 33' 42 E (northwesternmost point) and 50° 54' 50 N, 11° 36' 36 E (southeasternmost point). Difficulties for automatic footprint segmentation in the historical map are existing graticule lines,

---

[1] https://www.c4berlin.de/.

and text that is printed on top of some buildings. The building footprints in the original map are structured in two categories, where single buildings are filled with red color and building blocks are shaded in red (Fig. 3).

Fig. 3. Small part of the original map from 1936 of Jena showing the difficult properties for automatic building footprint segmentation. (Color figure online)

The map can be observed and downloaded via the Thuringian University and State Library (https://collections.thulb.uni-jena.de/receive/HisBest_cbu_00084559).

3   Methods

3.1   Generation of Historical 3D Models Using SfM

The calculation of camera parameters and reconstruction of a sparse point cloud using SfM is a necessary step for the generation of detailed 3D models using Neural Rendering approaches (see Sect. 3.2). It requires several steps which are shown in Fig. 4.

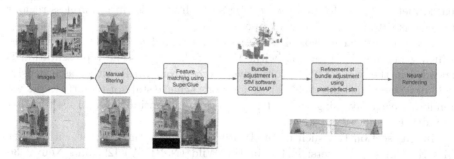

Fig. 4. The semi-automatic SfM workflow for filtering and orienting historical images necessary for Neural Rendering.

Initially, using historical photographs for Structure-from-Motion requires an appropriate pre-processing of the data. This implies, that the urban images retrieved in the competition need to be filtered.

As the images stem from the private property of citizens in Jena, usually no metadata is given and an automatic pre-filtering as in [28] is not possible. Therefore, the presented approach operates in a two-step semi-automatic way. In the first step, images that show buildings in the city of Jena are kept, while digitalisates of landscapes, close-up photographs, back of postcards, and multi-image postcards are removed by hand. In the second step, all of the remaining 635 images are processed using the SfM pipeline presented in [28]. As finding homologue points (feature matches) between historical image pairs is to be considered the main challenge for historical SfM [2,27,31], the proposed approach uses SuperPoint [8] & SuperGlue [39]. An issue that arises is, that the SuperGlue feature matching procedure is not fully rotational invariant [20] usually irrelevant for urban scenes. However, the digitized copies taken by the users are often rotated by 90°, 180°, or 270° which requires an initial correction using EXIF metadata.

All feature matches are imported into COLMAP [40] for estimation of camera orientation parameters using bundle adjustment and a sparse point cloud is generated. In addition, it has been observed that optimizing the accuracy of tie points is sometimes necessary when working with historical images. For the final reconstructed scenes a two-stage adjustment of keypoints and bundles is performed using the approach of [24]. As the complete dataset consists of many different buildings, COLMAP is used to generate single reconstructions (separate models) of those. Two of these generated reconstructions using exclusively historical images are used in the subsequent Neural Rendering approaches.

3.2   Generation of Historical 3D Models Using Neural Rendering

Working with historic imagery is challenging due to the sparse and uncalibrated nature of the data.

Running conventional Multi-View Stereo (MVS) algorithms on the oriented images from Sect. 3.1 usually results in incomplete models. The feature point-based methods used for dense matching suffer from holes in textureless regions or regions with an insufficient number of images.

Recently, neural network-based methods emerged for novel-view synthesis, which generates dense images without any holes. The scene representation is encoded in the weights of a Multi-Layer Perceptron (MLP) either as a density field or a signed distance field. These methods achieve state-of-the-art results via rendering each ray using volumetric rendering and optimizing all rays together in a dense manner.

In this section two such methods are investigated on their use with sparse historical image datasets: NeRF in the Wild (NeRF-W) [29] and Neural 3d Reconstruction in the Wild [42]. These methods have been developed with internet photo collections (*in-the-wild scenario*) in mind. These images are taken in uncontrolled conditions, with changing illumination and transient objects covering the subject matter.

We investigate how the performance of these methods degrades when reducing the number of images. Therefore, we create 6 additional splits (subset of images). In each split, half of the images from the previous split are removed. The number of images for the Brandenburg Gate scene becomes 1227, 613, 306, 153, 76, 38, and 19 for the respective split.

Both methods are qualitatively and quantitatively evaluated based on the generated novel views and the reconstructed geometry. To quantitatively evaluate the geometry we follow [42] and calculate the precision/recall and F1 scores against the ground truth lidar point cloud. We use the same three thresholds to describe the quality of the mesh at different scales. For the Brandenburg Gate scene, these are Low = 0.1, Medium = 0.2, High = 0.3 in meters.

The quality of the generated novel views is evaluated using the Peak Signal-to-Noise Ratio (PSNR) values on the validation images. For our objective, the quality of the sky is not important, therefore we calculate the PSNR values while masking out the sky as well. The sky masks, depth, and normal maps are rendered using BlenderProc [7] for evaluation. Since the appearance encoding of the validation images hasn't been used to train the appearance encoding, we use a zero vector for the embedding.

NeRF in the Wild. [29] is an extension of Neural Radiance Fields. It adds an appearance embedding to handle varying illumination conditions and a transient embedding to disentangle the static scene and occluders.

We use the implementation from [37] with 8 MLP layers with 256 features for the density layers and one layer for color. We apply the transient encoding to the coarse model as well in accordance with the original paper.

We use half-sized images for the reconstruction due to memory constraints but do inference at full size. NeRF-W is trained for 20 epochs, going through every image pixel in each epoch. The quantitative evaluation of novel views is shown in Table 1.

One image is selected from the validation set and visualized for qualitative comparison which can be seen in Fig. 5.

The PSNR values are lower than NeuS Facto (see next section) in all splits with sky mask. In splits three and four the PSNR values on the whole image are better for NeRF-W showing that it is better at representing the sky and background. Furthermore, a significant degradation is visible in the first three splits which is only true for the first split in NeuS Facto. This cannot be solved by simply increasing the hidden layer dimension to 512. This is caused by the more varied lighting conditions changing the appearance embedding, causing the pixel-wise difference to increase across the images. In splits three and four NeRF-W fails to correctly disentangle the transient parts. This gets resolved in the following splits with more images.

Table 1. Quantitative comparisons of NeRF in the Wild and NeuS Facto novel views synthesis via PSNR values

# images	NeRF-W		NeuS Facto	
	mask	full	mask	full
1227	12.32	11.97	**16.33**	**15.00**
613	15.22	14.70	**17.57**	**15.68**
306	15.09	14.34	**17.45**	**15.57**
153	16.22	**15.09**	**16.84**	14.92
76	16.09	**15.08**	**16.47**	14.92
38	15.02	14.14	**16.56**	**14.48**
19	13.37	13.27	**15.95**	**14.12**

To evaluate the geometry against the baseline, a mesh has to be extracted. This is possible via the marching cubes algorithm where a threshold has to be selected for the NeRF density to be considered the surface. This threshold is different for every training and the results wouldn't be satisfying as shown in Fig. 5(a). A way to bypass this issue is to reconstruct the mesh from the rendered depth images. As shown in [42] this also results in poor geometry, therefore we conclude that this method is not suitable for high-quality mesh generation and skip the quantitative evaluation of mesh quality.

(a) NeRF in the Wild   (b) NeuS Facto

Fig. 5. Extracted mesh using the Marching Cubes algorithm corresponding to the selected validation viewpoint

NeuS Facto. [47] uses volume rendering just like the previous method but at the end, it transforms the density into a signed distance field using a logistic distribution. This way there is always a clearly defined surface which is the 0-level set. This restriction means that transparent objects can no longer be represented but no ghosting artifacts can arise either.

According to Neural 3D Reconstruction in the Wild [42], the transient disentanglement in NeRF-W doesn't work with this method because everything gets represented as transient. Instead, semantic segmentation masks are used to ignore transient objects (such as people, vehicles, etc.) and the sky region is used to set the density loss to zero. A separate NeRF is used to represent the background. The SDF Studio [47] codebase is chosen for its convenient use and modularity. Here we use the $neus - facto - bigmlp$ model which contains several state-of-the-art optimizations. NeuS Facto is trained for 100k iterations and the pixels are randomly sampled at each iteration. Note that it is not guaranteed that all pixels are used.

Table 2 shows the quality of the reconstructed mesh with respect to the number of images used.

Table 2. Quantitative comparison of geometry with a reduced number of images on the Brandenburg Gate scene.

#images	Low			Medium			High		
	P	R	F1	P	R	F1	P	R	F1
1227	69.4	40.0	50.8	83.0	63.3	71.8	89.0	71.2	79.1
613	69.7	40.8	51.4	83.0	63.9	72.2	89.4	71.5	79.4
306	68.6	41.1	51.4	81.8	63.3	71.4	88.4	71.1	78.8
153	63.4	35.3	45.4	77.6	59.0	67.0	84.9	67.1	75.0
76	62.2	36.0	45.6	75.8	58.8	66.3	83.2	66.9	74.2
38	55.2	30.4	39.2	71.2	54.8	61.9	80.0	64.1	71.2
19	48.2	26.9	34.6	64.2	47.0	54.3	74.1	56.9	64.4

We achieve comparable, yet slightly worse results to the baseline Neural 3D Reconstruction in the Wild [42]. This can be attributed to the lack of surface-guided sampling. Reducing the images by half (from 1227 to 613) doesn't deteriorate the results at first. A potential explanation is that there are low-quality images in the 1st split or that the model reaches the model capacity. The supplementary material of Neural 3D Reconstruction in the Wild [42] contains a similar ablation study but only goes down to 25% of the images which is equivalent to our split two. For historic images, however, often even fewer images are available. As it can be seen from the plot, the quality starts to degrade in the subsequent splits. Figure 13 shows the rendered images for qualitative comparison of the splits.

Figure 5(b) shows the extracted mesh for the selected validation view. Additionally, we provide the meshes for viewing on the web[2]. The outer regions with few images and the roof/ground degrade the most. This is caused by the small angles between the optical axis of the cameras and the ground/roofs.

NeuS Facto achieves significantly better results in terms of geometry and PSNR values.

---

[2] https://sketchfab.com/dawars/collections/brandenburg-gate-ablation-study-935a0966ee92410caa746c0a9aba4235.

3.3   Generation of Historical 3D Models Using Old Maps

The historical map of Jena from 1936 has been obtained via https://collections. thulb.uni-jena.de/receive/HisBest_cbu_00084559. The map is exported to ArcGIS PRO software and adjusted via the alignment tool. The map is georeferenced by adding some control points as a reference from the base map [14]. These Control points having X, Y coordinates points are automatically added from the base maps reference data (Fig. 6). Georeferencing can help correct inaccuracies that are inherent in some aspects, such as the cartography of the raster, which causes it to be inaccurate from a geographical perspective [26].

Fig. 6. Collage of the necessary steps for automatic building footprint extraction. Starting point is a historical map (top left) that needs to be georeferenced (top right). Using different ArcGIS tools allows the extraction of footprints and evaluation of temporal changes between two maps.

The segmentation of historical maps aims to transform the image so that only the building footprints are visible. The building extraction of Jena in 1936 and 2022 has been done by using the *Detect Objects Using Deep Learning* tool automatically by using instance segmentation [21]. Using satellite images and the ArcGIS API for Python, one can train a deep learning model to extract these in a vectorized form. In order to extract building footprints, the trained model can be deployed on ArcGIS Pro or ArcGIS Enterprise. This workflow consists primarily of three stages:

1. Transfer Training Data
2. Train and Deploy a Model
3. Extract Footprints

ArcGIS Pro was used to generate the training data in the 'RCNN Masks' format with a *chip_ size* of 400px and a *cell_ size* of 30cm. The *prepare_ data* function creates a fastai databunch with the specified transformation, batch size, and split percentage from the path to the training data.

The map has been adjusted accordingly by visually identifying the geographic features that are clearly common between the raster data and the reference data. A layer of observed building footprints is what comes out of the model as the output. However, in order to complete the post-processing, the *Regularize Building Footprints* tool will be required to be used on the discovered building footprints (Fig. 6). This tool eliminates unwanted artifacts in the geometry of building polygons, which allows it to normalize the footprint of building polygons.

4 Results

4.1 Results of the SfM Processing

The depicted method for processing the filtered competition dataset yields a final number of 17 COLMAP models showing different buildings in Jena. These models consist of a varying size of 10 up to 170 images (Fig. 7 with a total number of 477 oriented photographs.

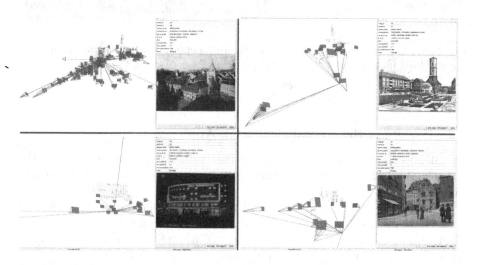

Fig. 7. Example for four different reconstructions generated by the modified SfM workflow using exclusively historical images.

For the exploration of the Neural Rendering approaches two medium-sized datasets are chosen. These include 48 photographs showing the Zeiss-Planetarium in Jena and 20 photographs showing the former Hotel International (Fig. 8). Initially, these images could not be oriented properly by using a conventional SfM workflow e.g., the default COLMAP settings or Agisoft Metashape.

Thus, the proposed method using SuperGlue feature matching and tie point optimization proves to be a reasonable strategy for preparing the data.

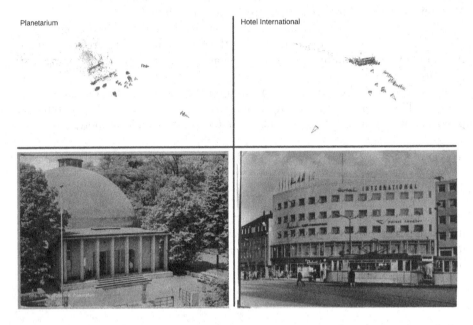

Fig. 8. COLMAP reconstruction of the Zeiss-Planetarium using 48 images and the former Hotel International using 20 images.

4.2 Results of the Neural Rendering Approach

To validate the findings in Sect. 3.2 we run NeRF-W and NeuS Facto on the two selected datasets from Jena. The resulting novel new renders can be seen in Fig. 9.

We make several changes compared to the experiment. We reduce the size of the hidden layers to 256 to avoid overfitting. For the hotel scene, we remove night-time images leaving 12 training images. With so few images the appearance embedding cannot represent large illumination changes correctly.

In this case, NeRF-W has clearer image renders and more detailed depth maps, except in the hotel scene where the color diverges.

Even though the experiment in Sect. 3.2 shows that high-quality results can be achieved with as little as 20 images using NeuS Facto, this requires images from various viewpoints and high-quality images. Furthermore, large illumination changes cannot be taken into account in this case.

Based on these findings we recommend the use of 40–80 high-quality photos with minimal illumination variation. It is also important to have photos from a

Fig. 9. Reconstruction of Jena datasets: observatory (top), international hotel (bottom) using NeRF-W and NeuS Facto methods respectively

higher altitude to get a good view of the roof for a complete mesh. The NeRF-W depth maps look very detailed which makes it a good candidate to use with TSDF [48] fusion if the NeuS Facto method doesn't give good results.

4.3 Results of the Segmentation of Historical Maps

Due to the nature of maps and how the training data appears, the *show_ batch()* method is used to arbitrarily select and visualize a few training samples. Masks depicting the structure footprints in each sample are applied. For the shaded image blocks, it is intended to create a binary mask with the areas representing buildings (Fig. 10).

On this image, Canny edge detection can then be performed, and the resulting contours can be vectorized. The method reveals the utmost production for the footprint detection of a building. It is intended to use the extracted footprint, extrude it to a 3D model and estimate the building height using oriented historical images of this point in time. The comparison of the 1936 and 2022 maps shows almost 60% of temporal change by the automatic footprint extraction. However, at the moment the manual labeling effort of footprints is quite extensive. For the 1936 map around 50% of footprints had to be labeled manually to retrieve the remaining building footprints automatically.

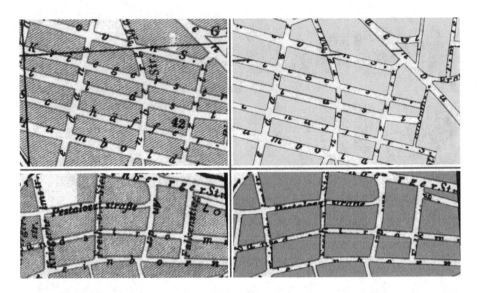

Fig. 10. The left part shows example patches of the historical map of 1936. The right part depicts the related automatically segmented building footprints.

5   Conclusions and Outlook

The presented research concludes with several findings when collecting and using historical images and maps for the generation of urban 3D models. Citizens can be well engaged to contribute to the enrichment of their city's history by providing their private images and postcards to the community. Due to the inhomogeneous quality of the analog originals and the varying digitization procedures, photogrammetric processing is still challenging and requires adaptations of the Structure-from-Motion workflow. This allows for estimating the camera orientation parameters of a large fraction of all uploaded images and the application of Neural Rendering approaches for specific buildings. However, this requires fine-tuning of existing strategies to enhance their capability for sparse historical datasets with vast image differences and uncalibrated cameras. The depicted approach is to the knowledge of the authors the first application of NeRF-based methods on exclusively historical photographs. Still, even with the participation of citizens, it is not possible to generate a 3D reconstruction of every building in the inner city of Jena because of a lack of existing photographs.

Therefore, a second strategy for a large-scale reconstruction of simpler 3D models is proposed using historical maps. Due to the extremely varying style of historical maps and the included textual elements, completely automatic segmentation is challenging. Thus, a semi-automatic approach is chosen which still requires extensive manual segmentation for subsequent automatic extraction of the remaining building footprints. Possible improvements are the transfer of one map segmentation to other historical maps or the use of novel image segmentation methods like Meta's Segment Anything [23].

With the aim of the publication generating reconstructions at a larger scale for further cities, a possible future solution could be the fusion of the image-based approach with the map-based approach in the future (Fig. 11).

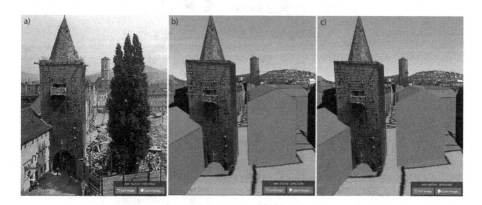

Fig. 11. Mockup for the combination of the developed map-based and image-based approach: a) Cropped original historical photograph around 1950 at the correct position in the 3D environment. b) The 3D scene behind the overlay of the historical photograph. c) Contemporary building model that should be removed in the 3D scene in 1950.

This includes the automatic extrusion of the segmented footprints and estimation of the building height using the oriented photographs. The texture could be derived from the historical images while detailed 3D structures are generated by the Neural Rendering approaches generating detailed urban 4D representations.

Acknowledgement. The research upon which this paper is based is part of the research project Jena4D which has received funding from the German Federal Cultural Foundation through the dive in programme for Digital Interactions. The authors gratefully acknowledge the FSU·Jena's support for this project by providing computing time through the HPC cluster *Draco*. We also thank Patrick Chilton from Benaco for his help in meshing the lidar scan of the Brandenburg Gate. [5]

Appendix A

Ground Truth

1227

613

306

153

76

38

19

Fig. 12. Qualitative comparison of NeRF in the Wild: color (left) and depth (right)

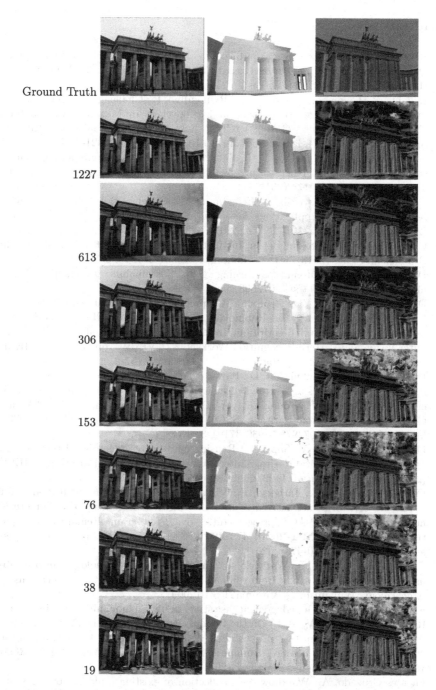

Fig. 13. Qualitative comparison of NeuS Facto: color (left), depth (middle), and normal (right)

References

1. Bekele, M.K., Pierdicca, R., Frontoni, E., Malinverni, E.S., Gain, J.: A survey of augmented, virtual, and mixed reality for cultural heritage. J. Comput. Cult. Heritage **11**(2), 1–36 (2018). https://doi.org/10.1145/3145534

2. Bellavia, F., Colombo, C., Morelli, L., Remondino, F.: Challenges in image matching for cultural heritage: An overview and perspective. In: Mazzeo, P.L., Frontoni, E., Sclaroff, S., Distante, C. (eds.) ICIAP 2022. LNCS, vol. 13373, pp. 210–222. Springer, Cham (2022). https://doi.org/10.1007/978-3-031-13321-3_19

3. Chang, Y.L., Hou, H.T., Pan, C.Y., Sung, Y.T., Chang, K.: Apply an augmented reality in a mobile guidance to increase sense of place for heritage places. Educ. Technol. Soc. **18**, 166–178 (2015)

4. Chatzidimitris, T., Kavakli, E., Economou, M., Gavalas, D.: Mobile augmented reality edutainment applications for cultural institutions. In: IISA 2013. IEEE (2013). https://doi.org/10.1109/iisa.2013.6623726

5. CyArk, Landesdenkmalamt Berlin, Institute For Photogrammetry, Iron Mountain: Brandenburg gate (2018). https://doi.org/10.26301/D51V-FQ77

6. Daniela, L.: Virtual museums as learning agents. Sustainability **12**(7), 2698 (2020). https://doi.org/10.3390/su12072698

7. Denninger, M., et al.: Blenderproc. arXiv preprint arXiv:1911.01911 (2019)

8. DeTone, D., Malisiewicz, T., Rabinovich, A.: SuperPoint: self-supervised interest point detection and description. In: 2018 IEEE/CVF Conference on Computer Vision and Pattern Recognition Workshops (CVPRW), pp. 337–33712. IEEE (2018). https://doi.org/10.1109/cvprw.2018.00060

9. Doukianou, S., Daylamani-Zad, D., Paraskevopoulos, I.: Beyond virtual museums: adopting serious games and extended reality (XR) for user-centred cultural experiences. In: Liarokapis, F., Voulodimos, A., Doulamis, N., Doulamis, A. (eds.) Visual Computing for Cultural Heritage. SSCC, pp. 283–299. Springer, Cham (2020). https://doi.org/10.1007/978-3-030-37191-3_15

10. Ferrara, V., Macchia, A., Sapia, S.: Reusing cultural heritage digital resources in teaching. In: 2013 Digital Heritage International Congress (DigitalHeritage). IEEE (2013). https://doi.org/10.1109/digitalheritage.2013.6744792

11. Fino, M.D., Ceppi, C., Fatiguso, F.: Virtual tours and informational models for improving territorial attractiveness and the smart management of architectural heritage: the 3D-IMP-ACT project. Int. Arch. Photogram. Remote Sens. Spatial Inf. Sci. **XLIV-M-1-2020**, 473–480 (2020). https://doi.org/10.5194/isprs-archives-xliv-m-1-2020-473-2020

12. Fisher, C.R., Terras, M., Warwick, C.: Integrating new technologies into established systems: a case study from roman silchester. In: Computer Applications to Archaeology, Williamsburg, Virginia, USA (2009)

13. Flaten, A.: Ashes2art: a pedagogical case study in digital humanities. In: Jerem, E., Redő, F., Szeverényi, V. (eds.) On the Road to Reconstructing the Past. Computer Applications and Quantitative Methods in Archaeology (CAA). Proceedings of the 36th International Conference, Budapest, 2–6 April 2008, pp. 346–352 (CD-ROM 193–199), Archeaeolingua, Budapest (2011)

14. Fuentes Cruzado, A.: Workflow data collection of existing buildings by 3D scanning process: (in modelling BIM). Ph.D. thesis, Universitat Politècnica de València (2017)

15. Gicquel, P.Y., Lenne, D., Moulin, C.: Design and use of CALM : an ubiquitous environment for mobile learning during museum visit. In: 2013 Digital Heritage

International Congress (DigitalHeritage). IEEE (2013). https://doi.org/10.1109/digitalheritage.2013.6744831

16. Haynes, R.: Eye of the veholder: AR extending and blending of museum objects and virtual collections. In: Jung, T., tom Dieck, M.C. (eds.) Augmented Reality and Virtual Reality. PI, pp. 79–91. Springer, Cham (2018). https://doi.org/10.1007/978-3-319-64027-3_6

17. Heinly, J., Schönberger, J.L., Dunn, E., Frahm, J.M.: Reconstructing the world* in six days *(as captured by the yahoo 100 million image dataset). In: Computer Vision and Pattern Recognition (CVPR) (2015)

18. Ioannidi, A., Gavalas, D., Kasapakis, V.: Flaneur: augmented exploration of the architectural urbanscape. In: 2017 IEEE Symposium on Computers and Communications (ISCC). IEEE (2017). https://doi.org/10.1109/iscc.2017.8024582

19. Ioannidis, C., Verykokou, S., Soile, S., Boutsi, A.M.: A multi-purpose cultural heritage data platform for 4D visualization and interactive information services. Int. Arch. Photogram. Remote Sens. Spatial Inf. Sci. **XLIII-B4-2020**, 583–590 (2020). https://doi.org/10.5194/isprs-archives-xliii-b4-2020-583-2020

20. Jin, Y., Mishkin, D., Mishchuk, A., Matas, J., Fua, P., Yi, K.M., Trulls, E.: Image matching across wide baselines: from paper to practice. Int. J. Comput. Vis. 1–31 (2020). https://doi.org/10.1007/s11263-020-01385-0

21. Jiwani, A., Ganguly, S., Ding, C., Zhou, N., Chan, D.M.: A semantic segmentation network for urban-scale building footprint extraction using RGB satellite imagery (2021). https://doi.org/10.48550/ARXIV.2104.01263

22. Kim, K., et al.: Augmented reality tour system for immersive experience of cultural heritage. In: Proceedings of the 8th International Conference on Virtual Reality Continuum and its Applications in Industry - VRCAI 2009, Yokohama, Japan, pp. 323–324. Association for Computing Machinery (2009)

23. Kirillov, A., et al.: Segment anything. arXiv:2304.02643 (2023)

24. Lindenberger, P., Sarlin, P.E., Larsson, V., Pollefeys, M.: Pixel-perfect structure-from-motion with featuremetric refinement (2021). https://doi.org/10.48550/ARXIV.2108.08291

25. Luna, U., Rivero, P., Vicent, N.: Augmented reality in heritage apps: current trends in Europe. Appl. Sci. **9**(13), 2756 (2019). https://doi.org/10.3390/app9132756

26. Lunetta, R., Congalton, R.G., Fenstermaker, L.K., Jensen, J.R., McGwire, K.C., Tinney, L.R.: Remote sensing and geographic information system data integration: error sources and research issues. Photogramm. Eng. Remote. Sens. **57**, 677–687 (1991)

27. Maiwald, F.: Generation of a benchmark dataset using historical photographs for an automated evaluation of different feature matching methods. Int. Arch. Photogramm. Remote Sens. Spatial Inf. Sci. **XLII-2/W13**, 87–94 (2019). https://doi.org/10.5194/isprs-archives-XLII-2-W13-87-2019. https://www.int-arch-photogramm-remote-sens-spatial-inf-sci.net/XLII-2-W13/87/2019/

28. Maiwald, F., Bruschke, J., Schneider, D., Wacker, M., Niebling, F.: Giving historical photographs a new perspective: introducing camera orientation parameters as new metadata in a large-scale 4D application. Remote Sens. **15**(7), 1879 (2023). https://doi.org/10.3390/rs15071879

29. Martin-Brualla, R., Radwan, N., Sajjadi, M.S.M., Barron, J.T., Dosovitskiy, A., Duckworth, D.: Nerf in the wild: neural radiance fields for unconstrained photo collections. arXiv:2008.02268, pp. 1–15 (2020)

30. Mildenhall, B., Srinivasan, P.P., Tancik, M., Barron, J.T., Ramamoorthi, R., Ng, R.: Nerf: representing scenes as neural radiance fields for view synthesis. In: ECCV (2020)

31. Morelli, L., Bellavia, F., Menna, F., Remondino, F.: Photogrammetry now and then – from hand-crafted to deep-learning tie points –. Int. Arch. Photogram. Remote Sens. Spatial Inf. Sci. **XLVIII-2/W1-2022**, 163–170 (2022). https://doi.org/10.5194/isprs-archives-xlviii-2-w1-2022-163-2022

32. Motejlek, J., Alpay, E.: A taxonomy for virtual and augmented reality in education (2019). https://doi.org/10.48550/ARXIV.1906.12051

33. Muenster, S.: Digital 3D technologies for humanities research and education: an overview. Appl. Sci. **12**(5), 2426 (2022). https://doi.org/10.3390/app12052426

34. Münster, S.: Militärgeschichte aus der digitalen retorte - computergenerierte 3D-visualisierung als filmtechnik. In: Kästner, A., Mazerath, J. (eds.) Mehr als Krieg und Leidenschaft. Die filmische Darstellung von Militär und Gesellschaft der Frühen Neuzeit (Militär und Gesellschaft in der frühen Neuzeit, 2011/2), pp. 457–486. Universitätsverlag Potsdam, Potsdam (2011)

35. Münster, S., Lehmann, C., Lazariv, T., Maiwald, F., Karsten, S.: Toward an automated pipeline for a browser-based, city-scale mobile 4D VR application based on historical images. In: Niebling, F., Münster, S., Messemer, H. (eds.) UHDL 2019. CCIS, vol. 1501, pp. 106–128. Springer, Cham (2021). https://doi.org/10.1007/978-3-030-93186-5_5

36. Ott, M., Pozzi, F.: Towards a new era for cultural heritage education: discussing the role of ICT. Comput. Hum. Behav. **27**(4), 1365–1371 (2011). https://doi.org/10.1016/j.chb.2010.07.031

37. Quei-An, C.: Nerf_pl: a pytorch-lightning implementation of nerf (2020). https://github.com/kwea123/nerf_pl

38. Sanders, D.H.: Virtual archaeology: yesterday, today, and tomorrow. In: Nicolucci, F., Hermon, S. (eds.) Beyond the Artifact. Digital Interpretation of the Past. Proceedings of CAA2004, Prato 13–17 April 2004, Archaeolingua, Budapest, pp. 319–324 (2010)

39. Sarlin, P.E., DeTone, D., Malisiewicz, T., Rabinovich, A.: Superglue: learning feature matching with graph neural networks. In: Proceedings of the IEEE/CVF Conference on Computer Vision and Pattern Recognition, pp. 4938–4947 (2020). arXiv:1911.11763

40. Schönberger, J.L., Frahm, J.M.: Structure-from-motion revisited. In: 2016 IEEE Conference on Computer Vision and Pattern Recognition (CVPR), pp. 4104–4113. IEEE (2016). https://doi.org/10.1109/cvpr.2016.445

41. Siddiqui, M.S., Syed, T.A., Nadeem, A., Nawaz, W., Alkhodre, A.: Virtual tourism and digital heritage: an analysis of VR/AR technologies and applications. Int. J. Adv. Comput. Sci. Appl. **13**(7) (2022). https://doi.org/10.14569/ijacsa.2022.0130739

42. Sun, J., et al.: Neural 3D reconstruction in the wild. In: Special Interest Group on Computer Graphics and Interactive Techniques Conference Proceedings. ACM (2022). https://doi.org/10.1145/3528233.3530718

43. Torres, M., Qiu, G.: Picture the past from the present. In: 3rd International Conference on Internet Multimedia Computing and Service, Chengdu, China. ACM (2011)

44. Tversky, B.: Visuospatial reasoning. In: Holyoak, K., Morrison, B. (eds.) The Cambridge Handbook of Thinking and Reasoning, pp. 209–240. Cambridge University Press, Cambridge (2005)

45. Vicent, N., Gracia, M.P.R., Torruella, M.F.: Arqueología y tecnologías digitales en educación patrimonial. Educatio Siglo XXI **33**(1), 83 (2015). https://doi.org/10.6018/j/222511

46. ViMM Working Group 2.2: Meaningful content connected to the real world. Technical report, Horizon 2020 Programme as Coordination and Support Action (CSA) (2017)
47. Yu, Z., et al.: SDFStudio: a unified framework for surface reconstruction (2022). https://github.com/autonomousvision/sdfstudio
48. Zeng, A., Song, S., Nießner, M., Fisher, M., Xiao, J., Funkhouser, T.: 3DMatch: learning local geometric descriptors from RGB-D reconstructions. In: CVPR (2017)

Visualization and Presentation

Digital Urban History Lab – Serious 3D in Research, Education and Popularization of Cultural Heritage

Piotr Kuroczyński[1]([✉]), Igor Piotr Bajena[1,2], and Peggy Große[1,3]

[1] Institute of Architecture, Hochschule Mainz – University of Applied Sciences, Mainz, Germany
`plotr.kuroczynski@lhs-malnz.de`
[2] Faculty of Architecture, Università di Bologna, Bologna, Italy
[3] University Library Heidelberg, Heidelberg, Germany

Abstract. The paper deals with the impact of the digital transformation on the research, documentation and dissemination of historical information, with a focus on the spatial development history of cities. The Digital Urban History Lab aims to exploit the challenges and opportunities of this digital transformation to move one step closer towards 'Serious 3D' in research, education and popularization of cultural heritage. The use of digital 3D reconstructions in scholarly projects, documentaries, and exhibitions has become increasingly common. However, unresolved issues have arisen regarding the scholarly nature of these reconstructions and their findability, accessibility, interoperability and reusability.

The Digital Urban History Lab addresses the above questions using the example of reprocessing, documenting, and communicating the latest findings about medieval cities: Mainz, Worms and Speyer. The focus is on the sustainability of research data and includes the development of a CIDOC CRM referenced data model and a virtual research environment using Linked Data technologies. The Digital Urban History Lab represents an exhibition space where the 3D models are presented along with interactive access to the knowledge behind them. The focus of the consideration is the working method of a source-based hypothetical 3D reconstruction of the past, which is hidden behind the concept of 'Scientific Reference Model'. Overall, the project illustrates the potential of scientifically based 3D models, supported by structured, semantically enriched, referenceable research data, which ensure accessibility and reusability, among others, for research, education, creative industries, etc.

Keywords: Serious 3D · Scientific Reference Model · Hypothetical 3d reconstruction · data modeling · CIDOC CRM

1 Introduction

August Bebel once said, 'Only those who know the past can understand the present and shape the future.' This quote underscores the significance of historical knowledge in shaping our understanding of the world. With the rise of digital transformation, new

S. Münster et al. (Eds.): UHDL 2023, CCIS 1853, pp. 131–144, 2023.
https://doi.org/10.1007/978-3-031-38871-2_8

opportunities and challenges have emerged in the realm of researching, documenting, and disseminating our past. The digital turn has revolutionized the way we approach historical research. It provides innovative tools and techniques that enable us to explore and analyze the past in unprecedented ways. However, along with these opportunities, there are also challenges to address.

Since the 1990s, the digital source-based 3D reconstruction has increasingly found its way into academic projects, documentary broadcasts and museum exhibitions [1], but also into the children's rooms of 'digital natives' with photorealistic images or in the form of immersive game worlds, like the Assassin's Creed series. But what about the scholar nature, in particular the traceability, accessibility, citability and reusability, of the digitally (re-)constructed 3D worlds?

This question reveals a long-standing desideratum in the field of digital research methods, which is mainly due to a lack of standards, interoperability and infrastructure regarding 3D models and the knowledge behind them. In the last five years, a broad examination of the issues, potentials, and challenges associated with 3D reconstruction as a method within object-based research has taken place within the domain community [2, 3].

According to the urban history, particular challenge lies in making the complex spatial development history of our cities comprehensible to a wide audience. Cities have intricate and layered histories, which can be difficult to convey effectively. Ensuring the accuracy, reliability and accessibility of digital historical resources is crucial to achieve a comprehensible communication of the history.

The Digital Urban History Lab is dedicated to tackling this challenge by utilizing digital technologies and methodologies. By leveraging digital tools, the lab aims to create interactive and engaging experiences that bring the historical development of cities to life. Through immersive visualizations, interactive interfaces, and accessible storytelling, the lab strives to make the rich history of our cities accessible and understandable to a broad audience.

Ultimately, the Digital Urban History Lab seeks to bridge the gap between the past and present by harnessing the power of digital transformation to deepen our understanding of history and shape a more informed future.

2   Digital Urban History Lab – Mainz, Worms and Speyer

Our institutions of cultural memory capture, research, manage and convey the past and thus secure the cultural heritage for future generations as a moment of identification in our society. How can the latest findings of urban archeology and building research be processed, documented and communicated?

The General Directorate for Cultural Heritage Rhineland-Palatinate (GDKE) asked itself this question as part of the preparation of the state exhibition "The Emperors and the Pillars of their Power - From Charlemagne to Friedrich Barbarossa" (September 9th, 2020 - June 13th, 2021). The state exhibition was related to the inclusion of SchUM-Cities, a historic center of Jewish culture in the medieval cities of Mainz, Worms and Speyer, in the UNESCO World Heritage List. One of the central cultural landscapes of Europe developed along the Rhine in the High Middle Ages. Mainz, Worms and Speyer in particular quickly rose to become the most important cities of the Holy Roman Empire and thus had far-reaching social and cultural significance, in particular for the Jewish community. The central position of the three imperial cities was reflected above all in the construction of large, representative sacred buildings commissioned by emperors and bishops. However, many monuments from this period have been lost due to later destruction and overbuilding and can only be traced today through modern building research, archaeological excavations or with the help of historical sources.

In order to explore the importance of Mainz, Worms and Speyer and to promote identification among the population, an application for the project "Mainz - Worms - Speyer. Three medieval cities in central Europe as Linked Data" was submitted to the Federal Government Commissioner for Culture and Media. The aim of the approved project was to create digital 3D models of the cities on the Rhine in close cooperation between GDKE and the Architecture Institute at the Hochschule Mainz – University of Applied Sciences (AI MAINZ) and to secure the digital processed knowledge on which these models are based in the long term. The curators and project managers of the state exhibition recognized the potential of digital 3D reconstruction and cross-media communication of the findings. In spring 2020, it was decided to present the results of the project to a broad public in an exhibition room specially set up for this purpose. The Digital Urban History Lab was conceived in cooperation between AI MAINZ and the media design department at the Hochschule Mainz, and opened in July 2021 in the Landesmuseum Mainz [4].

Fig. 1. View inside the DUHL. Interactive projection via touch screen on the white city model of Mainz 1250 AD in scale 1:1000. In the background the representation of the reconstruction processes (Hochschule Mainz/Olaf Hirschberg, 2021).

Two printed models of each city in the time Sect. 800 and 1250 AD, from Charlemagne to Friedrich Barbarossa, await visitors in the lab, as well as explanatory film animations on the hypothetical 3D reconstruction. The city models of Mainz contain a thematic compilation of different information, which is projected onto the physical model via an interactive interface on the touchscreen. In addition, the lab explains the process of digital reconstruction, variants and versions, and documentation within the Virtual Research Environment (Fig. 1).

3   Computer based Visualization and (re-)materialization

Linear narration and visualization in the form of film animations were chosen as a proven form of conveying medieval city history. The advantages of this format lie in the guided narrative, which directs the viewer's attention to what is being described through the chosen camera movement and focus. With regard to the 3D reconstruction and illustration of medieval city structures, the challenge lay in the wide-ranging hypothetical representation. Here, the character of a source-based 3D reconstruction comes to the fore, which always results in a hypothetical reconstruction. The linear form of mediation in the form of computer-generated images represents a result of the research work, which in most cases generate images of the past in the minds of the recipients without explaining the uncertainties and hypotheses. These strengths and weaknesses of the format need to be weighed. A reference to the hypothetical representation of the reconstruction should always be mentioned prominently.

Fig. 2. Computer-based visualization with the used color schema for architecture. View on Mainz 1250 AD, seen from the east bank of the Rhine (AI MAINZ/GDKE, 2020).

When working on the three medieval cities, only selective excavations were available and thus little archaeological and architectural documentation. The main work in the 3D modeling and visualization consisted of using the few solid clues (historical sources), the introduction of further analogies and a hypothetical closing of the knowledge gaps. In the linear form of mediation, an abstract representation of the city structures and the detailed 3D modeling of selected, significant and thus better documented buildings were agreed upon. Through a chosen color scheme, different building materials and structures should be recognizable in the film (Fig. 2). Following the schema Roman ruins are represented in pale yellow, medieval stone houses in white, wooden houses in pale brown and the cathedrals in their specific color of red stone.

Fig. 3. Attaching the printed elements of the model of the city of Mainz 1250 AD in scale 1:1000 to the underground (Hochschule Mainz/Piotr Kuroczyński, 2020).

As a second mediation format for architecture, which has also proven itself for centuries, physical models were used. As a result of the digital transformation, for more than two decades we have had a choice of several rapid prototype technologies for returning digital 3D models from bits and bytes back to physical substance.

The advantages of the format are a pleasant perception of spatial structures, a holistic view of the entire city and its components. In addition, the printed model offers the possibility to organize guided group tours on the model, for example, to convey the history to school classes. In the case of the three cities on the Rhine, the representation in the white model was chosen, which was produced in the stereolithography printing process consisting of hundreds segments with an edge length of 12 by 12 cm. This printing process made it possible to depict details, including people and farm animals, on a scale of 1 to 1000. The division of the segments resulted from the printing space of the 3D printers from Formlabs used. The division of the digital city models into a grid of 12 by 12 cm also brings with it the flexibility and possibility to exchange elements afterwards. In the case of the city models of Mainz around 1250 AD, the model consists of around 125 segments (Fig. 3).

An interactive mediation of the city history, consisting of the topography, the infrastructure, the functional use, the composition of the inhabitants as well as its important buildings and fortifications, was implemented by projecting the contents onto the white model. For this purpose, the content was compiled by the curators and presented on a touch screen for selection in collaboration with media designers. Visitors can explore the content on these and trigger the projection onto the model by making a selection of a topic on the touch screen (Fig. 1).

4   Scientific Reference Model and the Seriousness of 3D

The film animation and the 3D printing represent the mediation formats, as described before. They make use of the hypothetical reconstruction and the digital 3D models proceeding from it. As mediation formats, in most cases they want to tell a story, but due to their nature they do not allow the possibility of retracing their creation. The question of access to the source models, information about the authors of the models, the sources used, the uncertainties (hypotheses), the reusability (license) and so on remain unresolved. Thus, one of the main demands of the London Charter [5] and Sevilla Principals [6] regarding transparency and traceability of computer-based visualization remains unclarified.

The concept of Scientific Reference Model (SRM) aims to address this desideratum by structuring a 3D reconstruction as an applicable research method. The concept was developed in research and teaching at the University of Applied Sciences Mainz [7, 8] and is shown as Fig. 4.

The SRM starts from the indexing and interpretation of historical sources. This research activity is accompanied by the creative filling of knowledge gaps as a result of drawing analogies and/or logical deductions, in the most optimal case in close coordination with subject specialists.

As a representative of the source-based hypothetical 3D reconstruction, the documentation of the source material related to the 3D modeled objects is essential. To meet this need, the object to be reconstructed is divided into individual parts (segmentation) so that the sources can be referenced to the object (e.g. building elements). The project-specific segmentation allows for flexibility, and desired granularity in terms of information as needed.

This approach supports the explicit labeling of individual elements with information, such as the classification of the components and the link to the available sources. If one sets a classification of the sources, depending on reliability, information density, etc. in relations with the elaborated level of detail of the 3D objects, then alphanumerical uncertainty values for individual elements can be mapped on their equivalent in 3D model.

A comprehensive presentation of different concepts and value systems for the representation of uncertainties is provided by the currently submitted PhD thesis of Irene Cazzaro [9].

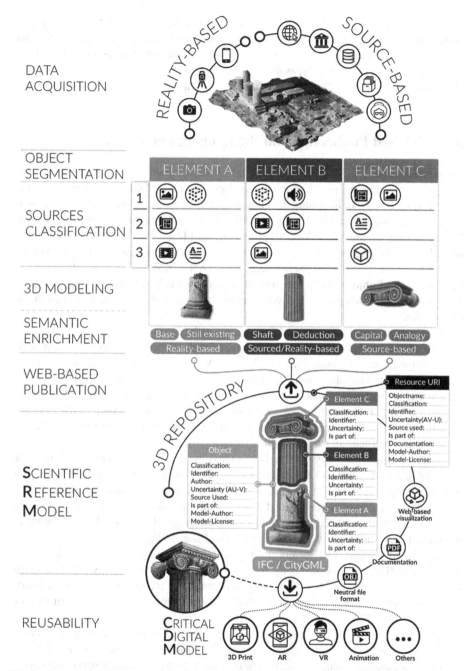

Fig. 4. Structural framework of the Scientific Reference Model (SRM) and its derivates. An overview (AI MAINZ/Piotr Kuroczyński and Igor Bajena, 2023, CC BY-NC-SA).

The SRM is seen as a reference model and starting/initial model for further applications, for example film animations, 3D printing, augmented reality, virtual reality, serious games, etc. The basic requirement of the concept is to publish the SRM on the web, to make it findable, traceable and reusable. Conversely, only a model that is findable, traceable and reusable can be considered a 'serious 3D' model for research, education and dissemination of cultural heritage.

5   Web based Publication and the Language of Serious 3D

The development of the Internet into mankind's leading knowledge repository also raises the question of how we should publish our digital research data on the Net. Since the beginning of the new millennium, the human- and machine-readable mapping of knowledge in graph databases has been understood as a solution approach in this context. Behind the names 'Semantic Web' [10] and 'Linked Data' [11] lies the desire to store formalized knowledge in a structured way and to link it to other data sets prepared in the same way. In the field of cultural heritage, the CIDOC CRM has become established as the 'language of objects' [12]. The formalization of knowledge here is based on about 200 relations and 100 entities with which event-based a subject can be described in the data model.

For the web-based indexing and publication of the 3D models in terms of SRM, the CIDOC CRM referenced application ontology OntScieDoc3D is used as data model. As a Virtual Research Environment (VRE), the WissKI software architecture with the available 'Pathbuilder Module' is used for the integration of CIDOC CRM referenced data models [13]. Here, it was the further development of the research results from the project of 'Digital Reconstruction of the New Synagogue in Breslau' – the detailed description of the documentation schema (data model) and the software architecture (WissKI) can be found in the project description [14].

The application ontology OntScieDoc3D lists the osd 73a 3D Reconstruction under the CIDOC CRM entity E73 Information Object to describe the digital 3D model. The 3D model originates from the research activity (osd 7a), which in turn uses sources (osd 31b) and is executed by a person (osd 21a). The digital 3D model (osd 73a) represents a man-made object (osd 22a) and is subject to clarified legal terms (osd 30a). The basic features of the data model can be seen in the hand sketch (Fig. 5).

The WissKI-based VRE offers the possibility to represent the complexities of a hypothetical 3D reconstruction using an underlying application ontology. The challenge was to adapt the VRE designed for the documentation of the reconstruction of a building, namely the New Synagogue in Breslau, to the requirements of a reconstruction of medieval cities [15].

In terms of SRM, the requirement was to identify and index the sources underlying the 3D model, as well as to integrate a value system for mapping the hypotheses.

Only outstanding buildings, such as the cathedrals, were included in detail as individual objects based on better sources. These were linked to defined areas (ensembles and neighborhoods) via 'part of' relationships. The value system in terms of uncertainties was mapped under the field entry 'plausibility' according to a three-level concept:

a) Models that were based only on analogies were assigned low plausibility,

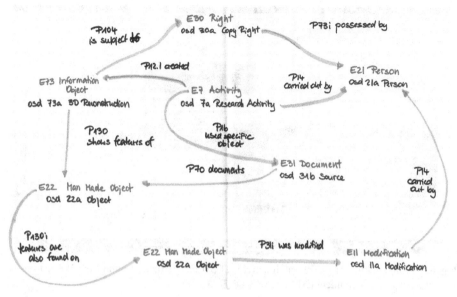

Fig. 5. Hand drawing of the OntSciDoc3D data model scheme (AI MAINZ/Peggy Große, 2020)

b) Models that were partially based on excavations and/or previous building research were assigned medium plausibility,

c) Models that could be based on extensive documentation, excavation and/or building research, were awarded high plausibility.

With this simple system, a low-threshold approach to the complex task of mapping hypotheses was achieved.

Sketchfab was used for web-based visualization of the 3D models uploaded to the VRE. Within the Sketchfab repository, the models were described as far as possible and the right question was clarified. All published models are available for further use under the Creative Commons license CC-BY-NC-SA 4.0.

In the sense of SRM, the VRE offers a comprehensive possibility to capture sources, objects, and the research activities, which are available in a structured way by means of the underlying data model. However, this requires a higher effort for the setup of the software architecture and for the data indexing in the system (Fig. 6).

For this reason, conventional 3D repositories are preferred for the web-based publication of SRM models. Repositories, where an upload of the model with descriptive and administrative metadata is possible and a low-threshold publication and accessibility is given. The importance and number of 3D models on the web is constantly increasing, resulting in a high pressure for solutions of reliable and sustainable archiving and accessibility of 3d content, especially in the context of cultural heritage [16]. A wide-ranging investigation of existing repositories and web-based viewers is underway at national and international levels [17]. A development including the requirements in the field of hypothetical 3D reconstruction is being investigated in the ongoing DFG-funded research project 'DFG-Viewer - 3D Infrastructure for Digital 3D Reconstructions' and is being

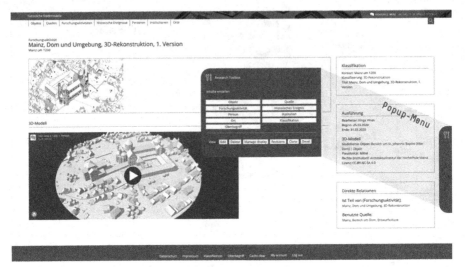

Fig. 6. Documentation of the research activity of 3D reconstruction within the WissKI-based Virtual Research Environment (AI MAINZ/GDKE, 2020).

used in research and teaching [18]. The issue of a common set of valid metadata for the 3D datasets is extensively addressed by the first two authors of this article in this publication (Ref. to be delivered).

6 Data Exchange Formats and the re-use of Serious 3D

The reusability of the digital 3D models requires the findability of the data sets, its documentation and the clarification of the rights of use, as well as the provision of 3D data sets that can be used independently of software in the best case. A key role is provided by the so-called data exchange formats, which ensure interoperability and sustainability of data sets. In the field of civil engineering and urban planning, these have been increasingly developed since the 1990s and 2000s, respectively, to drive digital transformation in the construction industry and urban administration.

The demand for digital representations of built environments is rapidly increasing and can only be met by enhancing software interoperability and data integration. To tackle this challenge, the joint working group of the Integrated Digital Built Environment (IDBE) has been established. The primary goal of this group is to unite experts from the Open Geospatial Consortium and buildingSMART to collaborate on the advancement of pertinent data standards [19].

Depending on the modeling method, the Industry Foundation Classes (IFC) data exchange format is available for Constructive Solid Geometry (CSG). This is used for object-oriented modeling within the planning method Building Information Modeling (BIM). The advantages of this modeling methodology from building construction were explained extensively in the project description for the reconstruction of the New Synagogue in Breslau.

The Boundary Representation modeling methodology is primarily used in urban planning. For this modeling method, the data exchange format CityGML has been developed for semantic enrichment of 3D data sets for about 20 years. In the case of 3D digital city models, in particular the hypothetical reconstruction of medieval cities, this format has been studied for the concerns of documentation and sustainability.

To mark up the models in the structure of the CityGML data model, add-on solutions for 3D modeling software are available, such as CityEditor for SketchUp [20]. With the help of these tools, individual surfaces can be marked up and saved as.gml or.xml files. Openings, walls, roofs, etc. can be classified. In the top hierarchy, the entire 3D object can be grouped and labeled with object-specific properties, such as name, dimension, year of construction or destruction, location, etc. (Fig. 7).

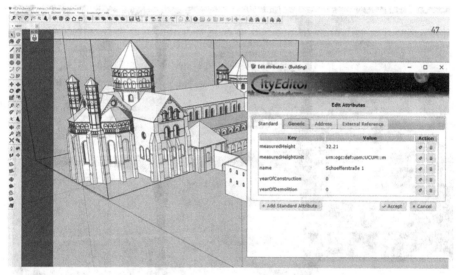

Fig. 7. City Editor tool for labeling geometry on the example of the Mainz Cathedral 1250 AD (AI MAINZ, 2019).

It is remarkable that the predefined structure can be extended by own attributes and external links can be added. This allows, among other things, the labeling of the objects with custom value systems for the uncertainties (hypothesis) and the setting of external links to controlled vocabularies, such as Getty AAT [21].

By 'Serious 3D' we mean the delivery of the results of a hypothetical reconstruction in semantically enriched data exchange formats. That means that a SRM requires a publication in the Web as well as the documentation of the model in the form of descriptive and administrative metadata as well as the distribution of interoperable 3D formats. This approach enables the reusability of the models for further applications.

An exciting reuse of the digital 3D reconstruction from the DUHL took place within the official MAINZ app. The app is considered a 'digital showcase' of the city, which has been developed since 2018 by the state capital Mainz, mainzplus CITYMARKETING and the Mainz Tourism Fund. The Mainz App shows diverse visualizations of historical eras and the cultural heritage of Mainz. For example, the integrated 3D reconstructions of significant sites and buildings give tourists and locals a vivid overview of "historical Mainz" using virtual and augmented reality. In the 'Emperor's year 2020/2021', the MAINZ app was supplemented with the new VR module 'Medieval Mainz', which includes 3D reconstructions of St. Martin's Cathedral, Leichhof, Liebfrauenplatz from the eras around 800 and 1250 AD (Fig. 8).

For the virtual reality application, the models were further processed in the software of Lumion3D, where a photorealistic representation of the mentioned places took place. These were rendered in spherical panoramas in high resolution and integrated into the MAINZ app with further historical information. The example shows a further use of the scientifically based results by the creative industry.

Fig. 8. Mainz-App. Comparison of the photo realistic visualization within the virtual reality application using the example of the marketplace in Mainz around 1250 AD (top), and around 800 AD (bottom).

7   Conclusion

The outcomes of the projects reveal the potential of serious 3d models based on scientific methodology delivering structured, semantically enriched research data ready to be (re-) used, accessed and assessed.

The Digital Urban History Lab represents the further development of the considerations on digital 3D reconstruction as a research method of object-related disciplines.

The presented Scientific Reference Model aims to address the issue of "serious 3D" models from the construction industry and to present an approach for the sustainable use of computer-aided reconstruction and visualization of the past, which has been widespread since the 1990s.

The focus is on the documentation of the decisions and the sources used as well as on the provision of the digital 3D models in interoperable formats. The authors see one approach to solving this problem in raising awareness for documenting the reconstruction, sharing the research results, and using the 3D repositories that are already available.

A promising further development of these approaches and the infrastructures is seen within the EU project 'Computer-based Visualization of Architectural Cultural Heritage' [22]. Here, the concept behind the Scientific Reference Model is to be introduced and tested in education. The successful establishment of a methodology as a common denominator of digital 3D models could mean the exchange and broad application of the results in education, research and in the dissemination of cultural heritage.

Acknowledgement. The Scientific Reference Model (SRM) methodology was developed in the course of projects and initiatives funded by the German Federal Government Commissioner for Culture and the Media, Academic Support Programme German-Jewish Lifeworlds in Eastern Europe (2017–2020), German Research Foundation (DFG), Funding code: MU 4040/5–1, DFG Viewer 3D - Infrastructure for digital 3D reconstructions (2021–2023), the German Academic Exchange Service (DAAD), Short- and long-term lectureships (2022) as well as through numerous discussions within the DFG funded project (Project identifier – 395536813), DFG-Network – Digital 3D reconstructions as tools of architectural history, (2018–2023).

References

1. Messemer, H.: The beginnings of digital visualization of historical architecture in the academic field. Virtual Palaces Part II Lost Palaces Their Afterlife, pp. 21–54 (2016)
2. Münster, S., et al.: Handbook of Digital 3D Reconstruction of Historical Architecture. Springer (in press)
3. Kuroczyński, P., Pfarr-Harfst, M., Münster, S.: Der Modelle Tugend 2.0: Digitale 3D-Rekonstruktion als virtueller Raum der architekturhistorischen Forschung. University Library Heidelberg (2019)
4. Digital Urban History Lab. https://landesmuseum-mainz.de/de/ausstellungen/digital-urban-history-lab/. Accessed 26 May 2023
5. Denard, H.: A new introduction to the london charter. In: A New Introduction to The London Charter, pp. 57–72 (2012)
6. Principles of Seville (2011)
7. Kuroczyński, P., Apollonio, F.I., Bajena, I.P., Cazzaro, I.: Scientific reference model – defining standards, methodology and implementation of serious 3d models in archaeology, art and architectural history. In: Proceedings of the CIPA2023 Symposium "Documenting, Understanding, Preserving Cultural Heritage: Humanities and Digital technologies for Shaping the Future." ISPRS Archives (in press)
8. Kuroczyński, P., Bajena, I., Cazzaro, I.: Scientific Reference Model. A methodological approach in hypothetical 3D reconstruction of architecture. In: Börner, W., Rohland, H., Kral-Börner, C. (eds.): Cultural Heritage – NextGen Innovative Approaches in Documentation, Research, Management and Education. Heidelberg: Propylaeum (in edition)

9. Cazzaro, I.: Digital 3D Reconstruction as a Research Environment in Art and Architecture History: Uncertainty Classification and Visualisation (2023)

10. Berners-Lee, T., Hendler, J., Lassila, O.: The Semantic Web - A New Form of Web Content that is Meaningful to Computers will Unleash a Revolution of New Possibilities **284**(5) (2001)

11. Berners-Lee, T.: Linked data. W3C - Des. Issues. 2–6 (2006)

12. Aalberg, T., et al.: Definition of the CIDOC Conceptual Reference Model (2015)

13. WissKI. https://wiss-ki.eu/de. Accessed 26 May 2023

14. Kuroczyński, P., Bajena, I., Große, P., Jara, K., Wnęk, K.: Digital reconstruction of the new synagogue in breslau: new approaches to object-oriented research. In: Niebling, F., Münster, S., Messemer, H. (eds.): Research and Education in Urban History in the Age of Digital Libraries. pp. 25–45. Springer International Publishing, Cham (2021). https://doi.org/10.1007/978-3-030-93186-5_2

15. Virtual Research Environment I Mainz-Worms-Speyer (800–1250). https://www.mainz-worms-speyer-3d.hs-mainz.de/. Accessed 26 May 2023

16. Fernie, K.: 3D content in Europeana task force. Europeana Network Association Members Council (2020)

17. Champion, E., Rahaman, H.: Survey of 3D digital heritage repositories and platforms. Virtual Archaeol. Rev. **11**, 1 (2020). https://doi.org/10.4995/var.2020.13226

18. Bajena, I.P., Dworak, D., Kuroczyński, P., Smolarski, R., Münster, S.: DFG 3D-viewer – development of an infrastructure for digital 3D reconstructions. In: Digital Humanities 2022. pp. 117–120, Tokyo (2022)

19. Gilbert, T., et al.: Built environment data standards and their integration: an analysis of IFC, CityGML and LandInfra. Open Geospatial Consort. Build. Int. 16 (2020)

20. City Editor, https://www.3dis.de/cityeditor/

21. Getty AAT (Art & Architecture Thesaurus). https://www.getty.edu/research/tools/vocabularies/aat/. Accessed 26 May 2023

22. Computer-based Visualization of Architectural Cultural Heritage. Supporting digital capabilities of the higher education sector and stimulating innovative learning and teaching practices. https://covher.eu/. Accessed 26 May 2023

Colouring Cities: A Citizen Science Platform for Knowledge Production on the Building Stock - Potentials for Urban and Architectural History

Robert Hecht[1]([✉]) [iD], Tabea Danke[1] [iD], Hendrik Herold[1] [iD], Polly Hudson[2] [iD], Martin Munke[3] [iD], and Theodor Rieche[1] [iD]

[1] Leibniz Institute of Ecological Urban and Regional Development, Dresden, Germany
r.hecht@ioer.de
[2] The Alan Turing Institute, London, UK
[3] Saxon State and University Library, Dresden, Germany

Abstract. Colouring Cities is an open digital platform that enables the collaborative collection and visualization of building data. The platform provides a unique opportunity to collect spatial information on the characteristics, performance, and evolution of building stocks, thereby bridging existing data gaps and supporting sustainable urban development. By harnessing the power of crowdsourcing, Colouring Cities allows researchers, architects, and urban planners to gather spatial information in a more efficient and cost-effective manner than traditional methods. The user-friendly interface and comprehensive data management capabilities make Colouring Cities a valuable citizen science platform, empowering everyone to collect, collate, visualize and share data. The paper reports on the platform and the worldwide activities as well as experiences in two case studies, Colouring London (UK) and Colouring Dresden (Germany). It highlights the platform's potential for knowledge production and transfer in urban and architectural history research, as well as digital humanities. While there is a need for further technical development and research on the impact of citizen science, the platform demonstrates great potential in these fields.

Keywords: Urban history · Platform · Citizen Science · Historical maps

1 Introduction

Buildings are of central importance socially, culturally, economically and ecologically. People spend most of their lives in buildings and also invest large sums of money in them. Buildings exist over epochs and shape our cityscape. Their construction consumes resources and impacts the environment. In terms of building materials, energy, and CO_2 emissions in general, buildings offer enormous potential for savings. This makes them particularly important in the context of climate protection and climate action [1]. Preserving existing buildings in the long term, constructing new buildings in such a way that existing materials are recycled and reused wherever possible—this is how building culture can be preserved on the one hand and a contribution can be made to decarbonize

S. Münster et al. (Eds.): UHDL 2023, CCIS 1853, pp. 145–164, 2023.
https://doi.org/10.1007/978-3-031-38871-2_9

the building stock on the other. In order to be able to understand and develop the building stock in a climate-friendly and resource-saving way, basic information is required, for example on the age, lifespan, construction, material and the concrete use of the buildings. This knowledge of buildings is also very relevant in the exploration and discovery of urban history in 4D [2].

However, it should be noted that detailed data on these building characteristics, necessary to support urban problem solving and climate change mitigation, is lacking in many countries or is not accessible or only accessible to a very limited extent [1, 3, 4]. In the last decade, a number of scientific studies have observed problems with the incompleteness, fragmentation, aggregation, inconsistency, inaccuracy and inaccessibility of many types of data on building characteristics needed to support sustainability research [5–9]. Difficulties with, and importance of access to building data, at international scale, were already being noted by Kohler and Hassler [10]. In many countries, scientific models of the behavior of the building stock are still based on assumptions rather than actual data, especially with regard to information on form, age and lifespan [11]. To assess the impact of changing conditions, it is necessary to identify what constitutes a particular building stock and understand its dynamic change by modelling the process based on actual data [12]. Reasons for difficulties in accessing information on buildings include the long-standing fragmentation of knowledge due to individual sectors' interest in or focus on particular building types (for example the state's in social housing owing to the scale of investment); the historical prioritization of new construction and technological innovation over adaptation and reuse by the construction industry, the architectural profession, the planning system, and by taxation frameworks. In addition, limited drivers have existed to encourage governments to invest in public auditing and monitoring of stocks as a whole, to systematically collect and publicly release spatial building attribute data, to investigate the relationship between physical characteristics of stocks and their socio-economic and environmental performance, or to study building longevity and positive and negative cyclical patterns over long periods of time.

In response to this situation and to close this data gap, in 2016 open-source code began to be developed for Colouring London, a prototype for open-source knowledge sharing platforms designed to collect, enrich and release open data on building stocks [1, 13]. In 2020 the Colouring Cities Research Programme (CCRP) was set up at the Alan Turing Institute – the UK's National Institute for Data science and AI – in order to support testing of Colouring London's reproducible open code across countries and to bring together an international interdisciplinary group to co-develop content and code. The Colouring Dresden initiative, currently being developed in Germany, is placing initial focus on the study of different citizen science actions and the integration of building attribute data and sources at local level [14].

In addition to gaps and fragmentation in relation to current building attribute data, lack of access to historical data has created barriers to understanding stocks as complex, slow-moving dynamic systems. It also has made it harder to engage local communities, where vast bodies of local knowledge lie, in collectively unpicking problems caused by current and historical changes to their local areas. In the age of digital libraries, historical documents, photographs, topographic maps and plans are an important public source of information for mapping and tracking changes in building stock over long periods of time. By making these sources accessible through digitization and making them openly available, they become particularly interesting for collaborative mapping using a citizen science approach. By participating in mapping initiatives, citizens can learn how to map building data using different methods, technologies and sources that suit their own interests and skills. They can also begin to better connect past, present and future action relating to the built environment and to understand the importance of understanding the past to better predict future patterns, and to create more sustainable trajectories.

In this paper, we focus on the introduction of Colouring Cities platforms, the citizen science approach, and on data integration and utilization of methods from urban history research. We then report on experiences with the platform in the two case studies London (UK) and Dresden (Germany) before finally highlighting and discussing the potential of the platform model for urban and architectural history research and digital humanities.

2   Colouring Cities Platforms

2.1   The Colouring Cities Research Programme (CCRP)

The CCRP currently works with international academic partners across nine countries – Australia, Bahrain, Britain, Colombia, Germany, Greece, Lebanon, Indonesia and Sweden – to develop and test reproducible open code for open Colouring Cities platforms. These map data on the composition, quality and performance, and dynamics of building stocks for all buildings, at building level. Key CCRP aims are to develop a global building attribute database (formed of networked international Colouring Cities platforms) to support UN Sustainable Development Goals (SDGs), to effect a step-change in the amount and type of building level attribute data available for use in scientific analysis and the application of AI and machine learning, and to integrate knowledge from science, the humanities and arts to improve understanding of the stock as a complex dynamic system.

2.2   The Colouring Cities Platform

Colouring Cities platforms are designed to engage built environment stakeholders from academia, government and industry, the third sector and the community in co-creating and maintaining high quality, open databases and visualization platforms about building stocks. These collect, collate, visualize, verify and make accessible different types of spatial data on buildings, which are structured within twelve subject areas covering building location, use, physical characteristics, age and history, energy performance, resilience, and quality and infrastructure context [15]. Data categories have been chosen to help increase the quality, sustainability, efficiency and resilience of stocks at local, national and global level, and to help communities and built environment professionals collectively tackle common problems of data silos and fragmentation, data quality aspects (e.g. accuracy, completeness), formatting, range, granularity, security and accessibility.

The platform enables four methods of data collection to maximize data quality, geographic coverage and accessibility for diverse stakeholders and audiences. The first, most straightforward method involves bulk upload by platform hosts of relevant existing open datasets. The second relates to live streaming of official datasets maintained on external servers where APIs are available such as planning application status or the conservation status of a building. The third relates to computational approaches that allow the creation of very large data sets that can be verified in a next step. This includes algorithms or computer vision systems to e.g. infer the number of floors, roof shape or building types based on morphological building properties derived from geospatial vector data or raster data sources such as digital historical maps or even street view images [4, 16–18]. The fourth form of capture is crowdsourcing the information at the building level using the platform. This is of particular interest because in the context of building research there is still little knowledge about how good the quality of crowdsourced building information is. Experience has been gained so far from the OpenStreetMap project [19] and isolated thematically focused crowdsourcing experiments [20]. Current work under the CCRP involves developing feedback loops between data capture methods to improve accuracy and coverage and to supplemented verification and source information features.

2.3 Why not OpenStreetMap?

The Colouring Cities platforms share similarities with OpenStreetMap (OSM) in that both map and visualize geospatial data, are hosted on freely accessible websites, release code and data under open licenses, include crowdsourcing features and use collaborative maintenance systems. Colouring Cities platforms have been influenced by OSM in each of these areas. However, the initiatives differ significantly in a number of ways. The CCRP is an academic research program, run by a national research institution involving a consortium of experts committed to common goals, and following agreed protocols. The CCRP collects comprehensive data on building stocks i.e. for every building, existing and demolished. It treats building footprints like biological cells where characteristics, operation and dynamic behavior are all needed to understand and optimize life cycles. It also tests a low cost academic governance, rather than an Open Foundation model.

The Colouring Cities platform has a much more rigid, defined data model which tests feedback loops between data capture methods including crowdsourcing. OSM's organic, bottom-up, freeform data model and tagging schemes focus on crowdsourcing and bulk uploads and the collection of a much wider range of data. The building attributes and categories in Colouring Cities are very specific and decided on through a lengthy, ongoing process of academic literature review and consultation with diverse stakeholders and experts. Over 100 building attributes have to date been selected based on value to diverse areas of research relating to the quality, efficiency, sustainability and resilience of building stocks. OSM represents physical features on the ground using tags. Thus, only current natural as well as man-made features of the real world can be mapped. OSM does not include opinionated data such as ratings, historical or hypothetical features. Building footprints on OSM have already reached a high level of completeness in European cities, though, building attributes of height or number of floors are missing for a large proportion of buildings [19, 21, 22].

An additional difference is that CCRP partners are not only involved and interested in capturing and releasing building attribute data using Colouring Cities platforms but also in areas such as: data analysis and results publication; data applications; data ethics; and engaging diverse stakeholders and input from science and technology, the humanities and the arts using multiple data capture methods. Nonetheless, OSM is an important source of information. The integration of the OSM unique identifier provides a link between the Colouring Cities data and the OSM data. This will maximize opportunities to use CCRP data within OSM, and foster collaboration with software engineers involved in OSM-related research.

3   Citizen Science Approach for Knowledge Production

Citizen science is the active participation of the public in scientific research projects and has taken shape in various disciplines [23, 24]. It is based on participatory principles that not only put the citizens in the role of data collectors (sensors) but also encourage volunteers to participate in solving scientific challenges [25]. People can voluntarily participate in research in a variety of ways [26] starting with contributing in data collection ('crowdsourcing') up to collaborative science ('extreme citizen science') where citizens are involved in problem definition, data collection and analysis [25]. Projects can require very different levels of knowledge and commitment from participants. Some require a high level of prior knowledge to understand the aims and objectives of the project and a high level of commitment to ensure that participants can be trained appropriately [23].

The Colouring Cities model offers various possibilities for initiating different participation formats for citizen scientists, such as:

- Building attribution and verification through the web-based digital platform where citizen scientists can do this individually due to the intuitive web interface, as well as being supported by training opportunities which can be tutorials, workshops, and hand-on-demos for mapping. Furthermore, these include outdoor activities ranging from city walks to scavenger hunts to coordinated mapathon that can initiate participation.
- Co-development of the platform (via co-creation workshops) and the possibility to contribute to the open code on GitHub (e.g. adding new issues to report bugs or feature requests, coding additional features, fixing bugs); and implementing own customized tools using the Colouring Cities API such as dashboards or import features for bulk uploads.
- Supporting the collection and processing of data sources (e.g. georeferencing maps, vectorization of historic buildings, annotating images, or completing digital collections on collaborative platforms). This can serve as a hub for Linked Open Data (LOD) and can be done on other community-oriented publication and communication sites for transcriptions, visualizations and/or software, such as the portals of the Wikiverse (Wikidata, Wikisource, Wikiversity, Wikimedia Commons, and Wikipedia) [27]. (Linked) Open Data functions both as a resource for and as a result of (many) citizen science projects [28].

In order to activate the citizen scientists, the relevant target groups need to be identified, for example people who are interested in architecture and (urban) history, cartography and urban planning, or children and young people on their educational path. The motivations of citizen scientists are, for example, to close knowledge gaps about the history of their city, their district or their neighborhood or to contribute to the further development of their own city in the sense of sustainable development. Their activation must then take place through targeted communication and participation formats [29]. Central tasks in citizen science projects are therefore communication, feedback and aspects of evaluation (activating existing communities for the project; building a communication structure that addresses the different needs and enables exchange on the different aspects of the project; defining appropriate tools for evaluation) [30, 31]. Furthermore, not inconsiderable amounts of data is collected and a data management plan needs to be developed that transparently and legally specifies what data is collected, who has what rights to the data and how to ensure long-term provision. The data and associated metadata (such as time, method or location of data collection) should be stored and managed permanently without violating data protection [32].

4 Integrating Data and Utilizing Methods from Urban History Research

The Colouring Cities platform requires a range of data and methods to operate effectively, some of which are commonly utilized in urban history research. The platform primarily leverages open geospatial infrastructures but can also benefit from existing data provided as Linked Open Data (LOD), which is freely usable, machine-readable, standardized, and referenceable through Uniform Resource Identifiers (URIs). This data can be sourced from various collaborative platforms and databases such as Wikipedia, Wikidata, and FactGrid that specialize in urban history. Additionally, many institutions make data available via their own LOD platforms. For instance, the interactive presentation of the renowned Nolli Map[1] is an example of a linked urban history research platform. Conversely, the data collected by CCRP can also be made available as LOD, benefiting other projects in the process. In the following, we present various data and methods that can be utilized in Colouring Cities.

4.1 Building Footprint Geometry

The current building footprints are the main spatial reference unit for building attribution, analysis and visualization within the platform. The building geometries can be official, commercial, scientific or user-generated. Various sources can be considered as the basis for the data, whereby the current building footprints should ideally be subject to a non-proprietary, open license that allows their use in the platform. This includes the user-generated OSM data under the ODbL license, for which, however, in some areas of the world, such as Asia or South Africa and outside the urban center or city, the known limitations in the completeness and quality of modeling still exist [33–35]. A very complete building footprint dataset is published by Microsoft[2] (MS), also under an ODbL license. This global dataset is generated using machine learning from various Bing Maps imagery between 2014 and 2022, although some quality issues have also been

---

[1] https://web.stanford.edu/group/spatialhistory/nolli.

[2] https://github.com/microsoft/GlobalMLBuildingFootprints.

reported, so it should be combined with other data [36]. In addition, there are building footprint data that were created in a scientific context and can be openly reused. These can be manual mappings or products derived from maps by means of remote sensing or image recognition, and are often provided for locations where building footprints have not previously existed, are incomplete or are hard to access. The most comprehensive, accurate and up-to-date building footprints can usually be found in official databases from National Mapping and Cadastral Agencies. These open state geodata on buildings are increasingly available in Europe and provide a good geometric basis [37].

4.2 Base Map

An essential component of the digital platform is a base map that displays topographical features, such as streets, street names, and landmarks. This map helps with orientation when mapping building attributes. OSM maps and official geoservices, which are available as standardized web services in many countries, are excellent resources for generating this base map. Additionally, high-quality ortho aerial images and very high-resolution satellite images can also serve as useful map backgrounds.

4.3 Historical Maps

To guide the annotation with regard to the historical evolution of buildings, old city plans and topographic maps are an indispensable source of information. Integrating these (georeferenced) maps – as provided for example in the Virtual Map Forum[3] containing numerous geo-referenced sources [38] – via standardized map services such as Web Map Service (WMS) as canvas images into the platform can support users in estimating characteristics such as the building age or original use of the building. Therefore, it is very welcomed that libraries and archives make their assets digitally available and give access to them via standardized interfaces. Moreover, computer vision techniques can be applied to extract the footprints, and other historical features from the historical plans and maps [4, 39]. The vectorized building footprints can support or even automate the annotation process but can also help to build historical urban 3D models [17]. Challenging in this regard are the inherent spatial, temporal but also thematic uncertainties resulting from the analysis process and depend on the quality of the available sources. Another challenge and current research topic is the spatio-temporal modeling of building objects in the case of demolitions, extensions, conversions and new construction.

4.4 Photographs

Further valuable sources of historical information on urban features are photographs and historic city scapes in paintings or copper engravings, which can be integrated for example from Deutsche Fotothek, Wikimedia Commons or individual repositories. The database of the Deutsche Fotothek[4] contains more than 112,000 entries (e.g. photographs

---

[3] The Virtual Map Forum (https://kartenforum.slub-dresden.de) contains numerous geo-referenced sources on Dresden, such as the Damage Map of 1946, which shows the different degrees of destruction of Dresden buildings after the end of the Second World War (https://slubdd.de/schadensplan).

[4] https://www.deutschefotothek.de.

and postcards) related to Dresden with the keyword 'architecture'. In addition, there are more than 1,000 historical views and just as many maps and plans. Providing an accurate count of the (historical and contemporary) sources present in the 'Dresden' category and its sub-categories on Wikimedia Commons[5] can be challenging due to the complex structure of the Commons categories. Nevertheless, the number of sources is significant, reaching well into the six-figure range.[6]

In contrast to other questions in historical scholarship, for which photographs can often only be used as a source with a certain degree of caution [40]. Due to their staged character, they offer an important database for the reconstruction of urban features by capturing a specific moment in a building's history. Of course, source-critical questions are necessary here as well, since, for example, postcards based on photographs have often been cropped or objects added afterwards. The process of finding suitable photos can be supported by the possibilities of AI-based image search on the Internet and the integration of social media.

4.5 Other Published Sources

Apart from visual sources, various text-based historical sources can also provide valuable information about the building stock, and many of these sources are available in digital form. One example is historical address books, from which it is possible to determine, for example, from when a building existed at a particular address and how it was used (e.g., as a residential or commercial building) at the level of the individual floors[7]. Gazetteers may also be used for example to determine construction and demolition dates. Historical drainage plans, individual images, and property ownership documents are examples of information from which attributes can be extracted from archive material on a building by building basis.

4.6 Expert Knowledge

Professional and amateur historians, civic societies, historic buildings organizations, and local community groups often hold a wealth of knowledge about buildings and local areas accumulated over extended periods. This knowledge is crucial to comprehend the inventory as a slow-moving system. Identifying and engaging with such individuals and organizations is a key goal, and project partners with expertise in these domains can assist in building relationships with these communities. For example, their knowledge about specific buildings could be gathered through guideline-based interviews or entered directly into the Colouring Cities platform after appropriate training, such as workshops or video tutorials. Additionally, this knowledge could include lifespan data on buildings, which could be entered into the Colouring Cities platform using features that transform text and image-based knowledge on construction and demolition dates into statistical

---

[5] https://commons.wikimedia.org/wiki/category:dresden.

[6] To get an automated count for four subcategories, please refer to https://petscan.wmflabs.org/?psid=24776495.

[7] The first address book for Dresden was published in 1702, from 1800 to 1944 they are available digitally almost without gaps (https://digital.slub-dresden.de/kollektionen/72).

data that can be readily utilized in scientific research. Therefore, this approach could help to leverage the vast body of historical knowledge available and enable community participation, thereby creating a more comprehensive and reliable inventory of the building stock.

5 Experiences from Two Selected Case Studies

In the following, we would like to report on the experiences of the first Colouring London prototype in the UK and the recently launched Colouring Dresden platform in Germany.

5.1 Colouring London

Colouring London[8] was developed as the prototype for the Colouring Cities Research Programme and builds on work at the Building Exploratory, London in the 1990s into free physical and digital tools, co-designed by diverse built environment stakeholders to facilitate knowledge sharing on building stocks [4], developed with heritage funding support (from the UK Department of National Heritage). From 2016 experimentation began at UCL, funded initially by Historic England, to integrate learning from this first iteration of Colouring London with advances in open data platform design, open code repositories, open licenses and collaboratively maintained systems. Between 2014 and 2015 building age data for 20,000 was manually mapped to provide building level data to experiment with, using art historical knowledge and multiple secondary historical sources including the Survey of London gazetteers, British History Online building entries, London local authority conservation areas appraisals, specialist historical websites, local historical guides and historical maps. Age was focused on owing to its relevance to energy modeling [41], building lifespan analysis and prediction [6], material and waste flow and survival tracking [42] and to set typology rules for procedural models able to be used in exploring 'What if?' planning simulations/scenarios [43]. Sources were discussed with representatives from a range of historical bodies. This method built on an approach to generating age data that was tested in 2010 with the London Borough of Camden, in the context of retrofit targeting using typology data, as part of work undertaken with the Centre for the Historic Environment at Oxford. It involved visually comparing digitized Ordnance Survey historical map tiles at twenty year intervals from 1860 to 1980, held by Camden, on a split screen, with current building footprints and then coloring current footprints according to the map intervals in which they were built. The process was carried out using GIS, in consultation with representatives of the historic environment, and used to inform the design of a range of Colouring London features specifically designed to support crowdsourcing from historic environment specialists and community groups. This included precise wording of questions, choice of colors and addition of copy and paste buttons. Through this process it became clear that the Colouring Cities platforms could also offer historians the opportunity to collaborate live on a new kind of mapping canvas through which knowledge could be added, gaps filled and links to collections and historical publications easily made by simply using building footprints. Intervals however did not necessarily relate to specific morphological periods and the method was

---

[8] https://colouringlondon.org.

found to be considerably less useful for applications noted above than data collected through building level research resulting in a more precise initial year of construction.

Since live testing began in 2018, over five million edits have been made of which around 250,000 have been from human users and the remainder computer generated/bulk uploads. Interestingly over 40,000 entries relate to age data have been added under a single username. This difference in the number of computational and manual edits, is largely explained by the nature of each method. However it is also due to limited resources for Colouring London prototype development being focused on work on system development, code reproducibility, sustainable, ethical programme governance model testing, and integration of data capture methods, rather than on engaging individual stakeholder groups in the crowdsourcing process.

Since 2020 a number of steps have been taken to improve historical data integration into core Colouring Cities open code[9] in response to recommendations and comments from the Colouring London Historic Environment Advisory Group and CCRP international partners and from findings emerging from prototype development (see Fig. 1 and Fig. 2). These include:

- Merging of 'Age' and 'Dynamics' Colouring Cities categories and renaming them as 'Age and History' to help collate related information and to make the interface easier for historians to use.
- Integration of initially three kinds of spatial data with the 'Age and History' section: i) building age, ii) number of, and lifespans of all demolished buildings ever built the site (capturing pairs of construction and demolition dates) plus web links to relevant sites holding historical information, and iii) survival maps.
- Introduction of 'survival maps' which allow contributors to compare historical and current footprints and color the latter by the degree to which footprints match with. Persistent identifiers are provided for each footprint to allow additional sources used in matching decisions to be added.
- Automated generation and upload of 750,000 age data entries inferred from vectorized historical street network data for London using vectorized data derived from Stanilov and Batty's, 2011 longitudinal study of London exploring underlying codes determining patterns of growth [44].
- Co-creation, within the 'Planning Controls' section, with Historic England, historic environment specialists, and communities, of a spatial dataset for all protected buildings in London. This allows for disaggregation of existing government point data and visualization using color coded footprints to increase access to information on protected areas of the stock. This process combines bulk upload of official data, automated address matching, and verification of geolocation by communities and historic building experts using crowdsourcing mechanisms. Platform contributors can add information on sites where they think unprotected buildings are under threat and color these if they feel these should be retained.
- Set up of an advisory group of national and regional historic environment organizations to help identify new features required to engage historians and communities, and to provide an efficient low-cost pathway to advertising to, and engaging, these

---

[9] https://github.com/colouring-cities.

groups in contributing data via membership newsletters, blogs and callouts. Large-scale publicity coordinated by this network will take place in June/July 2023 as part of a London data festival. Feedback from this, combined with work on Colouring Dresden and other consultation and engagement programs will inform new features and help refine data capture methods.

Future work will focus on feedback loops between automated uploads and crowd-sourced data to improve data accuracy. Plans to vectorize historical footprints using computer vision and use these to capture historical data from specific time points within Colouring Cities platforms are currently being explored with IOER, the Royal College of Art, and Turing's MapReader and SciVision projects.

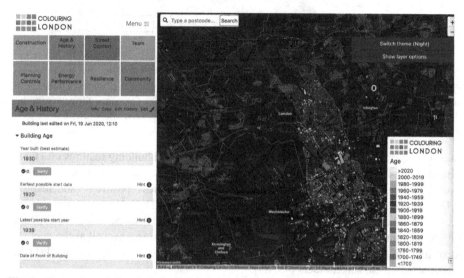

Fig. 1. Screenshot of the platform Colouring London in which the buildings from London are colored according to their year of construction (Screenshot taken from https://colouringlondon. org/).

5.2   Colouring Dresden

Building on the experience of the first prototype, Colouring London, the following section looks at the progress of the most recently launched platform in the Colouring Cities series: Colouring Dresden[10], the first platform in Germany launched in March 2023.

The project is coordinated at the Leibniz Institute for Ecological Urban and Regional Development (IOER) and is supported in its implementation by a local partner network from various fields such as architecture, research, education and culture. Since the first implementation idea in Germany and the launch of Colouring Dresden, transfer services

---

[10] https://colouring.dresden.ioer.info.

Fig. 2. Screenshot of the Colouring London platform demonstrating the possibilities of integrating historical topographic maps. In this case, a historical map from the Ordnance Survey from the 1890s is displayed (Screenshot taken from https://colouringlondon.org/).

became necessary. When translating the data categories and building features into German, the terms were adapted to the research needs in Dresden. The code for the Colouring Dresden implementation was forked from the Colouring Cities repository[11] and adapted to local needs and published under a GPL-3.0 license on GitHub. A proper environment according to hardware and software was set up following the documentation on GitHub. Before adapting the code, conceptual frameworks for the project as well as the content focus and the building characteristics to be surveyed were co-developed in workshops together with local stakeholders [45, 46].

In the implementation of Colouring Dresden, special focus was placed on basic building characteristics (such as building age, number of floors or current use), which form the basis for building typology. This enables a knowledge transfer for fragmentary building information on the platform by allocating each building into a building type for further analysis. By the date of publication, the project team was able to co-creatively sharpen its objectives. This resulted in the following goals for incorporation into the platform as a response from partners, citizen scientists and the administration of the city of Dresden:

- Various proposals for new or adapted features came up and will be implemented step by step to improve the platform and its code, like offering house numbers as an overlay or a geolocation function for a better orientation while collecting the data, new layout design for input elements especially for usage on mobile devices, or the opportunity to earn points as a reward for data collection in the context of a gamification approach. Adaptation of data category 'Resilience' to protect the diverse and valuable building stock in Dresden. In order to strengthen the resilience of buildings

---

[11] https://github.com/colouring-cities/colouring-core.

to climate change-related impacts, Colouring Dresden aims to close knowledge gaps about the historically grown building stock. A special focus was placed on aspects of the impacts of heat and heavy rain or flooding incidents, which have caused local damage and destruction on the building stock in the past as a global climate change consequence [47], or in the case of heat waves, health problems and excessive mortality rates, especially among vulnerable groups [48]. The data category 'Resilience' complements with the topics use of basement, inlet threshold of water or the historical water level in the area of heavy rain/flooding. On the subject of heat, the topics of adaptation measures, roof and facade features and perceived heat stress provide information.

- Testing citizen science formats with the aim of encouraging different target groups to "join in research". Digital regulars' tables, indoor and outdoor mapathons, actions in schools, hackathons and a dialogue series take place in various methods to explore crowdsourced mapping. For example, the community tests the outdoor application on the go in front of the smartphone (Fig. 3) in order to incorporate the results into a continuous improvement of the map's front end. In indoor mapathons, citizen scientists interested in history support the development of digital sources such as digital libraries, archives, photos or historical maps. Colouring Dresden will also be shown in an exhibition in the center of the city, schoolchildren could act as beta testers, open data availability involves Open Data specialists and elements of gamification have been used to increase the motivation of non-experts as well. Challenges lie in increasing the number of citizen scientists through targeted public relations via social media and direct contact. In this context, the development of a dashboard is planned to visualize mapping activities, but also to inform about the status and motivate citizen scientists. The citizen scientists thus help to jointly generate a large treasure trove of data that could not be generated in the project alone.

- Transfer of knowledge to increase the multiplication effect, which forms an added value for historical research. By involving schools and museums in the coloring of the map, children and young people are introduced to research by contributing to scientific knowledge. The increase in knowledge generated in the actions enables participants to further qualify and better understand the built environment.

- Creation of training materials to facilitate the use of Colouring Dresden. As some topics, such as construction or architectural appearance type, require a deeper understanding of building culture, training materials will be produced. In a co-creative process, the project identifies the needs of the citizen scientists and in which format the training material is most helpful. Furthermore, this allows for replication of other citizen science projects, as they can already draw on a pool of material.

- Enabling openly accessible and linked data in the field of 'Open Citizen Science'. The key is having persistent identifiers to realize unique links between different data items of several data sources. Next to others, increasing visibility is a relevant benefit of it and least to automatically derived statistics or visualizations like in the field of academia, e.g. Scholia[12]. Colouring Dresden follows an open science strategy. Thus, workshops or further events will be documented in reports uploaded on Zenodo[13] to

---

[12] https://scholia.toolforge.org/

[13] https://zenodo.org/search?page=1&size=20&q=keywords:%22Colouring%20Dresden%22.

share the experiences with other initiatives. Furthermore, citizen scientists are able to participate in the so-called Wikiverse, e.g. using the project page on Wikiversity[14] for a collaborative collected list of relevant digital sources for building-related knowledge within the city of Dresden and for collaborative development and publication of teaching materials on the use of these sources.

- Establishment of a network and digital infrastructure to link up with existing projects in the field of historical maps and urban history. In doing so, the local projects will increase their level of awareness. Furthermore, the project will strengthen networking with other citizen science projects in order to exchange local experiences (addressing target groups as well as communication and transfer).

While in London data is largely integrated via bulk uploads and automated generation, in Dresden crowdsourced mapping plays an important role at the start of the project: In citizen science actions the community tested the outdoor application in front of the smartphone on the move (Fig. 3). The results flow into an ongoing improvement of the front-end of the map. In addition, test events made it possible to improve the approach and motivation of the participants.

Fig. 3. Testing the platform Colouring Dresden in a mapathon event with citizen scientists (source: H. Hensel/IOER-Media)

Further research activities include on the one hand the evaluation of the motivation and learning success of the participants and the network partners and on the other hand the quality of the data collected by the citizen scientists. Initial surveys show that the project's knowledge acquisition and support are important to participants. In addition, the approach and motivation of participants could be improved through test events. Even though no evaluation results are available yet due to the short observation period, initial user statistics from Colouring Dresden show that the platform is attracting interest in the city and that the knowledge gap in the construction sector is being closed step by step. Future work could focus on further development of new topics, such as further development of the "Energy" data category. Of high relevance is also the improvement of the mapping of the temporal dimension with respect to building geometry and features,

---

[14] https://de.wikiversity.org/wiki/Projekt:Colouring_Dresden.

in order to be able to record historical forms and uses of buildings in a temporally related sense and to realize e.g. spatio-temporal map visualizations with a time slider.

6 Potentials for Urban History Research and Education

In the following, we address the added value of the Colouring Cities platforms, data, and visualizations that we see for urban history research and education.

6.1 Using the Platform in Urban History Research

Colouring Cities platforms provide a unique opportunity to integrate knowledge and data from diverse fields such as humanities, science, technology, and the arts, to facilitate comprehensive research on the architectural and building history of cities. By centralizing previously scattered information on building stocks and history, the platforms enable researchers to access data that was previously available in various research contexts and from different communities. This includes data that was only available in analog sources but is now accessible through the platform. With open access to this data, it can be utilized in a variety of contexts, including research on the history of individual city districts and streets for both architectural and building history, as well as social history studies.

The platform also allows historians to contribute their own knowledge and data to further enhance the research. By collaborating and filling in gaps in existing collections and historical publications, historians can contribute to a greater understanding of the rules and patterns of change operating within and across cities. Through such collaborations, opportunities arise to improve the quality, sustainability, and resilience of urban stocks.

In addition, data from these projects can be fed back into the platform, enriching the research opportunities for future historians. In summary, Colouring Cities' platforms provide a collaborative and dynamic environment for historians to contribute their expertise, connect with diverse sources of data, and advance the understanding of the history of cities.

6.2 Added Value for Education in Urban History

The value of urban history education is also enhanced through the use of Colouring Cities platforms. Citizens can increase their awareness and interest in the history of their city by accessing historical data on buildings in their own neighborhood. This process also allows them to gain insights into current research questions and methods of urban history. By participating in the processing of current research questions in their concrete surroundings, citizens can create tangible benefits for their own personal development and the development of their community. Examining the past of a place can lead to a greater identification with the surroundings, and may also create a sense of responsibility for preserving the history and character of the community [49]. This sense of responsibility could inspire citizens to engage in place-based community action. Ultimately, the Colouring Cities platforms have the potential to create a community that can be activated for research as well as for urban decision-making in other research questions and participation projects [50]. In summary, the Colouring Cities platforms offer not only research benefits, but also valuable opportunities for education and community engagement in the preservation and development of urban history and character.

7 Conclusion and Outlook

The Colouring Cities platform code is in constant development and is being tested in an increasing number of countries. In perspective, further research should be conducted on the contribution of Colouring Cities to support the measurement of the achievement of the United Nations Sustainable Development Goals and how it could be integrated into formal reporting mechanisms [51]. In order to make the platform even more attractive for urban historians, further discussion is required on how to achieve a balance between integration of further data sources within the platform itself – for example embedded photographs, maps and documents, and the use of links – i.e. to the collections of institutions managing these data. Though embedding will make platforms more interesting to use, creating links distributes the process of enriching and updating and storing data, as well as helping connect and promote archive/historical resources. In general, the potential of Linked Open Data (LOD) should be further exploited to improve data availability for users and to increase the visibility of existing related projects as well as the visibility of the results of organizations' and individuals' projects via open science communication [25]. For the long-term availability as well as for a broader use of the collected data, it seems important to connect to the relevant research data initiatives. For Germany, the consortia NFDI4Earth[15] for the geosciences and NFDI4Memory[16] for the humanities that use historical methods or that rely on data requiring historical contextualization are worth mentioning. NFDI4Memory, for example, is already planning to integrate platforms that also contain data based on citizen science projects - such as the data collections of the Verein für Computergenealogie[17] – or that are based on the software structures of the Wikiverse – such as the Wikibase instance FactGrid[18] operated by the Gotha Research Centre at the University of Erfurt [52]. In the planned 'Data Space' of the consortium, for which the aforementioned Virtual Map Forum of the Saxon State and University Library (SLUB) is to serve as one visualization instance, the data from the CCRP could also be brought together with other spatial data from these contexts.

With respect to citizen science as an approach, there are also specific challenges and risks (failed activation of citizen scientists, poor data quality, and digital vandalism) that still need to be explored in the context of applying the platform to urban history research. Recording historic building geometry would be desirable to obtain a historic city model. The geometrical acquisition of historic building footprints would be desirable to obtain a complete historic city model, but is also challenging. AI-based approaches to vectorize historical maps help to automatically reconstruct and classify historic buildings having great potential to expand the database and data annotation capabilities in the future.

---

[15] https://www.nfdi4earth.de/.

[16] https://4memory.de/.

[17] https://wiki.genealogy.net/.

[18] https://database.factgrid.de/wiki/Main_Page.

The CCRP is based on a culture of exchange between cities, which together can accumulate and share a huge common knowledge base and experience of collaborative practice. CCRP platforms are however all still at an early development. It therefore remains to be seen how successful platforms will be in terms of collaborative maintenance, and the degree to which they can serve as strategic instruments to promote collaborative governance of historical data [49].

Acknowledgments. The project Colouring Dresden is financially supported by prize money from the Citizen Science Competition 'Auf die Plätze! Citizen Science in deiner Stadt', funded by the German Federal Ministry of Education and Research and jointly coordinated by Wissenschaft im Dialog gGmbH and the Museum für Naturkunde Berlin. We would like to thank all our partners of Colouring London and Colouring Dresden. Special thanks go to the Colouring Cities Research Programme and the people of this international network. Mateusz Konieczny in particular is to be thanked for his valuable feedback related to OpenStreetMap.

References

1. Hudson, P.: Urban characterisation; expanding applications for, and new approaches to building attribute data capture. The Historic Environ.: Policy & Practice **9**, 306–327 (2018). https://doi.org/10.1080/17567505.2018.1542776

2. Münster, S., et al.: Where are we now on the Road to 4D Urban History Research and Discovery? ISPRS Annals of the Photogrammetry, Remote Sensing and Spatial Information Sciences. VIII-M-1–2021, pp. 109–116 (2021). https://doi.org/10.5194/isprs-annals-VIII-M-1-2021-109-2021

3. Sikder, S.K., Behnisch, M., Herold, H., Koetter, T.: Geospatial analysis of building structures in megacity Dhaka: the use of spatial statistics for promoting data-driven decision-making. J. Geovisualization Spatial Analysis **3**(1), 1–14 (2019). https://doi.org/10.1007/s41651-019-0029-y

4. Meinel, G., Hecht, R., Herold, H.: Analyzing building stock using topographic maps and GIS. Building Res. Inf. **37**, 468–482 (2009). https://doi.org/10.1080/09613210903159833

5. Tooke, T.R., Coops, N.C., Webster, J.: Predicting building ages from LiDAR data with random forests for building energy modeling. Energy and Build. **68**, 603–610 (2014). https://doi.org/10.1016/j.enbuild.2013.10.004

6. Aksözen, M., Hassler, U., Rivallain, M., Kohler, N.: Mortality analysis of an urban building stock. Building Research & Inf. **45**, 259–277 (2017). https://doi.org/10.1080/09613218.2016.1152531

7. Evans, S., Liddiard, R., Steadman, P.: 3DStock: a new kind of three-dimensional model of the building stock of England and Wales, for use in energy analysis. Environ. Planning B: Urban Analytics City Science. **44**, 227–255 (2017). https://doi.org/10.1177/0265813516652898

8. Miatto, A., Schandl, H., Tanikawa, H.: How important are realistic building lifespan assumptions for material stock and demolition waste accounts? Resour. Conserv. Recycl. **122**, 143–154 (2017). https://doi.org/10.1016/j.resconrec.2017.01.015

9. Biljecki, F., Sindram, M.: Estimating building age with 3D GIS. ISPRS Ann. Photogramm. Remote Sens. Spatial Inf. Sci. IV-4/W5, pp. 17–24 (2017). https://doi.org/10.5194/isprs-annals-IV-4-W5-17-2017

10. Kohler, N., Hassler, U.: The building stock as a research object. Building Res. Inf. **30**, 226–236 (2002). https://doi.org/10.1080/09613210110102238

11. Huuhka, S., Lahdensivu, J.: Statistical and geographical study on demolished buildings. Building Res. Inf. **44**, 73–96 (2016). https://doi.org/10.1080/09613218.2014.980101

12. Bradley, P.E., Kohler, N.: Methodology for the survival analysis of urban building stocks. Building Res. Inf. **35**, 529–542 (2007). https://doi.org/10.1080/09613210701266939

13. Hudson, P., Dennett, A., Russell, T., Smith, D.: Colouring London–a crowdsourcing platform for geospatial data related to London's building stock. In: Proceedings of the 27th Annual Gis Research UK Conference. pp. 23–26. , Newcastle University, Newcastle, UK (2019)

14. Hecht, R., Rieche, T.: Mit einer Citizen-Science-Plattform Gebäudewissen kartieren, erforschen und vermitteln und dabei klimagerechte Architektur unterstützen. gis.Business pp. 34–36 (2023). https://doi.org/10.26084/PGVC-TX74

15. Hudson, P. (ed): Colouring London and the Colouring Cities Open Manual, Wiki (2023). https://github.com/colouring-cities/manual/wiki/

16. Hecht, R., Meinel, G., Buchroithner, M.: Automatic identification of building types based on topographic databases – a comparison of different data sources. Int. J. Cartography **1**, 18–31 (2015). https://doi.org/10.1080/23729333.2015.1055644

17. Herold, H., Hecht, R.: 3D reconstruction of urban history based on old maps. In: Münster, S., Friedrichs, K., Niebling, F., Seidel-Grzesinska, A. (eds.) UHDL/DECH -2017. CCIS, vol. 817, pp. 63–79. Springer, Cham (2018). https://doi.org/10.1007/978-3-319-76992-9_5

18. Wu, M., Zeng, W., Fu, C.-W.: FloorLevel-Net: recognizing floor-level lines with height-attention-guided multi-task learning. IEEE Trans. on Image Process. **30**, 6686–6699 (2021). https://doi.org/10.1109/TIP.2021.3096090

19. Fan, H., Zipf, A., Fu, Q., Neis, P.: Quality assessment for building footprints data on OpenStreetMap. Int. J. Geogr. Inf. Sci. **28**, 700–719 (2014). https://doi.org/10.1080/13658816.2013.867495

20. Hecht, R., Kalla, M., Krüger, T.: Crowd-sourced data collection to support automatic classification of building footprint data. Proc. Int. Cartogr. Assoc. **1**, 1–7 (2018). https://doi.org/10.5194/ica-proc-1-54-2018

21. Alhamwi, A., Medjroubi, W., Vogt, T., Agert, C.: OpenStreetMap data in modelling the urban energy infrastructure: a first assessment and analysis. Energy Procedia. **142**, 1968–1976 (2017). https://doi.org/10.1016/j.egypro.2017.12.397

22. Biljecki, F.: Exploration of open data in Southeast Asia to generate 3D building models. ISPRS Ann. Photogramm. Remote Sens. Spatial Inf. Sci. VI-4/W1–2020, pp. 37–44 (2020). https://doi.org/10.5194/isprs-annals-VI-4-W1-2020-37-2020

23. Hecker, S., Haklay, M., Bowser, A., Makuch, Z., Vogel, J., Bonn, A.: Citizen Science: Innovation in Open Science. Society and Policy, UCL Press (2018)

24. Vohland, K., et al. (eds.): The Science of Citizen Science. Springer, Cham (2021). https://doi.org/10.1007/978-3-030-58278-4

25. Haklay, M.: Citizen science and volunteered geographic information: overview and typology of participation. In: Sui, D., Elwood, S., Goodchild, M. (eds.) Crowdsourcing Geographic Knowledge, pp. 105–122. Springer, Netherlands, Dordrecht (2013)

26. Shirk, J.L., et al.: Public Participation in Scientific Research: a Framework for Deliberate Design. E&S. 17, art29 (2012). https://doi.org/10.5751/ES-04705-170229

27. Bemme, J., Munke, M.: Digitale Wissenschaftskommunikation im und mit dem Wikiversum. Erfahrungen aus der SLUB Dresden. 027.7 Zeitschrift für Bibliothekskultur / Journal for Library Culture. **9**, (2022). https://doi.org/10.21428/1bfadeb6.4112166b

28. Mazumdar, S., et al.: Citizen science technologies and new opportunities for participation. In: Hecker, S., Haklay, M., Bowser, A., Makuch, Z., Vogel, J., Bonn, A. (eds.) Citizen Science - Innovation in Open Science, Society and Policy, pp. 303–320. UCL Press, London (2018)

29. Land-Zandstra, A., Agnello, G., Gültekin, Y.S.: Participants in citizen science. In: Vohland, K., et al. (eds.) The Science of Citizen Science, pp. 243–259. Springer, Cham (2021). https://doi.org/10.1007/978-3-030-58278-4_13

30. Schaefer, T., Kieslinger, B., Brandt, M., van den Bogaert, V.: Evaluation in citizen science: the art of tracing a moving target. In: Vohland, K., et al. (eds.) The Science of Citizen Science, pp. 495–514. Springer, Cham (2021). https://doi.org/10.1007/978-3-030-58278-4_25

31. Kieslinger, B., Schäfer, T., Heigl, F., Dörler, D., Richter, A., Bonn, A.: Evaluating citizen science - towards an open framework. In: Hekler, S., Haklay, M., Bowser, A., Vogel, J., Bonn, A. (eds.) Citizen Science - Innovation in Open Science, Society and Policy, pp. 81–95. UCL Press, London (2018)

32. Balázs, B., Mooney, P., Nováková, E., Bastin, L., Jokar Arsanjani, J.: Data quality in citizen science. In: Vohland, K., et al. (eds.) The Science of Citizen Science, pp. 139–157. Springer, Cham (2021). https://doi.org/10.1007/978-3-030-58278-4_8

33. Hecht, R., Kunze, C., Hahmann, S.: Measuring completeness of building footprints in openstreetmap over space and time. IJGI. **2**, 1066–1091 (2013). https://doi.org/10.3390/ijgi2041066

34. Zhou, Q., Zhang, Y., Chang, K., Brovelli, M.A.: Assessing OSM building completeness for almost 13,000 cities globally. International Journal of Digital Earth. **15**, 2400–2421 (2022). https://doi.org/10.1080/17538947.2022.2159550

35. Biljecki, F., Chow, Y.S., Lee, K.: Quality of crowdsourced geospatial building information: a global assessment of OpenStreetMap attributes. Build. Environ. **237**, 110295 (2023). https://doi.org/10.1016/j.buildenv.2023.110295

36. Roper, J., Hudson, P., Petersen, H., Pettit, C., Russell, T., Ng, M.: Colouring Australia: a participatory open data platform. ISPRS Annals of the Photogrammetry, Remote Sensing and Spatial Information Sciences. X-4-W3–2022, pp. 229–235 (2022). https://doi.org/10.5194/isprs-annals-X-4-W3-2022-229-2022

37. Biljecki, F., Chew, L.Z.X., Milojevic-Dupont, N., Creutzig, F.: Open Government Geospatial Data on Buildings for Planning Sustainable and Resilient Cities (2021). http://arxiv.org/abs/2107.04023

38. Stoltz, D.: Kartenforum und Virtuelles Kartenforum - Ein Werkstattbericht zum Refactoring. In: Munke, M.(ed.) Landes- und Regionalgeschichte digital Angebote - Bedarfe - Perspektiven. pp. 95–105. Thelem, Dresden (2022). https://doi.org/10.25366/2021.31

39. Hosseini, K., Wilson, D.C.S., Beelen, K., McDonough, K.: MapReader: a computer vision pipeline for the semantic exploration of maps at scale. In: Proceedings of the 6th ACM SIGSPATIAL International Workshop on Geospatial Humanities, pp. 8–19. ACM, Seattle Washington (2022)

40. Jäger, J.: Fotografie und Geschichte. Campus, Frankfurt /New York (2009)

41. Steadman, P., Evans, S., Liddiard, R., Godoy-Shimizu, D., Ruyssevelt, P., Humphrey, D.: Building stock energy modelling in the UK: the 3DStock method and the London building stock model. Buildings and Cities **1**, 100–119 (2020). https://doi.org/10.5334/bc.52

42. Tanikawa, H., Hashimoto, S.: Urban stock over time: spatial material stock analysis using 4d-GIS. Building Res. Inf. **37**, 483–502 (2009). https://doi.org/10.1080/09613210903169394

43. Roumpani, F., Hudson, P., Hudson-Smith, A.: The use of historical data in rule-based modelling for scenarios to improve resilience within the building stock. The Historic Environ.: Policy & Practice **9**, 328–345 (2018). https://doi.org/10.1080/17567505.2018.1517142

44. Stanilov, K., Batty, M.: Exploring the historical determinants of urban growth patterns through cellular automata: determinants of urban growth. Trans. GIS **15**, 253–271 (2011). https://doi.org/10.1111/j.1467-9671.2011.01254.x

45. Hecht, R., Rieche, T., Neumann, M.: Dokumentation des Workshops zum Ideensprint der Citizen Science Projektidee "Baukultur und klimagerechte Architektur in Dresden – Gebäudewissen kartieren, erforschen und vermitteln" (2022). https://doi.org/10.5281/zenodo.7101800

46. Hecht, R., Danke, T., Rieche, T., Gruhler, K., Kriesten, T., Schinke, R.: Dokumentation des "Workshops zur Ausarbeitung der Gebäudemerkmale und deren Erfassung" im Rahmen des Citizen Science Projektes "Colouring Dresden" (2023). https://doi.org/10.5281/zenodo.7624511

47. Maiwald, H., Schwarz, J., Abrahamczyk, L., Kaufmann, C.: Das Hochwasser 2021: Ingenieuranalyse der Bauwerksschäden. Bautechnik **99**, 878–890 (2022). https://doi.org/10.1002/bate.202200062

48. Oudin Åström, D., et al.: The effect of heat waves on mortality in susceptible groups: a cohort study of a mediterranean and a northern European City. Environ Health. **14**, 30 (2015). https://doi.org/10.1186/s12940-015-0012-0

49. van Noordwijk, T. (C.G.E.), et al.: Creating positive environmental impact through citizen science. In: Vohland, K., et al. (eds.) The Science of Citizen Science, pp. 373–395. Springer, Cham (2021). https://doi.org/10.1007/978-3-030-58278-4_19

50. Cappa, F., Franco, S., Rosso, F.: Citizens and cities: Leveraging citizen science and big data for sustainable urban development. Bus Strat Env. **31**, 648–667 (2022). https://doi.org/10.1002/bse.2942

51. Fritz, S., et al.: Citizen science and the United Nations sustainable development goals. Nat Sustain. **2**, 922–930 (2019). https://doi.org/10.1038/s41893-019-0390-3

52. Paulmann, J., et al.: NFDI4Memory. Consortium for the historically oriented humanities. Proposal for the National Research Data Infrastructure (NFDI) (2022). https://doi.org/10.5281/zenodo.7428489

Reviving the Sounds of Sacral Environments: Personalized Real-Time Auralization and Visualization of Location-Based Virtual Acoustic Objects on Mobile Devices

Dominik Ukolov[✉] [iD]

Research Center Digital Organology, Musical Instruments Museum of Leipzig University, 04109 Leipzig, Germany
dominik.ukolov@uni-leipzig.de

Abstract. The auralization of historical musical instruments and buildings is a field of research that is becoming increasingly important with the advancement of virtualization technologies. In the doctoral project MODAVIS, the methods and strategies are investigated using the example of the organ, as its acoustics are directly coupled to the surrounding building and multimodal data acquisition is essential. Sacred buildings in Central and Southern Europe are the main places where this instrument class is installed, but they remain mostly silent while the craftsmanship and cultural practices around them are threatened by several factors. The framework that is being developed in this project aims to standardize the virtualization of acoustical cultural heritage and to make its capturing processes accessible without any special technical or organological expertise. The result is a multimodal dataset in a special format, the virtual acoustic object, which can be used in a variety of ways, both for remote research and for audiovisual interactions. In this approach, it has been used to create a mobile application that makes a virtualized organ audible and visible by playing any work on the instrument while viewing it in AR or playing it oneself using virtual keys.

Keywords: Auralization · Musical Instruments · Mobile Application · Organology · Virtualization

1 Introduction

The proposed work focuses on the methodology of virtualizing and auralizing an organ positive for a mobile application with multiple interaction modes. Numerous processes are described, which can be reproduced using a specially developed open-source framework, in which not only audiovisual, but also cultural-historical information, measurement and analysis data can be integrated. The object is located in the Musical Instruments Museum of Leipzig University and

S. Münster et al. (Eds.): UHDL 2023, CCIS 1853, pp. 165–186, 2023.
https://doi.org/10.1007/978-3-031-38871-2_10

was digitized as part of the TASTEN project. It was made by Stephan Cuntz in 1610 and placed in the choir of the Nuremberg church until 1892, when, after several alterations between 1700 and 1860, it was acquired first by Paul de Wit, then in 1905 by Wilhelm Heyer, whose collection is substantial for the present collection. This object was used to generate a Virtual Acoustic Object (VAO), which was installed in a virtual church environment and which can be auralized, played and viewed in real-time from any position using a mobile application.

1.1 Cultural History

The pipe organ offers a rich cultural history that can be traced back to ancient Alexandria, which subsequently accompanied Greek and Roman events as well as royal and religious ceremonies. Its cultural significance is not only evident from its prominent placement in representative buildings throughout Central Europe, but also due to its influence on the European music history, which was shaped by composers and organists such as Johann Sebastian Bach, Antonio Vivaldi or Georg Friedrich Händel. For centuries, this instrument has been an integral part of not only musical but also cultural traditions, while it is even explicitly integrated into the architectural design of many buildings, deliberately reflecting magnificence or modesty. The acquisition of such an expensive and large instrument has a high identification value for a community, while the making of these instruments was recognized by UNESCO as a World Intangible Cultural Heritage in 2017 and is still recognized as identificatory for entire regions. The centuries-long existence of the same disposition of an organ in one place and the tradition of its playing make it possible to find an intergenerational sonic identity that is exceptionally rare. This is due to the fact that other classes of instruments with non-aerophonic sound production and wooden resonators can only be restored with materials and methods that are either not available, were produced under different conditions, or are largely unknown. In addition, the sound characteristics and their radiation are in contrast to other musical instruments; the actions of the player remain mostly invisible, while impressively low frequencies can be felt physically, whose spatial origin cannot be located aurally.

After the Baroque period had led to numerous regional variations of organs in both Catholic and Protestant churches, organ building experienced a new boom after secularization. This was also related to the increasing prosperity, advanced technologies and the availability of various metals resulting from colonial oppression and exploitation, especially but not limited to Southeast Asia by the Dutch East India Company. These colonial aspects and the provenance of the metals used need to be further investigated in order to assess their extent in European organ building, which is of great cultural importance. In the late 19th and early 20th centuries, pipe organs were increasingly found in entertainment venues such as theaters and cinemas, but also in civic buildings, hotels and wealthy residences. New technologies were introduced at this time, such as electro-pneumatic signals instead of complex mechanical action and even self-playing organs, but these costly installations became obsolete after the installation of loudspeaker systems and film music instead of improvisations.

This technological substitution continued in the 20th century, while the world wars led to a decline in organ building and the destruction of numerous objects and buildings, besides a significant decrease in organ building in the Soviet republics and the loss of objects due to the deconstruction of sacral buildings. As a result of the existing demand and the so-called organ movement - a widespread revival of baroque organs from the pre-Romantic period - a boom in organ building began after the Second World War, especially in the Federal Republic of Germany, which still reaches high levels of productivity. Despite an increase in the number of organ building companies since reunification, there are currently about 400 of them, more than before, but with fewer employees [1].

In the present situation, the organ as a deeply rooted and important cultural heritage is threatened not only by military actions and the consequences of climate change, but also by economic crises, a decline in the number of skilled workers, the rapidly advancing functional conversion of sacral buildings, as well as the accelerating decline of Catholic and Protestant congregations in Germany and the general population decline in rural areas.

1.2 Auditive Virtualization

The virtualization of musical instruments is an emerging field of digital organology that is currently still in its initial stages and requires the development of a comprehensive methodology, a task that is being addressed in the MODAVIS project [2] using pipe organs as exemplary objects of research. There are several factors that support this instrument class as a precedent, including not only the reliable availability of organological data, authentic playability and the need for remote research access due to their decentralized locations, but also the acoustical coupling of the instrument with the surrounding space as well as the methodological scalability due to its size and functional complexity. In the case of the pipe organ, virtualization research faces several challenges and difficult conditions that need to be solved and the approaches made available afterwards.

These challenges concern, for example, the photogrammetric capture of highly reflective materials and pipes reaching up to the ceiling under difficult lighting conditions, the recording of theoretically infinitely sounding pipes with complex behavior, the acoustical modeling of large spaces such as churches and cathedrals, or the simulation of the mechanical behavior on the auralized sound. In order to achieve scientific goals and to increase the authenticity of the virtual representation, e.g. by reducing divergences through the simulation of the acoustical behaviour driven by multimodal data, it is important that the data acquisition is as comprehensible and detailed as possible. Because of the omnidirectional perception and its effect on the spatial self-localization, the acoustic dimension is of high relevance for the perceptual relationship of the subject to a virtual representation, which can be disturbed by visual and auditory incongruencies leading to room divergence effects [3]. For this reason, the correct reproduction of the acoustical reflection behavior of a room is essential and must be taken into account, especially in the case of the organ as a coupled resonating body, an integral part of the unfolding sound. These aspects are addressed in the process of auralization, whose objective is to simulate the logical paths of the sound that is travelling from the emitting sound generator to the perceiving subject including its reflections. This can be achieved by the simulation of impulse responses (IRs), which can be described as audio data from which the sound pressure at a defined spatial position can be derived from a known signal, such as an impulse or a sweep through a frequency range that is being emitted from an arbitrary position. This audio data, usually obtained by playing a predefined signal through a loudspeaker and recording it with microphones, can be simulated using various techniques that will be discussed in a later section. In order for the results of such a simulation to be as close as possible to real-world measurements, several parameters must be known: the dimensions of the room and the surfaces, materials, and textures it contains, the radiation pattern of the outgoing signal, the characteristics of the receiver, and their exact positions and orientations in the room. These IRs can be generated from multiple positions and convolved with any sound that is as reverberation-free as possible, which can then be played back in a personal listening setup. However, in order to be able to perceive an authentic and logical spatial sound, the integration of further psychoacoustic signal processing methods is necessary to resolve some divergence effects. These methods include the integration of binaural synthesis and anthropometric features using Head-Related Transfer Functions (HRTFs), as well as head tracking to maintain the position of virtual sound sources, which is already possible with the latest generations of commercially available headphones.

These aspects of auralization have already been investigated by Vorländer [4] and Blauert [5], while the MODAVIS project aims to develop a framework and new standards for the generation of VAOs, consisting of multimodal datasets of musical instruments and internal relations to simulate their acoustical behavior; this standard is intended for both scientific and creative applications. The associated concepts are based on the experiences of the projects TASTEN and DISKOS [6], both funded by the German Federal Ministry of Education and Research and carried out by the research group DIGITAL ORGANOLOGY at the Musical Instruments Museum of Leipzig University. These projects focused, among other issues, on the acoustical recording, measurement and further digitization processes of various historical keyboard instruments, mechanical music automatons and their playback media, followed by analytical classifications and methodological evaluations. The concept of the VAOs, however, continues this preliminary work by also incorporating photogrammetric or reconstructed three-dimensional models, highly detailed documented audio recordings, acoustical models of instruments and environments, activation logics, as well as other object properties into consistent data structures and providing them with an internal relation system, while newly developed analysis and classification methods enable the dynamic synthesis of the audio material.

2   Object Information Gathering

Before an object is recorded, all available information is gathered, allowing not only the cultural significance, but also the time required, possible damage or malfunctions to be anticipated. This step also allows to identify potential information gaps that can be addressed when the object is accessed and digitized, e.g. missing information on couplers or unrecorded effects.

In the course of the MODAVIS project, a comprehensive and consistent database was created with information on approximately 60,000 of preserved and already destroyed objects, so that the various register stops, manual and dispositions are known and the dataset can be prepared for recording. Organological data was also consulted and linked, for example via the musiXplora [7] platform, for which a special intersection identifier was created; this can be used to retrieve information on individual organ builders, organ building companies or further literature and external identifiers, from which additional data on an object can be derived if necessary or cultural-historical contexts can be integrated. For the preparation of the recording, it is important that the dimensions of the manuals and pedalboards, the register stops, the names and addresses, the overall condition of the instrument, and the dimensions of the building and its surroundings are known. The database can be used to retrieve this information, including the position and the surrounding building of an organ. Using the OSM Overpass API, it is possible to determine the amount of noise to be expected at a location and to estimate the reverberation time for certain frequency ranges, which is partly determined by the dimensions of a building. Significant noise sources include, for example, building locations near major roads, tram and train stations, hospitals, construction sites or locations near airports. These factors can be determined including their distances and have a significant impact on the timing of a recording session, which may result in limiting the amount of pipes that can be recorded within the time available.

3   Recording

There are several things to consider when recording the sound of an organ for the purpose of transforming it into a VAO. These arise not only from the unique relationship between the sound source and the surrounding environment, but also from the mechanical triggering of the various types of aerophonic sound generators. For this work, the priority of the positioning was to capture the direct sound with a consistent sound width, but especially for the organ it is hardly possible to avoid a direct convolution with the reflections and the diffuse sound, so multiple techniques of dereverberation will be investigated in a later project phase. In order to be able to control each individual pipe, it is necessary to know which pipe is activated by which register stop and manual operation, as well as effects such as tremulands and gradually closing shutters, which can multiply the amount of sound to be recorded due to their variability. In addition, the keystroke is not binary, and both the velocity and the depth of the keystroke can affect the resulting sound, with the initial phase of a sound being quasi-chaotic and thus different from the previous one at each activation. For these reasons, detailed documentation of the recording is of paramount importance in order to make the recordings suitable for scientific purposes and authentic virtual reproductions; in addition to keystroke velocity and depth, humidity, temperature, and barometric pressure must also be captured, as these environmental factors affect sound propagation. Furthermore, to correlate the interaction and audio data for further pattern analysis, exact time synchronization of the recording devices and sensors must be ensured.

In order to correctly perform, monitor, and clearly manage these numerous parallel tasks, a software was developed that uses the available organ database to prepare the sounds to be recorded as an integrated roadmap. This roadmap also includes the combinations for their activation and guides through the entire recording process. In addition, real-time analysis is performed to detect noise or inconsistencies, or to monitor the progression of partials and the reverberation phase. An accelerometer and a gyroscope were used to capture the interaction data, and an interface was developed to allow the software to communicate with the sensor and synchronize the interaction data with an audio file. This project uses an MPU-6050 placed in a custom case and connected to an Arduino Uno, which is an inexpensive and open source method. The sensor itself is placed on a key, pedal or held during other interactions; when a recording is started, the case of the sensor is pressed, which transmits the acceleration and angularity information to the interface of the software via USB, where it is assigned to the recording event and stored in the interaction database.

The methodology behind the recording process itself is intended to be quite simple using the guided recording software: Each pipe is activated and held for a specified time, which can be extended by the real-time analysis of the fluctuation patterns that occur, afterwards some sequential and parallel activations are played and recorded to document the effects of the wind pressure distribution. Since the noises of an object are also an integral part of its auditory identification and authenticity, it is particularly important to capture these as well, such as the sounds of key releases, pedal actions or the pulling of register stops, but also the wind-related noises when an organ is turned on and off. The entire recording process is accompanied by consistency checks and audio analysis to verify that a recording has been assigned to the correct classification, for example by determining its fundamental frequency using crepe [8] as a faster and still accurate alternative to the [9] pYIN algorithm. The samples are recorded with the highest possible sample rate and bit depth, in this case 192 kHz and 24 bit, to provide more accurate data for the analysis section. After a recording session has been completed, a hash code is calculated for each audio file that serves as an identifier for further processing operations, which must be documented without exception.

4   Analysis and Classification

In order to prepare the digitally available audio data for virtualization, it is necessary to analyze it extensively for several reasons: it must be known when a key was pressed and at what exact time the initial phase begins and ends, and it must be determined how the fluctuation patterns behave and where potential loop segments can be located in the data. These allow a theoretically infinite continuation of the virtual sound with the same fluctuative dynamics, without any auditively perceivable repetitive segments. The timing of the keystroke and the initial phase is crucial not only to reproduce the temporal delay of a sound activation after the keystroke, but also to be able to synthesize further initial phases together with a convergent reflection behavior during their auralization, where the initial phase acts as a noisy impulse and thus has a significant effect on the spatial perception of the room. In addition, the analyses are used to identify irregularities by applying clustering techniques to different vector representations, including neural and various spectral representations. In this way, the recorded sounds can be prepared for quantifiable classification systems of pipe ranks by calculating spectral similarities, which will be helpful in categorizing the divergent register stop names.

To accomplish these tasks, an analysis and editing software has been developed that automatically applies all the processes to an audio dataset, slices the audio files based on interaction data or determinable acoustical parameters, generates graphical sound representations, and stores all analysis results in the form of a database (Fig. 1). By determining the fundamental frequency, it is possible to precisely tune the audio dataset, either to any historical tuning, or simply to correct the pipe sounds during the synthesis process, e.g. if the organ was not properly tuned before recording. The parameters used to determine the initial phase can vary depending on the frequency and type of pipe, so this process is carried out using a suggested selection until a pattern validity is achieved by the MODAVIS project. However, the gradients of the spectral bandwidth, rolloff and novelty could already emerge as essential parameters.

If non-integrated audio processing tools such as VST plug-ins are to be used, a parameter logging system already applied in midiAuralizer [10] will be activated. Here, the metadata of the plug-in such as the developer and the version as well as each individual parameter are saved and stored, so that the exact settings of the plug-in are not only available in the processing log, but can also be restored again within the plug-in. This is currently limited to VST plug-ins, but will be extended to AU (Audio Unit) and other formats.

5   3D Capturing and Model Editing

Since three-dimensional object and room models are also required for multi-modal capturing and acoustical modeling, several methods were evaluated for their suitability, technical requirements and time consumption with respect to the level of detail, including new techniques such as Neural Radiance Fields (NeRFs) [11]. Photogrammetry was found to be a suitable method for creating instrument models, especially for interactive elements such as manuals, register stops, and pedals, due to the level of detail achievable, low technical requirements, and stable reproducibility. This technique is also used to generate room models, but with the intention of transforming them into models that are suitable for acoustical simulations, not necessarily for virtual reality (VR) applications.

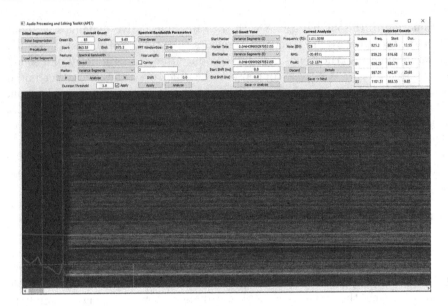

Fig. 1. The Audio Processing and Editing Toolkit (APET) performs several analytical operations to determine frequencies, segments and other parameters using various statistical algorithms. After an initial segmentation, the statistical parameters can be set to determine the phases, while the fundamental frequency and other acoustical information will be retrieved automatically.

5.1   Instrument

When photographing the instrument, special attention should be paid to the manuals, pedals and every single interaction element, as these will be mapped as accurately as possible and may be used to derive scientifically relevant measurement data. As far as possible, all parts of the instrument that are relevant for sound production should be photographed from several angles, if necessary also with telephoto lenses from a greater distance. However, this step may be less detailed if the principal pipes only serve the purpose of visual impression without any capabilites of producing sounds, which is not uncommon. However, since most of the pipes are hidden inside the case, further research will evaluate the suitability of endoscopic and other non-invasive methods for modeling the interior, as well as reconstruction methods based on restoration reports and construction drawings.

Various pre-processing tools have been developed to mask the instrument photos so that only the in-focus surfaces are included in the photogrammetric modeling process, provided that sufficient overlaps can be guaranteed. This is done using COLMAP's [12] calculation of the camera distances to specific surface points and matching them with the camera and lens specifications to mask the blurred pixels using back-projection methods, and then to mask overly strong reflections afterwards.

Once the model is created, the artifacts, distortions and exposure of the textures are corrected using Meshlab and Blender, with each step documented and stored via the logs. In the next step, the interactive elements were segmented according to a fixed naming scheme, so that the object names of each individual key contain the manual and MIDI note number, in order to be automatically addressable in the development engine. Next, the interactive object parts that intrude into the interior of the object are extrapolated using simple cuboid and cylinder primitives along with the textures, so that the edges of the neighboring keys or the register stops are not visually interrupted when they are held down or drawn. The edited and segmented model is then exported in .fbx format to prepare it for its import into Unity or other engines.

5.2   Room

Although this project used photogrammetry to generate room models, future work will evaluate the capabilities of volumetric techniques such as NeRF with respect to their distortions in auralizations. At the current stage of development, these models often tend to have high levels of artifacts and noise on their surfaces, but they can be substituted using the method of automated plane segmentation presented by Ukolov [13], as it can be applied to all models to obtain simplified geometric abstractions. Related to this, another technique is currently developed to integrate NeRFs with other room models to determine the position and orientation of variable objects such as microphones or object parts. This will make it possible to determine the distance and angle of a microphone in relation to a particular sound source.

For this work, the Bethanien Church in Leipzig-Schleußig was chosen as the target room for the auralization of the virtual acoustics, as it is easily accessible and is considered to have well-defined acoustics. Despite the very difficult lighting conditions on the day the photos were taken and the lack of high-performance hardware, a photogrammetric model was created and successfully transformed to be used for auralization purposes.

6   Acoustical Model Building

With the methodology used in this work, acoustical modeling essentially involves the generation of a simplified room model with annotated surfaces that can be derived from a photogrammetric model through semantic segmentations, point reprojections, and the assignment of coefficients that are relevant for acoustical simulations. For this purpose, the Photogrammetric-Acoustical Modeling Toolkit (PAMT) has been developed with a graphical interface to allow easy operation of the acoustical model building process at different levels of expertise. It is designed to provide a parameterizable pipeline for creating such models based solely on two-dimensional segmentations and classifications on photographs, which were used for model generation using COLMAP. This segmentation can be performed either manually using polygonal masking or automatically using

Mask R-CNN [14] and models that are trained to detect and segment objects on photographs.

Point Reprojections are based on the mapping of local 2D coordinates to global 3D point identities and vice versa, which can be applied to all coordinates contained within the set of a polygon mask using a pre-computed database. The toolkit also allows to define the material of a surface after setting a mask, either manually or by following the classifications of another neural network in two steps; these materials are relevant for the assignment of frequency-dependent absorption coefficients, using a specialized database with about 2,500 entries [15]. Inaccurate object appearances in the point cloud can be substituted by more detailed ones, even allowing the simulation of different room situations other than those captured. The result of this modeling process is an STL file and a referential database that points to the acoustical surface properties for each element.

7   Simulation of Impulse Responses

This annotated model can finally be used to simulate the IRs from any desired listener position, which is achieved using an interface to pyroomacoustics [16] that converts the encoded geometric and acoustical data into compatible structures. With the Image Source Method [17] and Acoustical Ray Tracing [18] an IR can be generated for the specified positions. This audio file can be convolved with any audio file that is contained in the VAO to reproduce the acoustical behavior at the corresponding position, including the frequency-dependent reverberation that occurs on the path from the sound source, e.g. an organ pipe, to the receiver, such as the virtual listening position.

In this work, these IRs were pre-generated for 16 positions and mapped to virtual locations; to create a smooth auditory experience, the IRs can be interpolated between the positions and auralized in real-time on the mobile application. Since the IRs are for positions in three-dimensional space, barycentric interpolation is applied to simplices of Delaunay triangulations, allowing interpolation in tetrahedrons within the coordinates that are contained in its shape. In a future approach, binaural impulse responses will be computed and combined with anthropomorphic transfer functions for a more authentic listening experience.

8   Virtual Acoustic Object Management

With the acquisition of object information, 3D models and audio data with the corresponding analysis results as well as an arbitrary acoustical room model, a VAO can finally be generated by importing the multimodal datasets using the specially developed VAO-Manager, in which the internal data relations can be defined to ensure an interactive behavior of the virtual object. This software is equipped with a GUI and is designed to validate all of the incoming data and structure them as consistent datasets (Fig. 2). Each individual file and data information entry is given a category-based identifier and a hash code in order to keep the modification logs traceable across any version.

To enable interoperability of the generated datasets, all databases are maintained in JSON format, as are the program's relevant functions. This allows for an easy overview, optimization, and further development of the software. Data consistency continues after content and format validation by validating all input information fields using specified regular expressions and renaming outgoing data according to predefined naming patterns. For example, for a single pipe recording, the filename would encode the register stop, manual and key number, variation, and recording number of a tone, so that it remains permanently identifiable even without the associated databases. Both the regular expressions and the patterns can be adapted at any time, while the categories and subcategories of the importable data are also designed to be expanded; this modular system is intended to allow the principles of VAOs to be adapted to the needs of individual projects with a high degree of flexibility. Each of the files encoded in the VAO can not only be exported separately, but also viewed, listened to, or otherwise opened directly within the interface. The filename schemes ensure that when imported into development environments, it is immediately clear which 3D model is intended for an implementation and which is not.

The software can also be used after the creation of a VAO to insert, modify or delete information and data, supported by an extensive versioning system that logs each operation, including metadata such as the software version used and the person or institution that performed the operation. This not only allows a virtual representation to be extended or corrected by multiple actors, but also ensures scientific traceability and reproducibility of data processing. Furthermore, protection mechanisms for undesired or illogical operations are integrated, such as the change of licensors or the subsequent definition of positions by unauthorized contributors. Each version of a VAO can be compared to another, and changes can be selectively applied or merged. The internal data relation system is designed not only to link data, but also to encode and infer functional properties from the data. Taking the organ as an example, a simple possible relation would be the object segment in the 3D model of a key, a register stop and that of one or more associated audio files as well as the interaction data; this relational network can be further extended at will, for example by reconstructed models of mechanical parts inside the organ, air pressure or dimensional measurements, material analyses, literature annotations and much more.

To handle such potentially complex networks, a relation structure has been developed that distinguishes between sound-causal relations, measurement data, metadata, and object information or literature data, with different relation types being defined. Provided that the model has been sufficiently segmented, several relations are automatically set after the consistency check of the imported datasets. This is made possible by defining functional dependencies and categorizations: In the case of the organ, the key would be the initial activator and pitch-determining element, the register stop the first-degree modulator, while effects such as tremulands and shutters are second- and third-degree modulators,

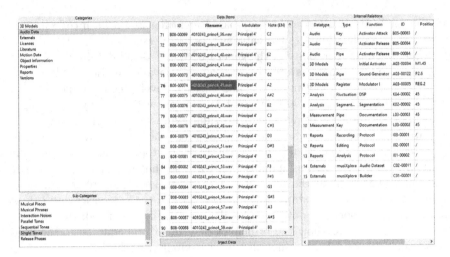

Fig. 2. The VAO-Manager allows the injection, extraction and editing of multimodal datasets including its internal relations. On the left side, the main and subcategory can be selected, while the files corresponding files appear in the middle section. On the right section, the relations can be set and viewed. Each data has an assigned identifier, while the terms and functions are related to predefined structures. This software is also used to encode and decode the VAO in multiple formats, in addition it is capable of performing various operations like the analysis of audio files, the view of 3D models or the conversion of MIDI files into animations.

the pipes are the resonators, and their exit holes are the sound emitters. Additional layers are energy sources such as wind machines and various types of transmitters, for example mechanical, electromagnetic, electrical or pneumatic transmitters. This system is generally applicable to all instrument classes that follow the principles of subtractive synthesis, with the exception of a missing material-bound and excitation-specific sound generator (e.g. strings, membranes, idiophones). In addition to segmented object parts, an upcoming version of the VAO-Manager will allow the addressing of annotations to integrate photos, literature, patents and other multimodal data into the relational system.

Another important point is the integration of already existing datasets that have not been generated with the MODAVIS framework and therefore have not been classified and processed. For this purpose, each imported file can also be analyzed and processed with the same methods as in the Audio Processing and Editing Toolkit (APET). In particular, the assignment of a register stop falls within the scope of the spectral assignment module of the software, if this is not recognizable from metadata or naming patterns. This module uses the methodology of LTAS according to Hergert [19] to assign the imported recordings of organ sounds to a probable pipe rank and the spectrally nearest register stop solely on the basis of the audio data encoded. However, if the corresponding information is available in some form, it can be assigned manually.

With this relation system and the Unity plugin described in a later section, it is not only possible to integrate various visualizations into the virtual representation of the organ, such as the highlighting of the pipe when a key is pressed or the overlaying of measurement data and literature, but also to transfer the depth of the keys from the interaction or measurement data directly into the model. In terms of literature integration, this system is particularly interesting because many organs have been equipped with pipes from different periods and by different organ builders; while some pipes are actually hundreds of years old, others are only a few decades old, have been repaired or restored. Not only can this be seen in the virtual representation, but listening comparisons or scientific analyses can easily be performed, for example of the diverging spectral characteristics or materials and dimensions. The various analysis methods, in which clustering algorithms on vector representations are particularly promising, will be investigated in a forthcoming project.

After all data sets have been structured and subjected to a final validation after processing, the VAO can finally be exported. The result is an archive file with the extension '.vao', which was compressed and contains all data in its intended structure with a special header as well as configuration files. This VAO file can be easily shared and imported to other computers in the VAO-Manager, or it can be extracted as an archive file with conventional tools, so that the data can be accessed even without the use of any specialized software. It can also be imported directly into development engines such as Unity using a special script. In a later version, it is planned to enable the compilation and export of VSTi/AU and standalone executables.

9   Musical Action Information Management

In order to be able to play musical pieces on the virtualized organ or to activate individual sounds, musical action signals are used, which are coordinated using the MIDI standard. This does not transport audio signals, but only the signals of musical actions - e.g. the pitch and velocity of a pressed keyboard key - and can function with low latencies in real-time, not least because of its extremely small data size. The Note On and Note Off signals can be used to control the activation or deactivation of a note with a specific pitch and volume (velocity), while the Program Change signal can be used to activate a timbre or instrument. MIDI signals can be communicated on 16 channels, so signals coming from predefined channels can lead to extended interpretations on the receiving virtual instrument. The signals are conventionally stored and retrieved as MIDI files with hexadecimal encoding or transmitted in binary form over MIDI cables, but can also be communicated via wired digital interfaces, Bluetooth and the Real-Time Transport Protocol (RTP). Since an organ often contains several manuals and also pedals to control the pitch of an intended sound, its Note signals are assigned to different MIDI channels in this work. The numerous different register stops, on the other hand, are assigned to Program Change signals, but since there is no Off signal here, unlike the Notes, the activation signals are assigned to odd numbers and the deactivation signals to even numbers, all of which are stored in a lookup database.

The interpretation of these MIDI signals is standardized for keyboards, electric pianos and other synthesizers and is performed without any problems, but for the virtual organs resulting from the VAOs it must be considered that the musical pieces that are encoded in MIDI files usually cannot be played correctly on them without further difficulties. Among the main reasons are the range of the manuals and pedals as well as the addressing of register stops of different lengths, so that the pitch addressed by a signal will not converge with the sounding pitch in every case if the stop differs from the 8' designation. For example, a piano piece played on an 88-key piano cannot easily be transferred to a 49-key manual; furthermore, a MIDI file in which e.g. electric guitars, strings or trombones are encoded cannot be played on simple flute stops, since this would completely miss the intended timbre. To solve these problems, a converter has been developed that can be used to generate a new MIDI file from any MIDI file in which the encoded input signals are assigned to the appropriate VAO based on the object and sound properties.

The core concept of this conversion process is that of spectral similarity, which is based on the fact that encoded information about the intended timbres is captured in the files and spectrally matched with those of the organ pipes. These encodings are done in the General MIDI (GM) standard, so a program number approximately corresponds to the same sound. Although these can be synthesized by some electronic sound generators with different procedures and tonal results, they still provide a suitable basis for spectral matching, since the standard sounds often generated by frequency modulation synthesis are widely used and bound to fixed program numbers. Consequently, the sounds contained in the GM standard were synthesized for the procedure using a standard library. An evaluation of the output similarities using a theater organ revealed that both the Euclidean distances between Mel-Frequency Cepstrum Coefficients (MFCCs) and the Frobenius norm of cross-correlations were most congruent with the perceptual impression. Here, MFCC distances performed better for pipe sounds and cross-correlations for percussive sounds and effects, while pitch changes, highly divergent spatial reflectance, and loudness differences negatively affected similarity matches, so they were adjusted prior to processing.

The result of the similarity evaluation is a list of suggested translations for the automatic conversion, with which e.g. a program number appearing in the incoming MIDI file can be converted to the program number of an organ stop and inserted into a new MIDI file. In this conversion process, the encoded metadata is first transferred to the new file, since it contains relevant time values as well as license data. In the next step, the note values are adapted to the note ranges and the MIDI channels to those of the proposed registers. Since the number of manuals in an organ is usually limited to a few, and MIDI signals can contain up to 16 channels, the assignment of the incoming note information to the manuals must be done using a pseudo-randomization algorithm in which octave shifts prevent spectral masking and thus overlapping sequences.

10   Integration in Development Engine

To integrate the VAO into a mobile application, Unity was chosen as the development engine, while the Vuforia [20] and Resonance Audio [21] SDKs were chosen for the implementation of AR and dynamic audio processing. A toolkit was developed to perform certain tasks in a pipeline, which firsts converts the 3D model into a compatible format, then it renders required graphics and compresses all audio files except the simulated IRs; in a final step it writes the new data structure and activation logic into scripts that can be used in Unity, which also manage the relations and links between the individual components (Fig. 3). At the core of the musical information processing are MIDI files interpreted by a specialized sampler whose behavior, such as running through seamless loop points, is defined by the data contained in a VAO. This real-time synthesis approach allows the file size of a musical piece to be kept between 10 and 200 kilobytes, depending on the amount of signals, eliminating the need for conversion on the mobile device.

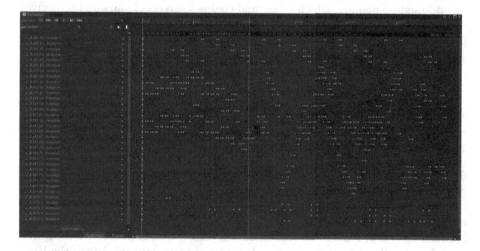

Fig. 3. This is an animation that has been processed by the MIDI to animation converter for Unity, where each object component is being addressed to perform certain transformations or rotations with the correct timing.

The basic principle of this interface for integrating VAOs is that the relevant data together with its relation leading to its activation is transferred into a structure that is accessible to Unity, and the activation parameters are implemented dynamically. This can be illustrated with an example: If a MIDI Note On signal is received after a register stop has been marked as active by a Program Change signal, the corresponding audio sample is played and an animation of the activated key and register stop are initiated. If a MIDI Note Off signal is received, the audio sample will continue until the next zero crossing point and then stop, while the animation back to the original positions are initiated and the reverb of the building can still be heard through the audio signal processors. The previously simulated IRs can be integrated into these processors, which can be interpolated or dynamically replaced in real time. A central point, however, is the conversion of MIDI files into an interpretable format, which is done here by tokenization, whereby absolute time information can be obtained from the complex serial time information of the MIDI format. During this tokenization process, the samples, animations and parameters to be addressed are also included per signal, so that the chain of commands can be executed in a correct order. To convert the resulting information into animation commands, a parameterizable program was developed in which the initial and target positions as well as the latencies of the action can be specified.

Seamless Loop Points consist of paired time points and define which segments of an audio sample are looped when a key is held if the hold time exceeds the duration of a sample. During the analysis process using the APET, several of these point pairs are determined and classified with respect to their variance and fluctuation intensity. These points can then be integrated into a loop process in a pseudo-random manner, which mixes and chains these point pairs and thus gives the impression of a dynamically sustaining sound without temporal limitations. In a future approach, the original sustain phases of a sample will be classified and predicted using neural networks to synthesize the fluctuative behavior into a looped segment using conventional audio signal processing.

11   Application

11.1   Structures and Modules

At the current stage of development, the general structure of the mobile application is divided into four main scenes; the first one allows the selection of the building, the user's predefined position within it, and the instrument that the user wishes to auralize. The second is the main screen and allows switching between the View, Player and AR mode, the song selection panel with a curated or alphabetically sorted list, and simple play and pause buttons. When the View mode is active, a graphical representation of the organ is displayed, while the AR mode allows the camera to be used and the organ action to be overlayed on a nearby floor. In this mode, the keys and register stops that are being addressed by the MIDI signals are animated according to their action signal, using the internal relations system. The third screen is active during the player mode and shows the orthographic front of the organ action with its interactive elements such as register stops and a keyboard true to the original to play them, while buttons allow to change the register stop and thus the pipe rank being addressed. The application has been developed for Android/iOS smartphones and tablets and is designed for use with headphones (Fig. 4).

Fig. 4. The View Mode allows to change the perspectives on the object by sliding the view on the touchscreen, while different musical pieces can be played and the virtual listening position changed by defining it in the room scene.

11.2   Use Cases

As this mobile application for the personalized auralization of acoustical cultural heritage is intended to be a proof of concept and further extensions will be implemented in later stages of development, the use cases are currently limited to the exploration of only one object. Nevertheless, some applications that can already be realized are the interactive mediation of the intangible cultural heritage of organ building and the endangered cultural practices around organs, the establishment of new relations to public sacral buildings through aesthetic experiences, the integration into local tourism projects, or to raise more attention for restoration donations. Another use case concerns the historical modifications made to an object or building over time; these can be reconstructed through modeling approaches and auralized after their conversion, which could be interesting for further research in acoustics and historical music performance practices. In addition, it is possible to perform a virtual installation of dislocated objects in their original locations, such as museum objects. The concept and methodology of this mobile application is intended to serve as a basis for further optimizations in terms of auditory and visual immersion, as well as for extension to other instrumental and architectural classes (Fig. 5).

Fig. 5. The Player Mode allows to play the VAO using the layout of the original keys and buttons to activate and deactivate the register stops, while the virtual listening position can be changed by defining it in the room scene.

12   Future Work

12.1   3D Audio and Position Tracking

The integration of HRTFs and Ambisonics in a binaural synthesis process, combined with the tracking of the user's position, allows the auralization of a three-dimensional sound field while walking through it in with up to six degrees of freedom (6 DoF). It is planned to record at least five organs with such a setup and to evaluate the accuracy of different tracking methods. It will be possible to display nearby buildings and their available instruments with links to the default navigation application. During the course of the project, the framework will be further optimized, in particular with respect to the dereverberation of audio data, the conversion into acoustical room models or the analysis and synthesis of fluctuation patterns and initial phases using neural networks.

12.2   Extended Visualizations

There are numerous plans to expand the visual components of this application, starting with the insertion of information bubbles, highlighting of activated pipes, and intersection through the organ model to show its hidden pipes. Additionally, the visualization of the MIDI file as a piano roll, the wave propagation paths and room modes are currently under development.

12.3   Shared Experience

To enhance the multisensory experience with an intersubjective component, it is considered to add a shared play mode, in which each building has a manually or randomly set program of musical pieces, so that users on site can listen to the same piece of music at the same time. With the provided MIDI converter, it is even possible to play arrangements of popular music on the virtual organ or on an organ with a MIDI interface, while performance recordings of organists in this format can be used to virtually replicate a concert.

12.4   Virtual Reality Applications

If professional photogrammetric models of the building interiors that are related to the virtualized objects can be provided, they will be combined within the engine and auralized in a VR application that will be extended by the aforementioned audio approach. These models will be acquired from cooperation partners and a suitable object for a case study is currently being evaluated.

12.5   Cooperations and Contributions

In order to implement more VAOs or to realize more extensive case studies, the framework will be published and its methodology will be mediated to interested persons and institutions at the final stage of the project at the end of 2023. One notable remote collaboration is with the Institute of Historic Organs in Oaxaca, Mexico, a region rich in unique objects but also threatened by regular earthquakes. It is also planned to introduce unique QR codes per building, which can be scanned in the entrance area and will either redirect to the respective app store or to the initialization of the available objects within the already installed app. An important aspect of the concept was to enable the implementation of these methods with low-cost devices in order to avoid excluding institutions with limited financial resources.

12.6   Virtual Placement in Original Locations

In the context of a planned case study, it will be possible to add or remove historical object or building modifications to approximate their state at a specific time period, but also to use and auralize reconstructions of completely destroyed buildings, providing a temporal dimension that could be of interest for educational purposes. In this study, several of the aforementioned aspects will be combined in an extended application. It focuses an organ by Gottfried Silbermann, which is prominently displayed in the Musical Instruments Museum of Leipzig University and was removed in 1907 from a church in Bobritzsch-Hilbersdorf near Freiberg in Saxony for a collection in Cologne. Since this church still exists in a relatively original state, it will be photogrammetically and acoustically modeled, after which a VAO of the museum's Silbermann organ will be virtually installed in its original location and auralized.

As the original wooden coffered ceiling was removed for the installation of another organ and replaced by an imitation vault, it will also be reconstructed based on photographic evidence and sketches to integrate it into the acoustical model. Using AR in the application, the organ will be visible in its original location by simply pointing at it with the device's camera, while a reconstruction can be viewed in VR. In the course of this work, comprehensive evaluations of the models will be carried out, e.g. by comparing the measured and simulated impulse responses. The project also aims at a demonstration and perceptual evaluation directly on site and in the museum, as well as an exploration of the cultural-historical and proveniental backgrounds including a visualization of spatio-temporal information about the origin of the materials and the various stations of the instrument. Since there are several objects in the mentioned museum that are no longer in their original locations, the developed methodology can be applied to other objects, regardless of whether the original buildings still exist or can be reconstructed.

13   Ethical Considerations

The ethical implications of digitization and the virtual object representation relate in particular to the danger that, in certain scenarios, they could be used as an argument to convert or dismantle buildings or objects, with reference to detailed digital preservation, virtual reproducibility and integration into cultural practices. It must be countered that digitization is already, by technical and perceptual means, only an approximation of a physical reality, and that unconsidered or unobtainable information would be irrevocably lost. The methods will be optimized with technological advancements, and it is necessary to preserve these objects, especially where there are intergenerational intersections in their cultural practices in its remaining form. In order to draw attention to the problem of the deliberate destruction of cultural heritage and the loss of the integrity of the objects installed in it, it is also planned to acoustically reconstruct the Church of St. Lambertus of Immerath and to auralize its original organ, since it was demolished in 2018 by the energy company RWE in favor of the coal mining in Garzweiler [22]. The organ was dismantled and sold to another parish in Poland, theoretically allowing it to be recorded and virtualized. A long-term goal of the MODAVIS project is to initiate a political commitment to digitize such historically significant buildings and instruments as comprehensively as possible before they are being destroyed or converted.

Another ethical implication is the potential manipulation of data to promote concerts, recordings, and the rental of recording locations. For example, audio data or processing parameters could be manipulated in a way that does not remotely correspond to the actual listening experience, which is not in the scientific intent of VAOs, but must be kept possible for creative purposes. These could include the integration of VAOs into the production of music recordings, including mixing processes, or the free and deconstructive artistic processing of audio data.

An important point to consider is the potential overrepresentation of VAOs in financially and materially privileged regions, with the consequence that mostly Central European and North American objects will be made available. Although the largest concentration of organs is located there, the numerous valuable objects, e.g. in Latin America, should not be excluded from the availability and feasibility of this standard and should be especially included. For this reason, the MODAVIS project aims at intercontinental cooperation in order to counteract such a development and to promote non-European object representations and their generation processes.

Acknowledgements. The author is supported by the German Academic Scholarship Foundation and by the association Netzwerk DIGITAL ORGANOLOGY e.V., preliminary work was carried out in the TASTEN and DISKOS projects, both funded by the Federal Ministry of Education and Research of Germany.

References

1. Eberlein, R.: Orgelneubauten sind selten geworden (2014). http://walcker-stiftung.de/Downloads/Blog/Orgelneubauten_selten_geworden.pdf. Accessed 26 Mar 2023
2. Ukolov, D.: MODAVIS (2022). https://modavis.org/. Accessed 26 Mar 2023
3. Werner, S., et al.: A summary on acoustic room divergence and its effect on externalization of auditory events. In: 8th International Conference on Quality of Multimedia Experience (QoMEX) (2016)
4. Vorländer, M.: Auralization: Fundamentals of Acoustics, Modelling, Simulation, Algorithms and Acoustic Virtual Reality. Springer, Heidelberg (2020). https://doi.org/10.1007/978-3-540-48830-9
5. Blauert, J.: The Technology of Binaural Listening. Springer, Heidelberg (2020). https://doi.org/10.1007/978-3-642-37762-4
6. Forschungsstelle Digital Organology. DISKOS. Komparation multimodaler Quellenkorpora der Musik, gefördert vom Bundesministerium für Bildung und Forschung (BMBF). https://organology.uni-leipzig.de/index.php/forschung/diskos. Accessed 26 Mar 2023
7. Khulusi, R., et al.: Visual analysis of a musicological encyclopedia. In: Proceedings of the 12th International Conference on Information Visualization Theory and Applications (2020)
8. Kim, J.W.: Crepe: a convolutional representation for pitch estimation. In: IEEE International Conference on Acoustics, Speech and Signal Processing (ICASSP), pp. 161–165 (2018)
9. Mauch, M., Simon, D.: pYIN: a fundamental frequency estimator using probabilistic threshold distributions. In: IEEE International Conference on Acoustics, Speech and Signal Processing (ICASSP), pp. 659–663 (2014)
10. Ukolov, D.: GitHub: midiAuralizer (2022). https://github.com/modavis-project/midiAuralizer. Accessed 26 Mar 2023
11. Mildenhall, B., et al.: NeRF: representing scenes as neural radiance fields for view synthesis. Commun. ACM **65**(1), 99–106 (2021)
12. Schönberger, J.L., Frahm, J.-M.: Structure-from-motion revisited. In: Proceedings of the IEEE Conference on Computer Vision and Pattern Recognition, pp. 4104–4113 (2016)
13. Ukolov, D.: Parameterizable Acoustical Modeling and Auralization of Cultural Heritage Sites based on Photogrammetry. arXiv:2302.05725 (2023)
14. He, K., Gkioxari, G., Dollár, P., Girshick, R.: Mask R-CNN. In: Proceedings of the IEEE International Conference on Computer Vision, pp. 2961–2969 (2017)

15. Physikalisch-Technische Bundesanstalt. The Room Acoustics Absorption Coefficient Database. https://www.ptb.de/cms/ptb/fachabteilungen/abt1/fb-16/ag-163/absorption-coefficient-database.html Accessed 26 Mar 2023

16. Scheibler, R., Bezzam, E., Dokmanić, I.: Pyroomacoustics: a python package for audio room simulation and array processing algorithms. In: IEEE International Conference on Acoustics, Speech and Signal Processing (ICASSP), pp. 351–355. IEEE (2018)

17. Allen, J.B., Berkley, D.A.: Image method for efficiently simulating small-room acoustics. J. Acoust. Soc. Am. **65**(4), 943–950 (1979)

18. Krokstad, A., Strom, S., Sørsdal, S.: Calculating the acoustical room response by the use of a ray tracing technique. J. Sound Vib. **8**(1), 118–125 (1968)

19. Hergert, F., Höper, N.: Envelope functions for sound spectra of pipe organ ranks and the influence of pitch on tonal timbre. Proc. Meet. Acoust. FVTMA **49**(1), 035012 (2022)

20. Vuforia Developer Portal. https://developer.vuforia.com/ Accessed 26 Mar 2023

21. Resonance Audio Homepage. https://resonance-audio.github.io/resonance-audio/. Accessed 26 Mar 2023

22. Welle, D.: Unused church torn down in Germany for coal mine. https://www.dw.com/en/unused-church-torn-down-in-germany-to-make-way-for-open-pit-coal-mine/a-42089253. Accessed 26 Mar 2023

From Archival Sources to a 3D-Visualization of Baroque Urban Topography: Vienna, Neuer Markt, C. 1760

Anna Mader-Kratky[1] , Günther Buchinger[1] , and Alarich Langendorf[2]([⊠])

[1] Austrian Academy of Sciences, Institute for Habsburg and Balkan Studies, Dr. Ignaz-Seipel Platz 2, 1010 Vienna, Austria
{anna.mader,guenther.buchinger}@oeaw.ac.at
[2] Archaeo Perspectives GesbR, Wilhelm Exner-Gasse 11/5, 1090 Vienna, Austria
alarich.langendorf@archaeo-perspectives.at

Abstract. This paper presents the preliminary results of a pilot study, in which the Viennese marketplace *Neuer Markt* was chosen as a model area to test the extent to which historic image data and written sources can be used efficiently for creating a digital 3D model of Baroque Vienna. Based on two examples (the town house *Neuer Markt 1* and the *Palais Schwarzenberg*), the reconstruction of a building that is very well respectively moderately well documented with images and plans is analysed and the handling of uncertainties is discussed.

The modelling is done in close cooperation between archival research, art historical expertise and technical implementation. The dialogue resulting from the intense reconstruction process inevitably raises questions that have been given little or no consideration in art historical assessment. In this sense, the pilot study sets fundamental art historical research in relation to a 3D-visualization, interpreting the process of modelling and its documentation as essential research tools. The project is being realised exclusively using open source software in order to ensure that the data set generated can be used as freely as possible in the long term. A first dissemination solution of the 3D model is being developed in cooperation with the *Wien Museum*, where the digital model is being made accessible to the public for the first time via a multimedia station as part of the reorganization of the collection in December 2023.

Keywords: Vienna's baroque topography · 3D modelling · archival sources

1 Introduction

Regarding the historical city of Vienna (today's *Innere Stadt*), a source-based interpretation and large-scale reconstruction of the cityscape from the 18th century onwards is possible. Based on still remaining buildings as well as an increasing number of image data (e.g. reliable historical maps) and written sources of aristocratic, ecclesiastical, municipal and civic building activities the imperial capital can be visualised through

S. Münster et al. (Eds.): UHDL 2023, CCIS 1853, pp. 187–203, 2023.
https://doi.org/10.1007/978-3-031-38871-2_11

digital modelling.[1] This paper presents the preliminary results of a pilot study, in which the Viennese marketplace *Neuer Markt* was chosen as a model area to test the extent to which this extensive and diverse stock of sources can be used efficiently for systematic reconstruction work.[2] The structural diversity of *Neuer Markt* gave rise to an ideal-typical urban space where the high and low nobility, the Capuchin order (with the imperial family as founder), the magistrate and the urban bourgeoisie met as builders. Although only two baroque houses and the Capuchin church remain of the 20 buildings to be reconstructed, historical depictions give us a good impression of all four sides of the square. Compared to these historical views, the digital 3D model enables realistic rendering of space without distortions, which allows for hitherto unseen perspectives and enables a new quality in the visualization of baroque urban topography.

The modelling is conducted through close cooperation between art historical expertise and technical implementation. As the modelling process encompasses both the square and small-scale architectural details, the resulting dialogue inevitably raises questions that have been given little or no consideration in art historical assessment – for example, on actual building heights or on the cubature and spatial relationship of buildings, i.e. on aspects that historical views usually show in an idealised way. In this sense, the pilot study sets fundamental art historical research in relation to a 3D-visualization, interpreting the process of modelling and its documentation as essential research tools.

2   The Historical Source Material

During this 14-month research project, the historical images and plans in the topographical collection of the *Wien Museum*[3], in the Municipal and Provincial Archives (*Wiener Stadt- und Landesarchiv*), in the picture archive of the Austrian National Library (*Österreichische Nationalbibliothek*)[4] and in the photo archive of the Federal Monuments Office (*Bundesdenkmalamt*) were systematically documented, such as paintings, engravings and drawings, building and situation plans as well as photographs. These historic images document the building stock and its changes.

In his multi-volume work *Wahrhaffte und genaue Abbildung [...]* (1724–1737), the engraver Salomon Kleiner recorded all important streets, squares and buildings of Vienna – including *Neuer Markt* [Fig. 1] – and in this way also documented the most modern architecture of the imperial capital at the time. More than 20 years later, the painter Bernardo Bellotto (named Canaletto) captured some of the city's squares in

---

[1] For the methodological considerations of reconstruction through computer-aided 3D modelling and a comprehensive summary of the wide field of research, see most recently: Münster, S.: Digital 3D Technologies for Humanities Research and Education: An Overview, Applied Sciences 12, 5 (2022), pp. 7–10.

[2] "Barockstadt Wien digital: Der Neue Markt, um 1760", a research project hosted by the Institute of Habsburg and Balkan Studies of the Austrian Academy of Sciences (Research Unit: History of Art) and funded by the City of Vienna (Stadt Wien – Kulturabteilung, MA 7), https://www.oeaw.ac.at/ihb/forschungsbereiche/kunstgeschichte/forschung/habsburgische-repraesentation/barockstadt-wien-digital, last accessed 2023/3/6.

[3] https://sammlung.wienmuseum.at/en/, last accessed 2023/3/6.

[4] https://onb.wg.picturemaxx.com/, last accessed 2023/3/6.

paintings, which are among the few colored sources from the period and thus provide essential information on the former house paint [Fig. 2].

The evaluation of the written sources served aspects of ownership and building history and led to a refined chronological classification of the historical building stock. The entries in the land registers in the Municipal and Provincial Archives provide reliable information about the acquisition dates and the circumstances of the purchase. The "Hofquartiersbücher" in the Finanz- und Hofkammerarchiv of the Austrian State Archives,[5] which record all houses subject to quartering, could unfortunately not be consulted for conservation reasons; only the "Hofquartiersbuch" from 1566 was made available digitally by the archive.[6] However, it was possible to view in full all applications for exemption from quarters, which in the case of building activity (mostly addition of storeys and re-facing of the house in question) have been preserved without gaps in the "Hofquartiersprotokollen" und "Hofquartiersresolutionen" (records and resolutions)[7] from the mid-17th to the late 18th century. All those protocols and resolutions provided evidence of builders and building data for each house to be reconstructed. In addition, house and building files in the Municipal and Provincial Archives provided a significant consolidation of the building-historical statements.[8]

The data pool was compiled for each property according to the following scheme: Various historical house or conscription numbers were linked to the current address in order to ensure a complete concordance and identification of the houses in the archival sources, which have all been assigned a unique identifier. Subsequently, the essential building data (owner, construction period, if known the master builder) were documented in brief. This is followed by an analysis of the predecessor buildings based on written and pictorial sources in order to trace functional continuities (craftsmen's houses, inns, aristocratic houses) as well as possible structural mergers of smaller plots. Subsequently, the building history of the stock that survived around the middle of the 18th century is analyzed. Finally, the data collection includes information on the further building history (alterations, demolitions, new buildings), cultural and socio-historical aspects that make the houses appear as "living" monuments, a stylistic classification and art-historical appreciation as well as a bibliography. All primary sources are clearly identified by permalinks to the websites of the corresponding archives, which are stored in the database, so that the information is comprehensible and transparent at all times.

---

[5] Austrian State Archives (ÖStA), FHKA (Finanz- und Hofkammerarchiv), Alte Hofkammer (AHK), HQuB (Hofquartiersbücher) 1–34.

[6] ÖStA, FHKA, AHK, HquB 3.

[7] ÖstA, FHKA, AHK, HquB 51–128, HquA (Hofquartiersakten) 1–16.

[8] Municipal and Provincial Archives (WStLA), Land Registers (Gb); WStLA, Municipal Departments 236 (MA 236), EZ series, old stock; WStLA, Subchamber Office (Unterkammeramt), Building consensus plans.

Fig. 1. Salomon Kleiner and Georg Daniel Heymann, *Die Kirche der Capuciner auf dem neüen Marckt*, view to the south, engraving, 1724 [© ÖAW, Sammlung Woldan]

Fig. 2. Bernardo Bellotto (named Canaletto), *Der Mehlmarkt in Wien*, view to the north, oil on canvas, 1759/60 [© Kunsthistorisches Museum Wien, GG 1668, https://www.khm.at/objektdb/detail/214/?offset=1&lv=list]

3   Technical Implementation: From Archival Sources to a 3D-Visualization

All materials from the art historical research were digitised as image and text data and transferred to a dedicated PostgreSQL/PostGIS-geodatabase. Using open geoinformation tools, the historical plan material was georeferenced into a nationally valid reference coordinate system. In particular, the city spanning maps executed for the inventory of pavement by the cartographer Anton Behsel (1823–1832) were suitable to fit in the numerous surviving building ground plans that could be collected from the archives due to their exact execution and thus their accurate spatial representation of the square [Fig. 3].

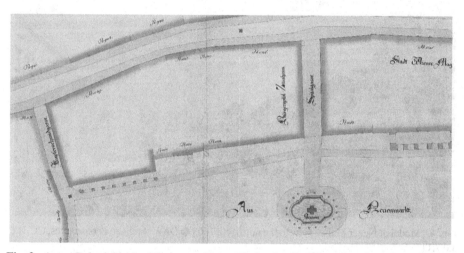

Fig. 3. Anton Behsel, block of Houses on Neuer Markt, detail of *Situationspläne der sämtlichen Plätze, Gassen und Basteien der Stadt* [...], 1832 [© Wiener Stadt- und Landesarchiv, Karten und Pläne, Sammelbestand, P1: 235G]

After matching this data set with Open Government Data (OGD) of the City of Vienna, a database object was created for each of the 20 buildings as a main entity with a Universally Unique Identifier (UUID), via which the referenced geometries (from simple 2D polygons for the use in geographic information (GI)-applications to complex 3D objects for visually complex renderings) as well as the respective image and text data could be linked.

Based on the data gathered in the geodatabase, each building object was first individually reconstructed; these single-building models with a detailed depiction of architectural features were then merged into the reconstructed square structure of the marketplace to form an overall 3D-scene. Within the scene selected 3D objects and specifically created 'empties' serve as reference points for the database entries holding the relevant Data.[9]

---

[9] For a similar approach, in which python scripts are used to link PostGIS database records to 3D objects directly in Blender, see: Scianna, A.: Building 3D GIS Data Models Using Open Source Software, Applied Geomatics 5, 119–132 (2013).

The majority of the digital processing was carried out in the open source software solutions QGIS and Blender,[10] which meant that a process based entirely on open data and software formats was used, intended to result in maximum traceability and reproducibility of the reconstruction. The basic goal was the digital reconstruction of all surfaces that could be perceived by fictitious contemporary visitors to the square around 1760; consequently, façades, roof surfaces on the square and street side, or windows were depicted in as much detail as possible, while courtyards, chimneys, etc. that could not be seen were depicted in a greatly reduced form [Fig. 4–5].

Fig. 4. Model of Neuer Markt, view to the north, c. 1760 [© ÖAW/Archaeo Perspectives, CC-BY 3.0 AT]

The reconstruction of the existing buildings and square elements consisted of the following steps:

1. 3D modelling of the objects based on the historical sources: This step, was by far the most time-consuming in the entire pipeline and was carried out in close consultation with art historians, whereby multiple rounds of discussions were necessary for each object in order to subject the implementation or the derivation from the (often contradictory) historical source material to a continuous plausibility check in terms of building history. The input from analogy comparisons, but not least also from empirical values of current (building) research, led to a gradual approximation to the spectrum of forms to be represented in each case. The resulting discussion not only served to verify the building history, but also repeatedly led to new scientific

---

[10] QGIS: https://www.qgis.org/de/site/, last accessed 2023/3/25; Blender: https://www.blender.org/, last accessed 2023/3/25.

Fig. 5. Model of Neuer Markt, view to the south, c. 1760 [© ÖAW/Archaeo Perspectives, CC-BY 3.0 AT]

findings.[11] The course of historical floor and storey levels, the design of detailed architectural forms, the spatial effect of building cubature and decorative furnishings are just a few examples from which new information can be derived through the modelling process. The core results of these discussions were recorded as text entries linked to the objects in the existing database in order to make the resulting model comprehensible and transparent. Where possible, the newly created geometries were supplemented with preexisting 3D data, e.g. in the case of repetitively occurring detailed shapes. Such pre-modeled data sets were primarily accessed via open and commercial 3D-libraries and inserted into the respective model, usually with only minor modification, in order to achieve a more efficient implementation-process. The fountain located in the center (*Donnerbrunnen*, 1738), which decisively shapes the entire square, was also inserted into the overall reconstruction based on an existing, photogrammetrically recorded model of the Wien Museum, where the original statues are to be found.[12]

2. Texturing of the surfaces: To increase the level of detail and visual fidelity, texturing (supplementing the 3D vector models with 'wrapped-on' raster or image data as a surface) of all objects was carried out in order to recreate the materiality of the

---

[11] Heike Messemer emphasises the aspect of knowledge consolidation that always accompanies the 3D reconstruction process: Messemer, H.: Digitale 3D-Modelle historischer Architektur. Entwicklung, Potentiale und Analyse eines neuen Bildmediums aus kunsthistorischer Perspektive, Heidelberg (2020), p. 23.

[12] The fountain figures are made of cast lead and come from Georg Raphael Donner. Currently the museum is being renovated; when the collection is reorganised, the original statues will become part of the permanent exhibition from the end of 2023; see: https://sammlung.wienmuseum.at/suche/?people=p11186, last accessed 2023/3/14.

objects to be reconstructed in addition to a higher visual fidelity. For this purpose, the combination of PBR (physically based rendering) materials were used, which enable a physically correct visualization of the scene lighting and its reaction to the material.

4   Documentation and Presentation of Uncertainties

Despite the solid source situation, it was not possible to completely reconstruct all the buildings of the baroque marketplace, especially since no or only insufficient plans have been preserved for a large part of them. To illustrate the uncertainties in the reconstruction, a gradation in the level of detail was applied. Thus, building elements that cannot be clearly derived from the sources were only reproduced in their building cubature, which already makes them stand out clearly in the model. Further visual labelling (e.g. color coding or transparent representation) was omitted in order to avoid an imparity in the overall effect of the baroque appearance. Any uncertainties or contradictions in the source material are documented in the database via linked entries, where a classification index number is stated alongside with further information, which reconstruction solution was chosen and for what reasons.[13] In addition to the visualizations showing the reconstructed historical material surfaces, the objects can also be displayed in false color uncertainty maps showing this information in further renderings.

The bird's-eye view by Joseph Daniel Huber (mapped in 1769–1772, printed in 1778) is the main source for the historical roofscape of Vienna, even if it shows the roofs in a slightly simplified form [Fig. 6]. Clearly recognizable at *Neuer Markt*, however, is the coincidence of large baroque four-tract buildings with hipped roofs and of narrow medieval plots with gabled houses whose gable roofs form ditches. The proportions are shown differently well: While the structural dominance of the Capuchin Church and the municipal flour pit (*Mehlgrube*) opposite is depicted according to reality, the *Palais Schwarzenberg*, which closes off the square to the south [top left corner in Fig. 6], is too large due to its status. The town house *Neuer Markt 1* [bottom right in the same figure, No. 1079], on the other hand, blends into the roofscape, even though it clearly towered over it in reality.

---

[13] The AU-VR (Average Uncertainty weighted on the Volume and the Relevance of the elements) Index will be used for the classification of the documented uncertainties: Apollonio, F. et al., The Critical Digital Model for the Study of Unbuilt Architecture. In: Niebling, F. et al. (eds.), Research and Education in Urban History in the Age of Digital Libraries, Cham (2021), pp. 3–24.

Fig. 6. Joseph Daniel von Huber, Neuer Markt, detail of *Scenographie Wiens und seiner Vorstädte*, engraving, 1778 [© ÖAW, Sammlung Woldan, https://viewer.acdh.oeaw.ac.at/viewer/image/ACO 4408812/1/LOG_0000/, last accessed 2023/3/24]

4.1   Neuer Markt 1 – An Unexpected Example of an Useful Starting Point

As an example of a solid source base, the previously unexplored town house *Neuer Markt 1* will be briefly presented here, bearing in mind that even in such cases uncertainties always remain in the reconstruction and that the latter is merely an approximation of the historical situation. Demolished in 1894 and replaced by a new house,[14] the baroque building was a remodelling of three renaissance houses, which were given a common façadein 1722/23.[15] The builder was the court pharmacist Johann Friedrich Günter von Sternegg, who added arcades in front of the house with a terrace on the first floor. The rebuilding created a town house of the highest representative standard on the threshold from the High to the Late Baroque. The wrought-iron grille on the arcade terrace, decorated with double eagles, referred to the owner's position as court pharmacist. A three-storey mansard roof emphasised the monumentality of the building.

---

[14] Dehio-Handbuch, Die Kunstdenkmäler Österreichs, Wien, I. Bezirk – Innere Stadt, Horn/Wien 2003, p. 743.

[15] WStLA, Gb., Gb. of Vienna, 1/18, fol. 19v, 1/19, fol. 171; Gb. Philipp and Jakobi-Chapel, 28/4, fol. 63. ÖStA, FHKA, AHK, HQuB 99, 1723/1724, fol. 13, 57.

The later changes remained marginal: before 1826, the arcades were closed diago-
nally towards the side street - before that, the arcade only stepped forward in the second
axis.[16] In 1840/42 a new attic was added and a hipped roof was erected.[17] Jakob Alt
documented this state of construction in two paintings (1842) [Fig. 7–8]. These, together
with Canaletto's view of *Neuer Markt* [Fig. 2] and the plan of the façade on the occasion
of its heightening, provide detailed models for the building's reconstruction. The first
step in the reconstruction of the baroque situation was the removal of the attic and the
sloping arcade end. For reasons of labour economy, the elaborate balcony decoration
with vases, putti and metal railings was provisionally reduced by the putti. For this we
used generic, pre-modelled shapes that were adapted in their form to the available image
sources.

Fig. 7. Left: Jakob Alt, *Der Neue Markt mit dem „Dreifrontenhaus"*, oil on canvas, 1842
[© LIECHTENSTEIN, The Princely Collections, Vaduz-Vienna, GE2560, https://www.liechtens
teincollections.at/sammlungen-online/der-neue-markt-mit-dem-dreifrontenhaus]; Right: Reconstruction of the same building, c. 1760 as 3D model [© ÖAW/Archaeo Perspectives, CC-BY 3.0
AT]

The first uncertainties arose with the openings on the ground floor behind the arcades.
Although they are clearly visible in the floor plan, the image sources unfortunately do
not show them. Therefore, the same openings were assumed and modelled here as are
pictorially preserved on the backside facing *Kärntner Straße*. Jakob Alt depicted basket
arches here, whereas the 1840/42 façade plan [Fig. 9] shows rather segmental arches. In
the reconstruction, we opted for the plan and recorded this uncertainty in the database.

---

[16] WStLA, MA 236, EZ series, old stock, file 1.3.2.236.A16., 1st district EZ 593.
[17] Ibid.

Fig. 8. Left: Jakob Alt, *„Dreifrontenhaus", von der Kärntnerstraße aus gegen die Kupfer-schmiedgasse*, oil on canvas, 1843 [© LIECHTENSTEIN, The Princely Collections, Vaduz-Vienna, Inv.-Nr. GE2561, https://www.liechtensteincollections.at/sammlungen-online/das-dreifrontenhaus-von-der-kaerntnerstrasse-aus-gegen-die-kupferschmiedgasse, last accessed 2023/3/20]; Right: Reconstruction of the same building as 3D model, c. 1760 [© ÖAW/Archaeo Perspectives, CC-BY 3.0 AT]

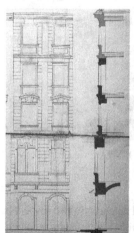
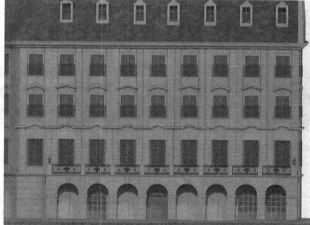

Fig. 9. Left: Neuer Markt 1, front elevation and vertical section on the occasion of heightening, 1840/42 [© WStLA, WStLA, M.Abt. 236, EZ-Reihe: Altbestand, 1.Bezirk EZ 593]; Right: Reconstruction of the front elevation towards Neuer Markt [© ÖAW/Archaeo Perspectives, CC-BY 3.0 AT]

One aspect that was quite essential for the overall model concerned the roof of the house, which has only been handed down via Canaletto's view and Huber's bird's eye view, which do not quite match in the presentation of the roof. The high mansard roof with its angles of inclination and with three rows of dormers could be traced well, but the type of termination of the roof to the south remained unclear. In the model, due to the lack of other reliable image sources, the solution according to Canaletto with a gable wall towards *Neuer Markt*, that means without a hipped roof – which can be seen on Huber's otherwise simplified presentation. Was also adopted for *Kärntner Straße*, resulting in a striking urban dominance of the house. Both at *Neuer Markt*, where the house steps forward around an axis in front of the building line of the neighboring houses, and at *Kärntner Straße*, which led from *Kärntner Tor* to *Stephansplatz*, the two mighty roof gables would have formed a façade-like, optical superelevation of the surrounding buildings, which today can only be made visible by the 3D model [Fig. 10]. Even if we can assume that both gables existed, this hypothesis is of course recorded as such in the database to enable a secure basis for discussion.

Fig. 10. Reconstruction of the two roof gables of Neuer Markt 1 [© ÖAW/Archaeo Perspectives, CC-BY 3.0 AT]

The result of the reconstruction is of interest to art historical research in two respects: On the one hand, the model introduces this monumental town house, which has not been preserved, with its high claim to representativeness, into the art historical discussion for the first time. The question of the unknown architect who designed the house arises, as does the significance of the house in comparison to contemporary palace architecture. The reconstruction of this and other houses will therefore enable a comprehensive stylistic analysis of Vienna's baroque architecture and lead to new insights. Second, the analysis of this and the neighbouring houses has shown that in the late 17th and early 18th centuries, the city of Vienna encouraged the construction of brick arcades instead of wooden arbors at *Neuer Markt*. This may have been primarily for fire prevention reasons, but – if fully implemented – would also have had an effect on urban planning. Thus, similar to the great squares in Spain or Paris, *Neuer Markt* would have been a square surrounded by arcades, surpassing all squares in Vienna in significance. This design intention could have been related to the Capuchin Church, whose crypt served as the burial place of the Habsburgs. The square could thus have been conceived as a dignified entrance to the crypt – an aspect that will now be brought into the discussion.

4.2 Palais Schwarzenberg – A Prominent Building with Contradictory Data

Several houses originally stood on the site of the later Schwarzenberg Palace on *Neuer Markt*, which Johann Baptist Count Verdenberg had remodelled into an early baroque palace after 1631.[18] In 1688, Ferdinand Wilhelm Prince Schwarzenberg acquired the building complex. In the period from 1701 to 1713, the Schwarzenbergs, who were one of the most influential families at the imperial court at the time, successively enlarged the area by purchasing additional properties and shortly afterwards received magisterial permission to rebuild the entire site.[19] Johann Bernhard Fischer von Erlach designed this remodelling in view of a difficult starting situation. While the wing overlooking *Neuer Markt* had three storeys, the front facing *Kärntnerstraße* had four. In addition, the owner obviously demanded that the existing building be largely preserved. In his façade designs, Fischer compensated for the disproportion of the different wings and proposed striking avant-corps facing *Neuer Markt* and *Kärntnerstraße*, where he also wanted to reduce the wing by one storey. But his ideas remained largely paper. Instead of the planned avant-corps, the central axes facing *Neuer Markt* received only a simple triangular gable and otherwise the plain façade retained its 17th-century structure with two portals [Fig. 11].[20]

Since the palace was demolished in the late 19th century, we have to consult historical sources for its reconstruction, but these provide divergent information about the façade decoration, which was mainly reduced to the window frames. Thus, only the appearance of the façade shortly before its demolition is really certain, because it is documented by photographs. At that time, the windows had plain frames and straight roofs, which might go back to a neoclassical remodelling of the façade around 1800. Even though this sleek design is almost unthinkable for a baroque building, we use it as the only dependable basis for our reconstruction [Fig. 12]. But on the first floor we did replace the straight roofs of the 19th century to alternating triangular and segmental gables with a disc or hemisphere set into them as decoration, because the baroque sources agree on this detail at least. However, in order not to create a falsifying impression, we decided to model a façade reconstruction on this basis, which also takes into account more elaborate window frames [Fig. 13].

---

[18] Fidler, P.: Architektur des Seicento. Baumeister, Architekten und Bauten des Wiener Hofkreises, Innsbruck (1990), pp. 367–368.

[19] Krummholz, M.: Vídeňské rezidence Schwarzenbergů a Johann Bernhard Fischer z Erlachu. In: Bezecný, Z., Gaži, M., Putna, M. C. (eds.), Schwarzenbergové v české a středoevropské kulturní historii, České Budějovice 2013, pp. 207–218, see pp. 213–214.

[20] Mader-Kratky, A.: Der Palastbau im Œuvre von Johann Bernhard Fischer von Erlach. In: Karner, H., Schütze, S., Telesko, W. (eds.), Johann Bernhard Fischer von Erlach (1656–1723) und die barocke Baukunst des europäischen Barock, München 2022, pp. 123–139, see pp. 136–137.

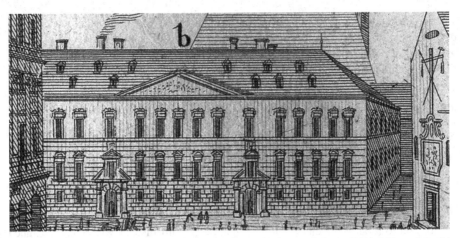

Fig. 11. Palais Schwarzenberg, detail from: Salomon Kleiner and Georg Daniel Heymann, *Die Kirche der Capuciner auf dem neüen Marckt*, engraving, 1724 [ÖAW, Sammlung Woldan]

The most relevant sources were an engraving by Joseph Emanuel Fischer von Erlach and Johann Adam Delsenbach (1715) and a drawing by Karl Schütz (1798). The engraving by Fischer/Delsenbach shows the front to Neuer Markt with the planned but not realised avant-corps [Fig. 14 B]. On the remaining façade, there are strikingly old-fashioned window frames on the second floor, as shown by Schütz in a similar manner [Fig. 14 C]. Again, we are facing alternating window frames, which on the one hand are reminiscent of blasted gables with a centrally placed sphere, and on the other hand might mean a segmental arched gable such as Fischer von Erlach planned for the avant-corps [Fig. 14 A]. If so, part of the 17th century décor would have been preserved when the façade was remodelled soon after 1713, supplemented by more updated design [Fig. 14 D].

Fig. 12. Palais Schwarzenberg, reconstruction of the façade with simple window frames and -roofs, c. 1760 [© ÖAW/Archaeo Perspectives, CC-BY 3.0 AT]

Fig. 13. Palais Schwarzenberg, reconstruction of the façade with more elaborated window frames and -roofs, c. 1760 [© ÖAW/Archaeo Perspectives, CC-BY 3.0 AT]

Research on Vienna's baroque architecture has so far paid too little attention to the question of maintaining tradition by perpetuating early baroque design forms in the 18th century. Moreover, *Palais Schwarzenberg* is a good example of how leading architects such as Fischer von Erlach were not only commissioned with new building projects, but often had to manage a balancing act between preserving inherited building complexes and introducing new ideas in order to add significance to the building, which was only possible by intervening in the façade decoration. The bas-relief in the tympanum should also be mentioned in this context: All historical images indicate a bas-relief in the tympanum without going into detail. The stucco bas-relief is also documented by black-and-white photographs before the palace was demolished, because its exceptional artistic quality meant that it should at least be preserved in this way.[21] As a very similar arrangement of the figures is already shown in a baroque drawing,[22] we assume that the relief dates from the 18th century, but may have been restored later and thereby reworked in a neo-baroque manner (e.g., in the head posture of some figures).

---

[21] Josef Löwy, *Neuer Markt 8, Schwarzenbergpalais, Giebel*, before 1895, Wien Museum, https://sammlung.wienmuseum.at/objekt/94264-1-neuer-markt-8-schwarzenbergpalais-giebel-fassadendetail/, last accessed 2023/3/6.

[22] Státní oblastní archiv v Třeboni (SOA), Oddělení Český Krumlov, Schwarzenberska ustredni kancelar, Hluboka nad Vltavou, Strední oddeleni, Inv.-Nr. 9016 – see: Krummholz, M.: „Zu unaussprechlicher Freude allerhöchsten Herrschaften wie auch zum höchsten Troste allhiesiger Inwohner." Zwei Illuminationen vor dem Wiener Stadtpalais Schwarzenberg anlässlich der Geburt der ältesten Söhne Maria Theresias. In: Kroupa, J., Šeferisová Loudová, M., Konečný, L. (eds.), Orbis artium: k jubileu Lubomíra Slavíčka, Brno 2009, pp. 539–553.

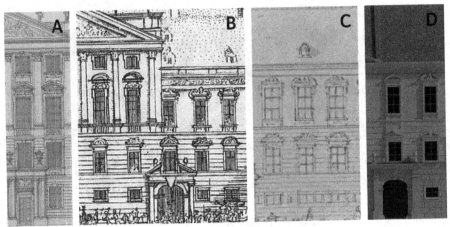

Fig. 14. Palais Schwarzenberg, comparison of different image sources: [A] Johann Bernhard Fischer von Erlach, Draft for the façade facing Kärntnerstraße, after 1701 [© Albertina Wien, AZ 9553]; [B] Joseph Emanuel Fischer von Erlach und Johann Adam Delsenbach, *Prospect des Wienerischen Ney = Marckts*, engraving, 1715 [© ÖAW/IHB]; [C] Karl Schütz, *Neuer Markt*, pen drawing, before 1798 [© Wien Museum, Inv.-Nr. 179.909]; [D] Realisation in the 3D model [© ÖAW/Archaeo Perspectives, CC-BY 3.0 AT]

5   Experiences Within the Pilot Study

In the sense of a feasibility study, the reconstruction of the marketplace around 1760 also served to test the modelling process for the reconstruction of larger city districts or to create a best-practice model in order to document the expenditure of technical resources in terms of hardware and software requirements as well as the required working hours:

Hardware: All models were created with the requirement that their visualization or embedding in an application should be largely hardware-independent and could be used for realistic renderings on high-end Desktop-Solutions as well as for visualization in applications running on low-End Systems. For the use in web-based or mobile applications the final geometries/meshes of certain models with heavy Geometry were remeshed to a limited number of polygons, materials were baked to 2K resolution textures and tested in relevant 3D web viewers to enable the models to be displayed in the render engines used here. The greatest challenge was finding a compromise between the richness of detail required from an art historical perspective and the limited creatable geometry in terms of hardware sufficiency and human resources. Thanks to the use of PBR texturing and texture baking however, even low-poly models allow high-quality visualization by means of complex light calculation or so-called ray tracing, which ensures the broadest possible spectrum of applications for the model.

Software: The use of the open-source software Blender has proven itself in all processing steps, thus avoiding time-consuming porting to other 3D applications.

From modelling and sculpting, retopology, UV editing, texturing and baking, the processing could all be carried out in the same software environment. Some weaknesses of the application could be ironed out by freely available addons and programmes (all based on Blender), which are made available by the open-source community. One example is the texture processing software in Armor-Paint,[23] which could be seamlessly integrated into this workflow.

The real-time render engine available here also allowed for a highly efficient texturing-pipeline compared to other applications. The large community and the independent Blender Foundation behind the development guarantee long-term support for the application and its data formats, which underlines the suitability of the software especially for research purposes and under the aspect of long-term archiving.

6 Dissemination and Long-Term Archiving

Although the creation of an educational scenario was not the primary goal of the project and the dissemination solution has yet to be determined, the model and its database give rise to multiple possibilities that were considered and prepared in the course of the data creation. In terms of visual fidelity, stand-alone offline applications are to be preferred, which can be created within game engines and are often used in the museum context via screens or VR stations. These systems are particularly suitable for the presentation of complex and, above all, interactive 3D content, which is why all the models created were optimised for use in this scenario and tested in it. A further possible application is the already mentioned browser-based solutions for example using pre-rendered scenes to make the models and content available online via html-based 3D viewers or as a web mapping application and thus to the widest possible audience. A first dissemination solution is being developed in cooperation with the *Wien Museum*, where our digital model is being made accessible to the public for the first time via a dedicated 3D multimedia station as part of the reorganization of the collection in 2023. In cooperation with the City of Vienna, the dataset is also to be disseminated in the future via the highly frequented platform "Wien Wiki",[24] whereby relevant entries on buildings would make the 3D data available via a web viewer.

The long-term archiving of the dataset will be carried out in cooperation with the Austrian Centre for Digital Humanities and Cultural Heritage of the Austrian Academy of Sciences (ACDH-CH). Storage on the open repository Zenodo is also planned in order to ensure an independent open and long-term accessibility.[25]

---

[23] https://armorpaint.org/, last accessed 2023/3/20.

[24] https://www.geschichtewiki.wien.gv.at/Wien_Geschichte_Wiki, last accessed 2023/3/20.

[25] https://www.oeaw.ac.at/acdh/, last accessed 2023/03/20; https://zenodo.org/, last accessed 2023/3/20.

Education

The Nuremberg Stations of the Cross. Enriching On-Site Experiences of a Historical Pathway by the "FAU GeoExplorer" App

Ute Verstegen[1]([email]) [iD] and Dominik Kremer[2] [iD]

[1] Lehrstuhl Christliche Archäologie, Friedrich-Alexander Universität Erlangen Nürnberg,
Kochstraße 6, 91054 Erlangen, Germany
ute.verstegen@fau.de

[2] Department Digital Humanities and Social Studies, Friedrich-Alexander Universität Erlangen
Nürnberg, Werner-Von-Siemens-Straße 61, 91052 Erlangen, Germany
dominik.kremer@fau.de

Abstract. In this paper we present the "FAU GeoExplorer" App, developed at Friedrich-Alexander University Erlangen-Nuremberg (FAU) as a tool that builds on existing solutions and combines the advantages of a didactically structured multimedia content hosted in a learning environment with the advantages of geo-visualization that can be used on site. As a prototypical use case from the domain of cultural and urban history, we present a route along the late medieval Nuremberg Stations of the Cross, a pathway with a series of seven sculptural art works leading from the Neutor city gate to the Johannis cemetery.

Keywords: Excursion · Education · Augmented Reality · Archaeology · Art history · Geography

1 A Geo-Visualization Tool to be used for On-Site Learning

At present, the provision of web-based site-specific content for particular 'real-world' locations is mostly limited to the technical possibilities of web publications while didactic concepts of mobile, location-based learning [1] provide major insights on the positive effects of learning on site [2]. On the other hand, current e-learning tools still are not able to support location-based content more than rudimentarily. A combination of both functions, however, is of high relevance for a multitude of use cases ranging from university excursions to nature trails and to participatory urban district apps.

At Friedrich-Alexander University Erlangen-Nuremberg (FAU), "FAU GeoExplorer" is being developed as a tool that builds on existing solutions and combines the advantages of a didactically structured multimedia content hosted in a learning environment with the advantages of geo-visualization to be used in self-organized, blended learning scenarios on site.

© The Author(s), under exclusive license to Springer Nature Switzerland AG 2023
S. Münster et al. (Eds.): UHDL 2023, CCIS 1853, pp. 207–219, 2023.
https://doi.org/10.1007/978-3-031-38871-2_12

1.1 Starting Point and Goals

During the COVID-19 pandemic, university excursions became a subject to severe restrictions. Particularly affected were those study programs in whose curricula excursions form an essential and didactically indispensable component, and in which participating in excursions is an obligatory requirement for graduation, such as in geography or archaeology. Since no university excursions were possible for more than two years, creative solutions had to be found in order to maintain the necessary excursions' experiences of the curricula. At FAU, we developed a range of virtual and virtually enriched formats of excursions: from purely digital site and museum visits to online map services, and to VR videos that encourage students' own explorations of a site during an online presentation. Already in 2018, FAU's chair of Christian Archaeology, with the climate debate and the requirements for climate-neutral travel in mind, had already launched the project "Virtual Excursions" [3, 4].

But why not be on site anyway? Even under lockdown conditions, it was not the outdoor experience itself that was prohibited. Only the size of the group was strongly restricted. With a suitable digital tool supporting self-organized learning and guiding the on-site experience according to didactic principles, an individual or small-group visit was well in line with common lockdown regulations. Such a tool also supports functionalities known from blended learning [5]: (1) working out the contents related to different sites in distributed visits in small groups, (2) collecting the information gathered in a Learning Management System (LMS, see [6]), geo-locating and linking them in the tool, (3) actually performing the excursion in small groups, and (4) reflecting on the on-site experiences in an (online) meeting afterwards.

We quickly learned that our approach can also be useful in other than just academic settings in the future. The medium-term goal of our project is to develop an application that can be used both in academic teaching as well as in school, and to stage public archaeological or geographical trails.

1.2 Setting the Scene: Didactical Considerations

As current approaches are often technology-based or explorative and lack concepts and evaluations approved by didactics and education sciences [1], in a first step, we will provide a short introduction on findings in these fields and derive related requirements from them. In general, mobile, location-based learning signifies learning aided by mobile devices at a place of interest [1]. In contrast, place-based learning often relates to learning merely *about* places with the help of common E-learning tools [7]. Approaches of self-organized learning cover mediating processes of learning with certain degrees of freedom or including students in the preparation process of knowledge [8]. This is a promising option already in school [9]. In addition to both aspects, we also address self-scheduled visits alone or in small groups on site.

[10] shows a high potential of mobile, location-based learning. Learning on site at the same time visualizes, contextualizes and exemplifies the topic of interest and thus allows for achieving learning objectives in both a more motivating and a more sustainable manner. At the same time, as a typical high risk/high reward scenario, mobile, location-based learning provides two challenges: (1) Lecturers need special training themselves

to stage a controlled, yet inspiring and engaging setting [2]. (2) Reusability is key to compensate for the intense preparation efforts [1].

Both challenges can be addressed systematically by technical means, as generating, maintaining and publishing content is a workflow already well supported by learning content management systems [6]. A workflow model reducing complexity to didactically approved templates can address the first challenge. In our intention to provide more support for creating on-site-learning content, we identified two essential requirements: (1) We need a light-weight content management and content delivery system adapted for the geospatial domain. (2) The tooling has to act as an overlay platform that provides an easy to follow workflow model that allows for (a) integrating different types of media including 3D, AR and VR content from distributed sources as well as (b) linking in established functionality from other E-learning apps.

1.3 Design and Implementation: Geo-content Management

As content creation is an essential part of the workflow in self-organized learning, we decided to provide a light-weight standalone platform guiding a reduced and task-oriented preparation of content for different types of media. As we did not want to bind ourselves to specific software, we aimed for an overlay platform allowing for integrating media from distributed storage and additional functions from linkable E-learning apps.

We evaluated a solution architecture based on native mobile apps and one based on progressive web apps. Native mobile apps usually perform best regarding map frameworks and cached offline content, but (despite frameworks like flutter [11] or react native [12]) still need adaptations for each platform in completely different software development environments. Progressive web apps on the other hand offer at least limited offline cache functionality and allow for easy linking of other web applications by using shared sessions between different browser tabs, but have the disadvantage of multi-browser testing. Eventually, we decided for the progressive web app because we were able to use the same technology stack for all software components. The application consists of two components, a content creation layer and an on-site presentation layer.

In the content creation process, projects maintained by specific content owners are composed of (1) routes, and (2) excursion sites related to specific routes and (3) pages associated with each excursion site. Decomposing the content associated with each site to multiple pages reduces the information load and thus the distraction when interacting with the presentation layer. Each page contains a (1) small introducing text, (2) one single piece of media maximum and (3) a clear task to follow. This retains the focus on the engaged on-site exploration. As the content creation layer mirrors exactly this pattern, the creation process of creating an easy-to-follow excursion is strongly assisted.

Configurable media ranges from imagery, video and audio to 3D and AR models. Media is described by appropriate metadata. A table of content provides easy access to the input draft at any stage. To support HTML-enabled content, we integrated a simple markdown editor. Figure 1 gives an impression of the input form.

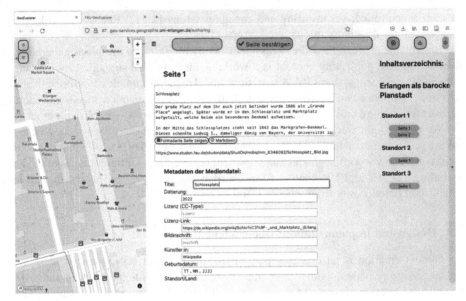

Fig. 1. FAU GeoExplorer input form.

Key components of the presentation layer are a map view that always focuses on the context of the current site and a panel containing the pages associated with this place. By following a step by step presentation of the associated pages, the tool mediates an on-site experience and learning process. As the route segment leading to each site may be an essential part of the task to solve, we support the optional configuration of a recommended path to the next stop.

Figure 2 and 3 visualize the main interface. The map and the content panel are arranged side by side in a landscape view following the 'mobile first' paradigm. The menu bar on top provides two buttons: easy access to (1) the routes available in the specific project and (2) a list of all media of the currently selected route. The footer shows a breadcrumb path of the exact position of the current page within the content hierarchy. The right panel contains media (a historical image of Nuremberg in Fig. 2 and a 3D model of the first Bamberg Station of the Cross in Fig. 3) and related tasks, highlighted by a dotted box. Specific buttons below can be used to switch both pages and sites. The left panel shows a map centered to the current site. If configured, the recommended path from the previous site to the current one is visualized as well. Common pan and zoom functions are provided. Given user consent has been stated, the current position of the user is shown as well.

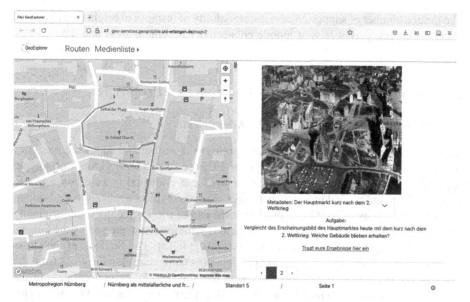

Fig. 2. FAU GeoExplorer interface covering an excursion site including a proposed route and one photo integrated in an comparative image task.

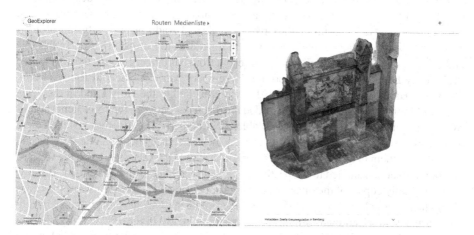

Fig. 3. FAU GeoExplorer interface covering an excursion site including 3D content.

1.4 Getting Feedback: Early Evaluation Results

First evaluation of the FAU GeoExplorer [13] proved the positive effects of mobile, location-based learning. When acting as co-creators of the content, especially young students appreciated the high motivation gained from working with novel media on contemporary digital platforms. Well-known limitations cover the extra effort needed to provide successful on-site learning experiences [2], which is balanced by increased reusability of content. Other impediments cover well-known limitations of mobile devices in general like limited number of supported devices, readability of displays in bright sunshine, low battery runtimes, partial lack of mobile connectivity in remote areas and data privacy [10].

2 The Nuremberg Stations of the Cross as a Prototype

2.1 Nuremberg's Way of the Cross by Adam Kraft

Building on preliminary work on digital learning with virtual and augmented realities at FAU's chair of Christian Archaeology, in 2022 we started to work on a prototypic application for the FAU GeoExplorer to be used and evaluated in an urban scenario and including outdoor and indoor experiences. The prototypical application leads along the Nuremberg Way of the Cross, erected at the end of the 15th century and originally consisting of seven high reliefs and a sculptural crucifixion group created by the famous Nuremberg sculptor Adam Kraft (c. 1460–1509) [14, 15]. The Stations of the Cross were a series of Christian religious images depicting Christ carrying the cross from the place of his judgement and condemnation at the house of Pilate in Jerusalem to the place of his crucifixion at Golgota, and finally showing the lamentation of Christ and his entombment [16].

In Jerusalem, in the course of the Middle Ages, a route was established through the city along the sites that were supposedly associated with various episodes of Christ's Carrying of the Cross, some of which have a foundation in New Testament narratives, others were based on extra-biblical sources, legends and Tradition [17]. Pilgrims brought knowledge of these places and the itinerary in Jerusalem to Europe [18–20]. In the 14th and 15th centuries, numerous pilgrims also set out from Nuremberg to visit the holy places in the Holy Land. Among them were the Nuremberg patricians Sebald Rieter (1426–1488) and Hans VI. Tucher (1428–1491), who travelled to the Holy Land in the years 1479 and 1480 [21], and who even recorded the distances between the Jerusalem stations by steps and made this information available at Nuremberg. The itinerary installed there at the end of the 15th century precisely reflects these distances between the stations and also includes them in its inscriptions. The original Way of the Cross started at the western city portal (Neutor) and led to the pestilence cemetery at Sankt Johannis outside the city.

Today, only copies of the original art works are displayed at the Stations of the Cross along the historical road (Fig. 4). Most of the original stations have been transferred to the Germanisches Nationalmuseum in Nuremberg already in the 19th century, the last one (station 7) after World War II. Remains of the sculptural crucifixion group belonging to the entire ensemble, which was formerly placed in front of the entrance to the Johannis cemetery, can be seen at the Heilig-Geist-Spital in Nuremberg, and a sculptural group showing the Entombment of Christ is still present on site at the Holzschuher Chapel at the Johannis cemetery.

Fig. 4. Nuremberg, Way of the Cross. Station 7 "Lamentation of Christ", modern copy after Adam Kraft. Photo: Falk Nicol, LS Christliche Archäologie, FAU, 2022.

The Nuremberg Stations of the Cross, which were once painted in color, were supposed to enable the faithful to experience Christ's suffering as authentically as possible in their own everyday environment, also for those who could not travel to the Holy Land themselves. They are an impressive example of the so-called Passion piety at the end of the Middle Ages and an important testimony of Nuremberg's cultural heritage. In order to involve the faithful physically and emotionally in a particularly strong way, various artistic methods were used by Adam Kraft: For example, the composition of the reliefs follows the distance people walk along the path, and the direction of movement is always from right to left. The faithful thus line up in the direction of movement as they walk along and always take exactly the same number of footsteps as Jesus in Jerusalem. In addition, the figures surrounding Jesus on the reliefs are dressed in contemporary 15th century clothing. In doing so, the events were transposed for the people at that time into their present time and into their own everyday environment in Nuremberg. Moreover, the Nuremberg Stations of the Cross are also particularly important because they became the model for similar Ways of the Cross in the wider area and in Germany, including the Way of the Cross in Bamberg installed at the beginning of the 16th century, whose reliefs have been preserved at their original locations to this day [20].

2.2 Nuremberg's Way of the Cross as a FAU GeoExplorer Project

The FAU GeoExplorer project "Nuremberg Stations of the Cross" aims to enrich individual encounters as well as group learning activities related to this important historical cultural heritage ensemble in Nuremberg's urban space by a smartphone app, while visitors walk along the route in Nuremberg's urban space. As a basis, the route from the so-called Pilatushaus via the Neutor along the individual stations to the Holzschuher Chapel in the Johannis Cemetery was entered in the GeoExplorer map interface. The stations of the Way of the Cross as well as other important locations (like city gates or houses) define excursion sites. Didactically structured textual information or multimedia content is added to each site. The multimedia content is mainly stored on the ILIAS-based Learning Management System "studon" operated at FAU, and loaded into FAU GeoExplorer via a link. The storage at a site secured by login is necessary because, for copyright reasons, some images cannot be shown freely on a website, but must comply with special restrictions for instructional use at universities and schools. 360-degree photos and videos are available on the YouTube channel "INVESTIGATIO_CA" [22] of the Chair of Christian Archaeology, and are streamed as part of the FAU GeoExplorer interface from there.

While the texts contain background information on the historical context, the biblical and extracanonical textual sources, and the artist Adam Kraft, the images show historical depictions of relevant places at Nuremberg (Fig. 5) and of the original installation contexts, or contemporary drawings and paintings with Nuremberg costumes or armor, which can be compared with details in the reliefs. Users are asked to rediscover these elements on the reliefs by means of didactically integrated tasks (Fig. 6).

Fig. 5. FAU GeoExplorer. Nuremberg, Neutor. To demonstrate the topographical situation in Nuremberg's surroundings in the late Middle Ages or Early Modern period, the Neutor city gate is shown in a historical painting (c. 1690).

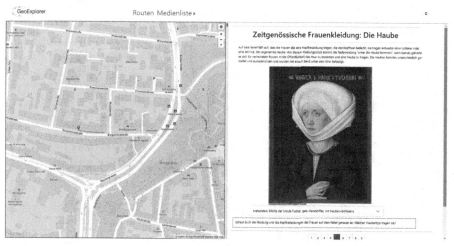

Fig. 6. FAU GeoExplorer. Nuremberg, Way of the Cross, station 3 "Daughters of Jerusalem", after Luke 23, 28–31. Users are given the task of comparing the headdress on the contemporary portrait of Ursula Tucher, the wife of Hans Tucher, with the relief on site.

In cooperation with the Germanisches Nationalmuseum and the City of Nuremberg (owner of the original artworks), 3D models of the original reliefs in the Germanisches Nationalmuseum were created and uploaded to the online repository "kompakkt" (Fig. 7). Again, the Geo-Explorer provides a player component for the individual stations to enable comparisons with the copies and the state of preservation of the original reliefs (Fig. 8).

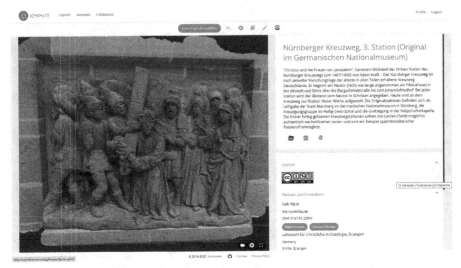

Fig. 7. Nuremberg, Way of the Cross, station 3 "Daughters of Jerusalem". Original sandstone relief by Adam Kraft. Nuremberg, Germanisches Nationalmuseum. 3D model at the repository "kompakkt": Alissa Dittes, Falk Nicol, LS Christliche Archäologie, FAU, 2022.

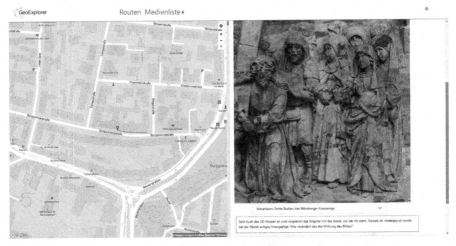

Fig. 8. FAU GeoExplorer. Nuremberg, Way of the Cross, station 3 "Daughters of Jerusalem". Users are given the task of comparing the copy on site with the original artwork by Adam Kraft kept at the Germanisches Nationalmuseum Nürnberg by using the 3D model.

A special highlight are 3D models of the Bamberg Way of the Cross (Fig. 9), which can also be compared with the Nuremberg stations on site in front of the respective relief. In this way, it becomes clear that the Bamberg reliefs, with a reduced repertoire of figures but similar compositions, are to be regarded as simplified copies or variations of the Nuremberg reliefs. By using an augmented reality functionality, FAU GeoExplorer allows these reliefs to be virtually placed next to the reliefs on site at Nuremberg, in order to enable a more realistic visual comparison.

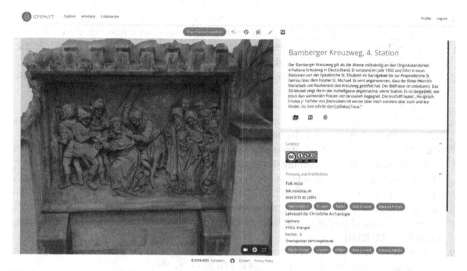

Fig. 9. Bamberg, Way of the Cross, station 4. Original sandstone relief, 1503, located at Aufseß-gasse in Bamberg. 3D model at the repository "kompakkt": Falk Nicol, LS Christliche Archäologie, FAU, 2022.

3 Future Perspectives

In the context of self-organized mobile, location-based learning, our approach explores a teaching concept through the integration of an engaging and integrating geovisualization combined with modular on-site learning content, which enables the implementation of guided excursions alone or in small groups. In terms of blended learning, the format can be complemented by pre- and post-discussions in co-presence and the participants can already be involved in the creation of the content, a task natively supported by the input form provided with the platform. With this approach, we aim not only to make learning situations at school and university more appealing, but also to provide regular training for teachers and the interested public. In the future, the "FAU GeoExplorer" will be further developed to act as a public, site-specific digital educational tool.

References

1. Feulner, B., Ohl, U.: Mobiles ortsbezogenes Lernen im Geographieunterricht. Praxis Geographie **44**(7/8), 4–8 (2014)
2. Lude, A., Schaal, S., Bullinger, M., Bleck, S.: Mobiles, ortsbezogenes Lernen in der Umweltbildung und Bildung für nachhaltige Entwicklung. Schneider, Hohengehren (2013)

3. Mührenberg, L., Verstegen, U.: Christliche Archäologie im 'inverted classroom' und auf 'virtueller Exkursion'. In: Döring, K., Haas, S., König, M., Wettlaufer, J. (eds.) Digital History. Konzepte, Methoden und Kritiken Digitaler Geschichtswissenschaft. Studies in Digital History and Hermeneutics 6, pp. 281–302. De Gruyter, Oldenbourg (2022)

4. Verstegen, U., Mührenberg, L., Nicol, F., Abura, J.: Virtual Reality in der Christlichen Archäologie. Zur Konzeptionierung virtueller Exkursionen und ihrem Einsatz in der universitären Lehre. In: Pirker, V., Pišonić, K. (eds.): Virtuelle Realität und Transzendenz. Theologische und pädagogische Erkundungen, pp. 191–221. Herder, Freiburg (2022)

5. Rovai, A., Jordan, H.: Blended learning and sense of community: a comparative analysis with traditional and fully online graduate courses. The Int. Rev. Res. Open Distance Learning 5(2), 1–13 (2004)

6. Turnbull, D., Chugh, R., Luck, J.: Learning management systems, an overview. Encyclopedia of Education and Information Technologies, pp. 1052–1058 (2020)

7. Aßbichler, D., Eckmeier, E., Dühnforth, M., Küppers, U.: GEOWiki@LMU – ein interaktives und interdisziplinäres E-Learning-Tool zur Vermittlung praxisnaher Lehrinhalte. In: Frey, D., Uemminghaus, M. (eds.) Innovative Lehre an der Hochschule, pp. 147–148. Springer, Heidelberg (2021). https://doi.org/10.1007/978-3-662-62913-0_15

8. Selmbill, D., Seifried, J.: Selbstorganisiertes lernen und unterrichtsqualität. In: van Buer, J., Wagner, C. (eds.) Qualität von Schule: Ein kritisches Handbuch, pp. 401–412. Peter Lang, Frankfurt a.M. (2007)

9. Schlieder, C., Kremer, D.: Geogames als medium: schüler entwickeln inhalte für ein ortsbezogenes spiel. Praxis Geographie 44(7/8), 31–35 (2014)

10. Feulner, B.: SpielRäume. Eine DBR-Studie zum mobilen ortsbezogenen Lernen mit Geogames. Dissertation. Dortmund (2021)

11. Google LLC, The Flutter SDK. https://flutter.dev/. Accessed 24 Mar 2023

12. Meta Platforms, Inc., React Native. https://reactnative.dev/. Accessed 24 Mar 2023

13. Kremer, D.: WebGIS meets E-Learning. Werkzeuge für digital unterstützte geographische Exkursionen. In: Bröll L., Erdmann J., Egbert B. (eds.): Bildung auf Distanz: (Medien-) Technologie, Politik und Lebenswelten in aktuellen Lernprozessen. e-culture (29), pp. 43–54. Trafo, Berlin (2022)

14. Adam Kraft – Der Kreuzweg. Ausstellung im Germanischen Nationalmuseum vom 22. März bis 7. Oktober 2018. Ed. by F. M. Kammel. Verlag des Germanischen Nationalmuseums, Nuremberg (2018)

15. Zittlau, R.: Heiliggrabkapelle und Kreuzweg. Eine Bauaufgabe in Nürnberg um 1500. Nürnberger Werkstücke zur Stadt- und Landesgeschichte 49. Stadtarchiv, Nürnberg (1992)

16. Sternberg, T.: Und lass mich sehn dein Bilde. Der Kreuzweg als liturgisches und künstlerisches Thema. In: Liturgisches Jahrbuch 53(3), 166–191 (2003)

17. Bieberstein, K.: Jerusalem. In: Markschies, C. (ed.) Erinnerungsorte des Christentums, pp. 64–88. Beck, München (2010)

18. Wegmann, S.: Der Kreuzweg von Adam Kraft in Nürnberg. Ein Abbild Jerusalems in der Heimat. In: Mitteilungen des Vereins für Geschichte der Stadt Nürnberg 84, 93–117 (1997)

19. Timmermann, A., Die bewegliche Stadt. Jerusalem in der städtischen Imagination des Mittelalters. In: Köster, G., Link, C. (eds.) Faszination Stadt. Die Urbanisierung Europas im Mittelalter und das Magdeburger Recht, pp. 318–330. Sandstein Verlag, Dresden (2019)

20. Kühnel, B., Fiktion und Treue zum Original. Europäische Jerusalementwürfe. In: Dietl, A., Schöller, W., Steuernagel, D. (eds.) Utopie, Fiktion, Planung. Stadtentwürfe zwischen Antike und Früher Neuzeit, pp. 175–195. Schnell & Steiner, Regensburg (2014)

21. Herz, R.: Die "Reise ins gelobte Land" Hans Tuchers des Älteren (1479–1480). Untersuchungen zur Überlieferung und kritische Edition eines spätmittelalterlichen Reiseberichts. Wissensliteratur im Mittelalter 38. Reichert, Wiesbaden (2002)
22. YouTube channel: INVESTIGATIO_CA. https://www.youtube.com/channel/UCaD687K1-gMm5PXf_VHjfcA. Accessed 24 Mar 2023

Designing Learning Tasks and Scenarios on Digital History for a Research Lab for Pupils
Trends, First Implications and Perspectives

Dora Luise Münster[✉] and Sander Münster

Friedrich-Schiller-Universität Jena, Leutragraben 1, 07743 Jena, Germany
{dora.muenster,sander.muenster}@uni-jena.de

Abstract. Digital literacy and technologies are becoming increasingly important not only in university teaching but also in lifelong learning [1, 2]. Currently, most teaching activities in digital humanities aim at university students [3] or vocational education. The article highlights (1) current trends concerning digital humanities education on EU level, (2) analyses digital history activities in Germany which so far mainly takes place within prototypic academic projects, (3) highlight practice driven implications and (4) present how we integrate this in the lab design in Jena.

Keywords: Urban history · cultural heritage · research-discovery learning · interdisciplinary · Teaching and Learning Lab · digital methods · virtual city tours

1 Introduction

Digital literacy and technologies are becoming increasingly important not only in higher education teaching, but also in lifelong learning [3, 4].[1] Currently, most courses in the field of digital humanities are aimed at students at universities [2] or in vocational training programs. Educational opportunities for pupils on this topic are currently primarily covered by non-school institutions such as museums and libraries. Pupils research labs in the fields of digital humanities and digital cultural heritage are nearly non-existent. These are almost exclusively in STEM fields.[2] The goal of this paper is to (a) survey frameworks for digital education in the humanities (b) present the current state of teaching labs in the field of digital history, and (c) exhibit initial results of establishing a Digital History and Humanities Lab and engaging pupils in digital history projects. Special emphasis will be placed on differentiated assignments suitable for working with heterogeneous groups.

---

[1] Parts of this article has been published in [1,2].
[2] Last status of Google research: 02.06.2023.

2 Current State of Educational Programs in Digital Humanities and Cultural Heritage

Globally, Digital Cultural Heritage (DCH) is an emerging field. Cultural heritage refers to traces and expressions from the past that have lasting value in contemporary society [5]. It traditionally focuses on tangible objects, but a broader understanding that incorporates intangible heritage and computer-based material has gained significance over the last decade. Digital heritage, technically intangible, comprises resources of human knowledge or expression (e.g., cultural, educational, scientific) as well as cultural heritage materials including texts or images which are created digitally or converted into digital form [6]. Although there are many university programs and courses focusing on DCH, there is no comprehensive overview of programs. One reason may be that many study courses are driven by traditional fields such as digital archaeology, digital curation or digital conservation as well as related areas as digital humanities (DH) [7]. Discourse about its role and position within the humanities is ongoing, and educational programs for DCH vary on international, national, and local levels. While organizations, institutions and funding agencies are increasingly focused on DH and DCH pedagogy [8] and curriculum development [9]. DCH education in the EU is more comprehensive, with more concrete efforts at standardizing competencies than for example in the US.

2.1 Core Curricula and Competency Frameworks

Core curricula as an overarching body of knowledge and competencies in a specific domain sum up conditions for learners, learning processes as well as outcomes and therefore define requirements for education. They record competencies for students in several sectors (subject-specific, social, etc.) and show the content of modules and their objectives. Furthermore, they point out organizational aspects and offer methods for university lecturers to design courses that achieve the desired learning outcomes. These outcomes include appropriate digitization processes related to teaching, learning, and curriculum development. Within DH and DCH, emerging methodological and technical changes continue to greatly impact the development of core curricula [10]. In particular, the wide array of digitization techniques require transformations not only in digital content but also in teaching digital pedagogy and curricular-based digital skills [11].

    Competency Frameworks provide agreed definitions, descriptions, and implementation methods according to the demands, standards, and guidelines of specific sectors [12]. The DigComp framework [13] considers digital literacy as a critical, future skill for citizens. Frameworks that include recommendations for educators are for instance the digital literacy framework [14] that addresses university-educators in the Anglo-Saxon world and covers media literacy, communications and collaboration, professional engagement, digital resources, teaching and learning, assessment, empowering learners, and facilitating learners' digital competency, ICT-literacy, learning skills, formal and informal digital-scholarship and information literacy [15].

2.2 Educational Programs in Digital Humanities

Syllabi and core topics in DH are mostly analyzed on university level. Sahle designates digital society, culture and science (1), special research field areas (2), theories, methods and questions addressing them (3), digital transformation and tools (4) as well as resources for single research fields as main areas of study programs [16]. Sula et al. specify more precisely topics like enrichment, capture, and storage as prevalent in European analysis, meta-activities such as project management and creation (designing, programming, writing) as special features in anglophone programs [17]. These approaches also mention the significance of teaching content, methods, and skills in combination with practical formats like case-studies, projects, evaluation [16] or project-based-learning [18].

What are major findings?

- Throughout Europe there is a multitude of educational programs in DH and DCH
- Target group is so far almost exclusively students at universities
- Framework programs and core curricula are strongly competence-oriented

3 The Digital Laboratory Approach in School Education on Humanities

3.1 Digital Cultural Heritage Education in Schools

As the aforementioned frameworks primarily target university students and postgraduate education, school education is currently mainly the target of heritage institutions, although the European Heritage Strategy for the 21st Century [18] includes a call for the inclusion of heritage education in school curricula. "The young generation in particular is an important target group for World Heritage education, as only they can guarantee the preservation and sustainable use of World Heritage sites in the long run" [19]. The aim is to convey knowledge about cultural heritage as well as its history and value for today's society. The World Heritage Site itself is seen as the starting point of any cultural heritage education. An important goal is that the pupils "can experience World Heritage Site as a historical place, but also as a place of change and creativity" [19]. Crucial to the success of teaching cultural heritage in schools is the knowledge and contacts of teachers, but also their digital skills, as the multiple layers of meaning of cultural heritage can best be accessed through interactive methods [19].

One way to motivate and empower prospective teachers to teach digital cultural heritage in history classes is the university's teaching-learning lab. In a protected setting, students can develop, implement, and reflect on digitally supported teaching opportunities for historical learning with pupils.

3.2   Results of a Literature Review

A current state of student laboratories in DH was studied via a keyword-based survey in 10/2022 via Google Scholar.[3] The filter-based investigation was limited to German-language articles published between 2012–2022. The search initially revealed 200 articles, 15 of which dealt with digital history education and has been selected for further analysis (Table 1) For those articles a qualitative content analysis based on Mayring [19] was conducted.

As preliminary results, teaching-learning labs have so far been located primarily in STEM fields. Increasingly, they are also establishing themselves in the humanities and social sciences. This innovative teaching concept is defined as follows: "Student teachers develop theory-based learning opportunities (…) in a (university) teaching-learning lab seminar, which are then tested, reflected upon, revised, and retested with students in the university classroom." [20, p. 94].

The interdisciplinary topic of digital history education is hardly present in the German-speaking world so far. Due to the rapid digital change, however, the integration of the teaching of digital competencies is also considered necessary in history didactics. "As public historical culture becomes increasingly digitally professionalized in the form of press articles (…) and, yes, even school-based teaching and learning materials, enabling and promoting "digital" (…) historical research, interpretation, communication, and presentation skills becomes a central task of any history course." [30, p. 137] Demantowsky sees potential in the reception and production of digital media. Both the expansion of the learning space through the internet, the multimedia forms of presentation, possibilities of mobile, but also self-directed and cooperative learning play a role. Increased subject-oriented learning promotes the development of an individual awareness of history. Collaborative learning formats, on the other hand, provide insight into the construct character of historical narratives and the discursivity of historical interpretations [34].

Teaching-learning labs with a focus on learning history using digital media have not yet been established or investigated as a research topic in the German-speaking world. Only 1 of 15 relevant publications is dedicated to this topic [21]. Similarly, only one publication on labs with a focus on digital learning was identified, with learning workshops highlighted in this context as a didactic alternative to digital learning in the classroom [22].

A few publications (3/15) are dedicated to the subject of professionalizing prospective history teachers in teaching-learning labs with a purely history didactic topic [20, 23, 24]. In Rehfeldt's case, mainly interdisciplinary effects of already conducted teaching-learning lab seminars were investigated and adapted for the subjects English, and history. Somewhat more detailed research is devoted to digital history didactics (4/15). Digital history didactics is thereby defined as "(…) integral part of history didactics and deals with the conditions and effects of digital change on historical consciousness, historical learning, history and memory culture" described [26]. In this context, digital historical offers are primarily examined as a learning occasion, location, or object in history classes and a case is made for the use of digital media in teacher training and continuing education [25–28].

---

[3] Keywords: History didactics, history learning, digital, digital media, teaching-learning labs.

Table 1. Results of the literature review on digital history learning in the teaching-learning laboratory

Keywords	Topics	Articles
Learning History Digital media	Influence of the digital transformation on history learning Opportunities and challenges in the use of digital media in history-related teaching and learning Use of virtual and augmented reality technologies in history teaching	Christoph Pallaske (2015): Die Vermessung der (digitalen) Welt. Geschichtslernen mit digitalen Medien. [30] Marko Demantowsky (2015): Die Geschichtsdidaktik und die digitale Welt. [29] Ingo Oliver Pätzold (2021): (Digitale)Medien im Geschichtsunterricht. [31] Elena Lewers (2022): Medienkritische Auseinandersetzung von Virtual Reality im Geschichtsunterricht. [32] Marko Demantowsky, Christoph Pallaske (Hrsg.) (2015): Geschichte lernen im digitalen Wandel. [34] Daniel Bellingradt, Claudia Heise (2022): Die App Hidden Hamburg als erlebbare Geschichte und Digital-Public-History Experiment. [33]
Digital history didactics	Digital historical offers as a learning occasion, place or object in history lessons Use of digital media as a necessary component of teacher education and training	Silja Leinung (2021): Perspektiven für eine digitale Geschichtsdidaktik. [27] Daniel Bernsen et al. (2012): Medien und historisches Lernen. Eine Verhältnisbestimmung und ein Plädoyer für eine digitale Geschichtsdidaktik. [26] Bettina Alavi (2015): Lernen Schüler/innen Geschichte im Digitalen anders? [25] Christoph Kühberger (2015): Geschichte lernen digital? Ein Kommentar zu mehrfach gebrochenen Diskursen der Geschichtsdidaktik. [28]

(continued)

Table 1. (*continued*)

Keywords	Topics	Articles
Teaching-Lear-ning-Laboratory History Didactics	Professionalization of prospective history teachers	David Seibert (2020): Lehrer werden für das Fach Geschichte – im Labor! [24] Daniel Rehfeldt et al. (2017): Fächerübergreifende Wirkungen von Lehr-Lern-Labor-Seminaren: Adaption für die Fächergruppen Englisch, Geschichte und Sachunterricht. [23] Daniel Rehfeldt et al. (2018): Mythos Praxis um jeden Preis? Die Wurzeln und Modellierung des Lehr-Lern-Labors. [20]
Teaching-learning laboratories Digital Media	Learning workshops as a didactic alternative to digital learning in the classroom	Werner Wiater (2020): Lernwerkstätten in Zeiten des digitalen Lernens. [35]
Teaching-learning laboratories History didactics Digital Media	Research-based history learning with digital media in the context of a university Learning Workshop	Malte Klein (2021): Durch Forschendes Lernen kennenlernen, was Digitalität mit Geschichte macht. [21]

Conditions for the success of a teaching-learning lab are mentioned by Seibert and Wiater. They investigated whether teaching-learning labs contribute to improving teacher training at a university and which pre-professional competencies are acquired. For them, research that accompanies practice plays a role, as does the close integration of theory, practical implementation and reflection. In the protected setting of the teaching-learning lab, students can test themselves and develop teaching-specific n competencies. Regular feedback from the teachers provides them with a realistic self-image [36]. Wiater sees an opportunity above all in the fact that teaching-learning labs are extracurricular institutions and thus independent of curriculum and grading. Hence, they create a fault-tolerant, motivating, and anxiety-free learning environment without pressure to perform or compete. In the teaching-learning lab, the individual abilities, knowledge and interests of the learners can be addressed and opportunities for independent learning, planning and reflection can be created. Individual learning needs, learning goals and progress are recorded and made visible. Students are accompanied by tutors who support and guide them and prevent them from being overwhelmed [35].

What are major findings?

- Digital cultural heritage education is not yet anchored in school curricula yet
- So far, no adaptable handouts exist for the digital teaching of history
- In the german-speaking world, there is little research and experience on working in a humanities teaching-learning lab

4   The Jena Digital History and Humanities Lab

4.1   Preliminary Project with Elementary School Children: Creation of Virtual City Tours of Churches in Jena

Initial experience in the area of digital learning in a humanities subject was gained in the religion history project Virtual Children's City Tour of the Churches in Jena. This was carried out in June 2022 in a Jena elementary school with a time frame of 3 times 60 min with five 3rd grade and six 4th grade pupils. The goals of the project included improving the pupils' digital literacy, addressing the religious and urban historical topic of churches in Jena, and training teamwork skills. The final result was two virtual city tours for children, which were to be inserted into the existing application 4dcity.org and thus made available for independent use (Fig. 1).

In a qualitative survey conducted after the project, it was found that working with a computer and working independently on a topic of their own choice were particularly motivating factors. In addition, the personal reference to some churches and the digital method of the virtual city tour motivated the students to deal with the topic of city history. Filtering out and formulating the most important information from texts and understanding the task formulations could be identified as hurdles.

Fig. 1. Screenshot of the 4D mobile browser application with pupils' contributions

4.2 Differentiated Task Settings as the Basis for Learning in Heterogeneous Groups

While the preliminary project involved only two grades, a teaching-learning lab brings together a very heterogeneous group of pupils. In order to enable as many students as possible to gain knowledge, acquire competencies and experience self-efficacy, the tasks must be formulated so that students can work at different levels. Two proven options are to either give students multiple tasks to choose from or to formulate tasks in a way that allows for varying depths of work. (Table 2) [37].

Table 2. Options for formulating differentiated tasks

(1) Choices	
Or tasks	Choice between a complex or easier task
Star tasks ***	The tasks are offered in three difficulty levels
Tasks with different levels	Only after a task has been successfully completed can pupils attempt a task with a higher level of difficulty
Various degrees of openness	First offer a very open task, as an aid reduce the openness
(2) Differentiation in task formulation	
Different difficulty levels	Tasks with different levels of complexity Low: name, state, describe, summarize High: justify, judge, interpret, create
Slope	Tasks differ in terms of content or approach
Learning aids	Strategic or content-related input, if uncertainties arise about the procedure or the content of the task Examples: Patterns, repetition tasks, visualizations, guiding questions
Learning product	Differentiation with regard to the quality, number and type of the targeted learning products
Learning objective	Tasks differ in the degree of complexity, type and number of aids, form of securing results and reflection

4.3 Project to Test Digital Laboratories in the Humanities

In order to test and establish digital labs in the humanities, the DH Lab, funded by the Stiftung für Innovation in der Hochschullehre, started in 2022 at the University of Jena, involving the departments of Digital Humanities and Didactics of History as well as the Thuringian State Library. The teaching-learning lab involves students of history teaching to develop digital history lessons and to test and reflect on them with pupils in class as well as in the context of extracurricular activities (Fig. 2). In the process, the prospective teachers gain practical experience in teaching cultural heritage, which they can build on in their later professional lives. The focus is on Jena's city history and is intended to motivate the children and young people to deal with the cultural heritage, famous personalities and historical events of their hometown in a creative way (Fig. 3). To this end, a range of digital methods are used, for example to create virtual city tours (Table 5), 3D scan historical everyday objects (Table 4) or interview contemporary witnesses (Table 3). The first results of the project are three courses designed by students of art history and history teaching, which will be offered once a week as an extracurricular workshop for students in grades 5–10 within the framework of the DH Lab over a period of six weeks.

Fig. 2. A student presents her digital project to pupils

Fig. 3. 3D scan of the miniature version of a monument

Table 3. Description of the oral history project

---

(1) Tell us what it was like: oral history project
Eyewitness accounts are often the most authentic way to immerse oneself in history. The goal of this project is to provide students with the necessary skills to create these oral history contributions. We create articles about the history of the GDR, including its impact on younger generations. The students learn about the various digital tools and how to use them, delve into legal issues surrounding oral history, and receive support in creating, editing, and using the contributions

---

Table 4. Description of the 3d digitization project

---

(2) Objects tell stories, we listen
What does a microwave have to do with history? Can I learn anything about earlier life from the tools in the barn? What furniture did the inhabitants of our town own a hundred years ago? The big and small events of the past are not only found in old books. History surrounds and encounters us every day. We only have to be prepared to see and hear these stories. Together, we look for objects and try to decipher what we can learn about history through them. By making 3D scans of the treasures we find, we want to take a close look at them and learn how to work freely in an exploratory way

---

Table 5. Description of the Stolpersteine digitization project

---

(3) Culture of remembrance rethought: digitization of Stolpersteine
We see them regularly on our way to school, when we meet friends in town or when we go for a walk with our eyes open: *Stolpersteine*. They are memorial stones that remind us of the people who were persecuted, deported and murdered under National Socialism. In this course, they are brought into the digital world. On 4dcity.org, pupils list the locations on a virtual city map, learn about the stories of the people behind the *Stolpersteine*, and tell their stories through own texts that are later published on the website

---

Next steps of the project: The Teaching-Learning Hub: Digital History in Jena provides the practical implementation, reflection and revision of the courses and materials on a publicly accessible platform. The research topics monitored in the teaching-learning lab are the development of pupils' and students' digital literacy, the investigation of suitable teaching concepts when using digital tools and options for long-term establishment of teaching-learning labs in the field of DH.

What are major findings?

- Digital history education can be implemented as early as at primary school age
- Working in heterogeneous groups of pupils requires differentiated task definitions
- Prospective teachers are motivated to develop, try out, and reflect on digital history provision for pupils in a teaching-learning lab

5 Summary

At EU level, digital history education is based on competences. This is taught mainly at universities and is regulated by core curricula. Digital history education in schools is currently only provided in small pilot projects; there is no overarching integration into the curriculum. Labs are pursuing both reflection on media and creation (e.g., creation of VR experiences), partly with the aim of improving teacher training and teaching. However, despite several projects, there is currently no coordinated knowledge base for creating digital history courses for students.

The first experiences from our project show that as digital education is limited, especially at younger ages, dealing with heterogeneity is a major issue. Our approach is therefore to.

- record individual (digital) knowledge and skills,
- work in a project-oriented and interest-driven way,
- provide tutors to give students individual support,
- formulate differentiated tasks,
- use and reflect on different digital tools.[4]

6 Next Steps

The focus of the analysis so far has been a review of the literature dealing with digital history learning in the context of teaching and, in particular, teaching-learning labs. A further step would be an analysis of the conditions for success of long-established STEM student labs and the possibilities for transfer to a learning lab in the humanities. For example, the opportunities and limitations of interdisciplinary cooperation in the academic monitoring of teaching-learning labs, as well as concepts for long-term funding and establishment, could be investigated and compared. Furthermore, it would be interesting to find out what technical equipment and introductory courses in the use of digital tools are needed in digitally focused Teaching and Learning Labs in order to be able to implement methodological and content-related ideas without technical barriers.

The opportunities and limitations of the focus on regional history could be investigated and compared with other thematic foci.

Since so far only German-language articles have been evaluated; a next important step would be to analyse publications in English-speaking countries and their experiences with teaching-learning labs in the field of DH.

Acknowledgements. This study was carried out in a project funded by the Stiftung für Lehrinnovation (DH Labor: grant number Freiraum2022_FRFMM-334–2022). The authors want to thank Dr. Katrin Fritsche for her input on the EU. They want also to thank to Marlene Kropp, Bastian Schwerer and Eric Wiegratz for the design and realization of the pupils' workshops.

---

[4] A selection of digital tools suitable for teaching history can be found in [1].

References

1. Muenster, D., et al.: Digital history education for pupils. First steps towards a teaching learning lab. In: ISPRS Archives (in press) (2023)
2. Muenster, S., et al.: Teaching digital heritage and digital humanities – a current state and prospects. Int Arch Photogramm Remote Sens Spatial Inf Sci XLVI-M-1-2021, pp. 471–478 (2021)
3. European Commission. Orientations towards the first Strategic Plan for Horizon Europe (2019)
4. European Commission. European Cultural Heritage Strategy for 21st century (2017)
5. UNESCO. Draft Medium Term Plan 1990–1995 (1989)
6. UNESCO. Concept of Digital Heritage (2018)
7. Muenster, S., et al.: Digital cultural heritage meets digital humanities. The International Archives of the Photogrammetry, Remote Sensing and Spatial Information Sciences XLII-2/W15, pp. 813–820 (2019)
8. Hirsch, B.: Digital Humanities Pedogogy: Practices, Principles and Politics (2011)
9. Locke, B.: Digital humanities pedagogy as essential liberal education: a framework for curriculum development. DHQ: Digital Humanities Quarterly **11**(3), 116–123 (2017)
10. Schulz, J.: Auf dem weg zu einem DH-curriculum digital humanities in den geschichts- und kunstwissenschaften an der LMU Munich. In: Klinke, H. (ed): #DigiCampus. Digitale Forschung und Lehre in den Geisteswissenschaften. Universitaetsbibliothek der Ludwig-Maximilians-Universit?t, Munich, pp. 77–101 (2018)
11. Grünewald, S.: Studiengänge in der Digitalisierung: Baustelle Curriculumentwicklung. Hochschulforum Digitalisierung **52** (2020)
12. Corr, S., et al.: Fostering innovation in heritage professions: the effect of the eych. Scires-It-Scientific Res. Inf. Technol. **9**(1), 49–60 (2019)
13. European Commission. The Digital Competence Framework 2.0 (2019). https://ec.europa.eu/jrc/en/digcomp/digital-competence-framework
14. JISC. Strategic perspectives on digital literacies (2014). https://www.jisc.ac.uk/guides/developing-digital-literacies/strategic-perspectives-on-digital-literacies
15. Eichhorn, et al.: Entwicklung eines Kompetenzrasters zur Erfassung "Digitaler Kompetenz" von Hochschullehrenden. Paper presented at the GMW 2017 (2017)
16. Sahle, P.: Auf dem Weg zu einem Kern- und Referenzcurriculum der Digital Humanities (2013)
17. Sula, C.A., et al.: A Survey of Digital Humanities Programs. Journal of Interactive Technology & Pedagogy (2017)
18. Kröber, C., et al.: An App for the Cathedral in Freiberg - An Interdisciplinary Project Seminar. In: Sampson, D.G., et al. (ed.): Proceedings of the 11th International Conference on Cognition and Exploratory Learning in Digital Age (CELDA 2014) Porto, Portugal. Oct. 25–27th 2014. pp 270–274 (2014)
19. Mayring, P.: Qualitative Content Analysis. Forum Qualitative Sozialforschung 1 (2), Art. 20 (2000)
20. Rehfeldt, D.: Mythos Praxis um jeden Preis? Die Wurzeln und Modellierung des Lehr-Lern-Labors. die hochschullehre, pp. 90–114 (2018)
21. Klein, M.: Durch Forschendes Lernen kennenlernen, was Digitalität mit Geschichte macht. Ein Kommentar zum Projektbericht Forschungswerkstatt zur Erstellung einer Digitalen Edition von Bianca Frohne und Swantje Piotrowski. In: Think! Historically. Geschichts-didaktische Perspektive auf die Vormoderne. Universitätsverlag Kiel, Kiel, pp. 127–136 (2021)
22. Wiater, W.: Wissensmanagement. Eine Einführung für Pädagogen (2007)

23. Dea, R.: Fächerübergreifende Wirkungen von Lehr-Lern-Labor-Seminaren: Adaption für die Fächergruppen Englisch, Geschichte und Sachunterricht. In: Maurer, C. (ed.) Implementation fachdidaktischer Innovation im Spiegel von Forschung und Praxis, GDCP-Tagung 2016, pp. 556–559. Universität Regensburg, Regensburg (2017)

24. Seibert, D.: Lehrer werden für das Fach Geschichte – im Labor! Professionalisierung angehender Geschichtslehrer~innen durch Entwicklungsaufgaben in Lehr-Lern-Labor-Seminaren als Einstieg in eine theoriegeleitete Unterrichtspraxis. (Dissertation) (2020)

25. Alavi, B., et al.: Lernen Schüler/innen Geschichte im Digitalen anders? In: Demantowsky, M., et al. (eds.) Geschichte lernen im digitalen Wandel, pp. 3–16. De Gruyter, Oldenbourg, Berlin, München, Boston (2015)

26. Bernsen, D.: Medien und historisches Lernen. Eine Verhältnisbestimmung und ein Plädoyer für eine digitale Geschichtsdidaktik. Zeitschrift für Digitale Geschichtswissenschaften **1**, 1–27 (2012)

27. Leinung, S.: Discovering Greek & Roman Cities - Perspektiven für eine digitale Geschichtsdidaktik. In: Barsch, S., (ed.) Geschichtsdidaktische Perspektiven auf die 'Vormoderne'. Fachwissenschaft und Fachdidaktik im Dialog. Kiel, pp. 51–56 (2021)

28. Kühberger, C.: Geschichte lernen digital? Ein Kommentar zu mehrfach gebrochenen Diskursen der Geschichtsdidaktik. In: Demantowsky, M., et al. (ed.): Geschichte lernen im digitalen Wandel. DeGruyter, Oldenbourg, Berlin, München, Boston, pp. 163–168 (2015)

29. Demantowsky, M.: Die Geschichtsdidaktik und die digitale Welt. In: Demantowsky, M., et al. (eds.) Geschichte lernen im digitalen Wandel, pp. 149–162. De Gruyter, Oldenburg (2015)

30. Pallaske, C.: Die Vermessung der (digitalen) Welt. Geschichtslernen mit digitalen Medien. In: Demantowsky, M., et al. (eds.) Geschichte lernen im digitalen Wandel, pp. 135–148. De Gruyter, Oldenbourg, Berlin, München, Boston (2015)

31. Pätzold, I.: (Digitale) Medien im Geschichtsunterricht. Eine empirische Untersuchung zu Einstellungen und Nutzungen Lehrender des Fachs Geschichte an unterschiedlichen Schulformen. Masterarbeit (2021)

32. Lewers, E.: Durch Raum und Zeit? Medienkritische Auseinandersetzung mit Virtual Reality im Geschichtsunterricht. Medienimpulse **60**(2), 1–41 (2022)

33. Bellingradt, D., et al.: Eine Stadttour durch Hamburg im Jahr 1686. Die App Hidden Hamburg als erlebbare Geschichte und Digital-Public-History-Experiment (2022)

34. Demantowsky, M., et al. (eds.): Geschichte lernen im digitalen Wandel. De Gruyter, Oldenbourg, Berlin, München, Boston (2015)

35. Wiater, W.: Lernwerkstätten in Zeiten des digitalen Lernens. In: Stadler-Altmann, U., et al. (eds.) Spielen, Lernen, Arbeiten in Lernwerkstätten, pp. 135–147. Verlag Julius Klinkhardt, Bad Heilbrunn, Facetten der Kooperation und Kollaboration (2020)

36. Seibert, D.: Theoretisches Wissen gleich träges Wissen? Praxisrelevanz von fachdidaktischem Wissen in Lehr-Lern-Labor-Seminaren. die hochschullehre **5**, 355–382 (2019)

37. Bildungsserver Rheinland Pfalz. Wahlmöglichkeiten geben (2023). https://heterogenitaet.bildung-rp.de/materialien/differenzieren/wahlmoeglichkeiten-geben

Virtual Experiences Using Digital Technologies for South Tyrol Heritage Education

Francesca Condorelli[(✉)] [ID], Giuseppe Nicastro[ID], and Alessandro Luigini[ID]

Faculty of Education, Free University of Bozen-Bolzano, Bolzano, Italy
{francesca.condorelli,giuseppe.nicastro,
alessandro.luigini}@unibz.it

Abstract. This paper reports on the experiences of the EARTH_LAB of Free University of Bozen-Bolzano that has been working in the field of digitization of heritage for years with the aim of realizing educational paths, both in schools and museums, of art education and the study of graphic and visual sciences in the field of architectural representation, education and visual studies. In particular past and present projects about virtual and augmented reality for heritage education will be presented with a particular focus on the enhancement of South Tyrol heritage, especially of the two cities of Brixen and Bozen. A workflow will be presented to make digital the urban environment with the aim to develop digital services for heritage education and didactics. In particular the first step concerns the acquisition of urban data of the historical centers of Brixen and Bozen with architectural survey campaigns of the monuments and urban heritage that have been selected using 3D laser scanner, drones, 360° HDR photos. After the second step of data processing, the third steps consists in the production of navigable models of the heritage stored in an extensive digital catalogue of the heritage that could be used for different purposes such as simple visualization, geometric study, static verifications, protection. In particular there are used for the construction of educational paths through VR and AR navigation for implementing enhancement projects dedicated mainly to citizens but also to tourists. Moreover, the same models are used for the design and implementation of the serious game for heritage education in schools and the high degree of interdisciplinarity (scholars of graphic science, digital heritage, interaction design, art history, pedagogy and psychology are involved in the research) provide the project with a wide scope of application and accuracy of the design process.

Keywords: Digitalization · Heritage Education · Virtual Reality · Augmented Reality · Urban Heritage

1 Introduction

In the age of ubiquitous digital media, the educational world is seeking to significantly expand the scope and range of subjects in which formal settings, especially schools, and informal settings, especially museums, are transforming from spaces of codified

S. Münster et al. (Eds.): UHDL 2023, CCIS 1853, pp. 233–245, 2023.
https://doi.org/10.1007/978-3-031-38871-2_14

knowledge to laboratories of knowledge acquisition to become fully personalized participation. Art and heritage contexts between schools and museums, in particular, can make an important contribution to this transformation [1].

An educational approach to art and heritage must include explaining the processes that make up works of art and help everyone, especially the youngest, acquire new languages rooted in knowledge of expressive codes that belong both to the present and to other eras and cultures. From this point of view, art education in schools and museums is fundamental, as it provides each individual with "a basic grammar" to navigate a reality increasingly permeated by visual codes. People should not passively absorb the numerous stimuli of the various media, whether traditional or innovative. In this sense, experimentation with new digital tools and technologies in the context of the creative process and the construction of new meanings is of great importance.

1.1 Virtual Reality and Augmented Reality as Education Tools

Virtual reality and augmented reality are far from new in the educational landscape [2], and although everything related to them is now receiving enormous attention in the general and specialized media and is undergoing a complete paradigm shift and unprecedented change, mainly due to the market and the pressure of technology companies, it is important to emphasize that even the "latest promising educational technology" has not emerged recently, especially when considered as an educational tool. The first applications of virtual reality appeared in the late 1980s, and apart from some unsuccessful experiments in the entertainment industry, as could be expected, it was clear from the beginning that its most promising applications would sooner or later be found in education. However, it would be even more risky and superficial to forget the short-lived but still relevant past of virtual reality application if we did not take into account the current, enormous and seemingly unstoppable boom of the consumer electronics market and its promises of an incredible range of innovations in both the professional and entertainment sectors.

The education sector, along with the gaming industry, seems to be the most affected. VR digitally recreates a real-world scenario using a variety of software and hardware platforms; AR, on the other hand, overlays digital VR elements with the real world. Both offer interactive experiences, but are different in nature: with VR, the user is immersed in a digital world and the experience is fully controlled; AR, on the other hand, overlays and supplements the real-world experience with additional information.

VR and AR systems can be used to enable immersive, game-based learning by creating a digital narrative, providing authentic resources, and integrating contextual information [3]. AR and VR in the teaching process, especially with regard to the teaching of cultural heritage, make it possible to create scenarios that go beyond a theoretical description; to combine theoretical information with hands-on experimental activities, including through a more playful method; "learning by doing", without real consequences in case of mistakes; use tags and hotspots to create connections, including visual ones, that are easier to share and understand; model objects in different scenarios; and use museum/archaeological projects to carry out learning activities and tours with an immersive experience [4–8]. A key pedagogical option of VR that is critical to cultural heritage studies is the ability to reproduce virtual objects and environments that allow students to better understand the properties and relationships of objects and environments that would be difficult to understand in everyday life (Fig. 1).

Fig. 1. Students test some of the serious games designed by Earthlab. Bolzano, November 2022.

Virtual reality is a powerful tool, and not just in its immersive variants, because augmented methods are also potentially disorienting [9]. In educational programs the critical question concerns the natural entertaining capacity of virtual and augmented reality applications, which should caution against the danger of gamification that could easily turn such an application into a "simple video game." Therefore, VR and AR must be carefully integrated into well-defined programs with clear objectives and procedures, and we can therefore rightly expect to successfully use a new source of inspiration, discussion and comparison. For this reason, the approach of VR/AR as a didactic tool is above all perfect for the research and study of art objects, it becomes not only useful but also potentially panic and potentially dangerous, especially when seen from the perspective of Italy and South Tyrol.

The possibility of exploring valuable and rare artifacts "from anywhere," the idea of literally being able to manipulate and experiment with them in different ways, using masterpieces as do-it-yourself tools, explicitly points us to a completely unexplored landscape and a new, very interesting field of research. Research. This promising field of research, while not entirely new, as mentioned earlier, is still in its infancy, and very few realities are geared toward testing immersive and extended approaches to art education. We can easily predict that this will change very quickly, in part because of market pressures and the support and attention given to this topic in mainstream media. Observe and provide initial evidence of tools, resources, and processes that engage diverse teachers and learners will be a valuable opportunity for the local, national, and international education and learning landscape.

2 Methodology

This paper reports on the experiences of the EARTH_LAB of Free University of Bozen-Bolzano that has been working in the field of digitization of heritage for years with the aim of realizing educational paths, both in schools and museums, of art education and the study of graphic and visual sciences in the field of architectural representation, education and visual studies.

In particular past and present projects about virtual and augmented reality for heritage education will be presented with a particular focus on the valorization of South Tyrol heritage, especially of the two cities of Brixen and Bozen.

A workflow will be presented to make digital the urban environment with the aim to develop interactive environments for heritage education and didactics.

2.1 Data Acquisition and Data Processing

The first step concerns the acquisition of the historical centers of Brixen and Bozen with different architectural survey campaigns of the monuments and urban heritage. The technological evolution that has affected survey instruments in recent years now allows us to conduct digitization campaigns of real environments by acquiring a considerable amount of different information in a short time. The information datasets generated in this way become an essential tool for describing all the relevant characteristics of the environment or architecture to digitize the usual two-dimensional restitutions, conducted with the use of drawings, photos and videos, it is now possible to carry out advanced restitutions of the data that are increasingly immersive, thus offering new points of view on the research's object.

The data acquisition operations conducted therefore see the use of some of these technologies, including terrestrial laser scanning for point cloud acquisition, terrestrial and aerial SfM photogrammetry and panoramic photos taken with 360 degree cameras.

Once all the operations related to the architectural survey campaigns were completed, in the second step of the project it was possible to proceed with the interpretation of the data and their subsequent processing according to the planned restitution and utilization methods. Working with an extensively consolidated workflow in the field of integrated digital surveying, all the operations of scans registration acquired by terrestrial laser scanning and SfM were carried out in order to achieve an optimal level of overlapping between the different types of data and thus be able to proceed to the subsequent phases of data interpretation. By operating on the acquired point clouds, it was possible to generate metrically defined, high-resolution orthogonal images; these planes constitute the reference basis for the critical interpretation of the surveyed geometries and the subsequent phases of the project.

2.2 3D Modelling and Digital Environment Design

The third step consists in the production of navigable 3D models in an extensive digital catalogue that could be used for different purposes such as simple visualisation, geometric study, static verifications, protection. In particular they are used for the construction of educational paths through VR and AR navigation for implementing enhancement projects dedicated mainly to citizens but also to tourists.

For the creation of the 3D models to be used in static renderings, it was necessary to filter the point clouds in order to reduce the noise generated by unwanted measurements and to lower the density of the points in the presence of excessive redundancy; once the acquisitions had been optimised, it was possible to carry out the meshing of the points and the texturing of the three-dimensional surfaces. The 3D restitution, in this phase, was oriented towards the creation of high-density polygon models whose characteristics were suitable for the accurate and detailed description of the surveyed geometries. In the design phases relating to the dynamic 3D models, it was necessary to perform mesh reduction operations on the three-dimensional models by operating a simplification that could, while reducing the number of polygons, maintain an appropriate level of geometric accuracy of the elements described.

Moreover, the same models are used for the design and implementation of the serious game for heritage education in schools and the high degree of interdisciplinarity (scholars of graphic science, digital heritage, interaction design, art history, pedagogy and psychology are involved in the research) provide the project with a wide scope of application and accuracy of the design process.

The transition from the survey of an artefact to its digital visualisation therefore presupposes making design choices that consider hardware and software technologies, the type of narrative one wishes to undertake, and not least the types of users one wishes to involve. If in the past the purpose of a 3D product was mainly to produce static renderings, today we have to look at those same models as assets that can be used in different contexts: digital reconstructions make it possible to display complex information in a more complete visual manner, building a communication channel aimed at a wide and diversified audience of users.

The possibility of using digital data acquired in different applications (virtual tours, virtual or augmented reality applications) has therefore allowed us to design diversified user experiences that can meet the needs of a heterogeneous audience while managing to contain costs and production times. Rendering engines such as the Unreal Engine or Unity simplify the adoption of this design process, and being highly customisable programming environments in which one can combine one's own assets, they guarantee the designer the possibility of efficiently exploiting all the output generated during the return phases of the survey campaign.

3 EARTH_LAB - Ongoing Projects and Results

3.1 B_Digital – Bozen und Brixen Digitisation for Heritage Education

Project credits – PI: Alessandro Luigini; Co-I: Waltraud Kofler (Heritage Platform unibz); research team: Alessandro Basso, Demis Basso, Letizia Bollini, Francesca Condorelli, Giuseppe Nicastro, Monica Parricchi, Barbara Tramelli. Partners: Politecnico di Torino, University of L'Aquila, Universito of Camerino. Fund by Free University of Bozen-Bolzano.

The Project B_Digital, - Bozen und Brixien Digitisation for Heritage education, envisages the digitisation of the most important architectural emergencies of the historical centres of Bozen and Brixen for documentation and enhancement purposes [10]. One of the main focuses of the project is the realisation of immersive digital environments as narrative tools to tell the story of the territory and its cultural heritage: the project envisages the realisation of applied games that can foster the transmission of value with a view to heritage education.

The step launched in 2020 saw the working group engaged in an integrated digital survey campaign conducted on the most relevant religious architecture in the city of Bressanone. In particular, data were acquired on the Cathedral of Santa Maria Assunta and San Cassiano, the city's main place of worship, and the nearby Church of San Michele: the TLS acquisitions covered both the interior and exterior parts of the two complexes.

Currently, the cloister of the cathedral was digitised and the frescoes were studied in real size through an unwrapping operation. The 3D model was implemented in Unreal Engine to create the environment in which to structure the narrative.

A short distance from the two churches is the Major Seminary, seat of the Theological Study of Brixen and the adjoining library. The complex was surveyed in two phases: the first L.S. acquisitions (carried out in parallel with the Cathedral and St. Michael's Church) concerned the main fronts on the namesake square, the inner courtyard, the Church of the Holy Cross and, finally, some of the main rooms on the first floor including the ancient library. A second acquisition campaign covered all the remaining external fronts, the courtyard and the roofs, which were entirely digitised through aerial photogrammetry operations conducted with a Dji Mavic Mini 2 drone. The use of a drone with reduced weight characteristics (<250 g) allowed us to fly not only in the external parts of the buildings, but also in the internal environments, and to be able to acquire high-resolution photos and videos useful for offering the users of the platforms under development new points of view of the acquired objects.

All the point clouds acquired therefore describe the main geometric and material characteristics of the buildings: for the parts with frescoes and valuable architectural details (such as the church or the library), scanning parameters were set to guarantee an adequate point density as well as the acquisition of the colour data.

The next step of the project, once the data processing phase of the point clouds has been completed and the subsequent phases of meshing the 3D models and applying the textures, will see the import of the 3D models into the dynamic rendering engines (Unity, Unreal) required to create the interactive environments (Fig. 2).

By the end of 2023, the working group plans to complete all the acquisitions that are currently in progress: the surveys will focus in particular on the urban facades facing on the main streets of the city and on the connecting paths of the architectures that have already been surveyed.

Fig. 2. B_Digital – Bozen und Brixen Digitisation for Heritage education: digital acquisitions of the main religious architecture in the city of Bressanone (BZ).

3.2   Experimenting VR Gaming with Children – The VAR.HEE. Project (Virtual and Augmenter Reality for Heritage Education Experience

Project credits – PI: Alessandro Luigini; research Team: Alessandro Basso, Demis Basso, Bruno Fanini; Monica Parricchi. External partners: MOdE – Museo Officine dell'Educazione, University of Bologna Alma Mater Studiorum, Università of L'Aquila, Universty of Camerino, CNR-ISPC. Fund by Free University of Bozen-Bolzano.

In heritage enhancement and education paths implemented with gamification content, a testing phase is planned on elementary school children.

For this reason, serious games created in VR were tested by children aged 5 to 12 years old. In particular, the results of two different tests are reported. The first game was viewed via high-definition VR HMD (head-mounted display) viewers Oculus Rift.

An educational path, and the relative experimentation, was implemented on the cultural heritage focused on the production of the typical bread of the Val Pusteria area - and the rural life around it. The project was aimed at primary school children and was based on a serious game in Virtual Immersive Reality. For this reason,the game is about the discovery of a maso, an architectural type that is very common in South Tyrol [11].

Through tests, the children were able to discover the functions of the various rooms and objects within the farmstead and used for bread making. From the point of view of structure, the game consists of a series of multiple-question quizzes in which the child can answer by laying eyes on the answer he or she wants to choose. If it is correct, they move on to the next room and question. The second game was developed to be visioned by cardboard viewers.

In this case this experimental serious game is based on the integrated use of 360° equirectangular imagery to create the illusion of being in real space. Through the use of virtual reality visors, immersive inputs are provided to impress users without triggering too many interactive visual stimuli that are potentially destabilizing during initial exploratory experiences to focus on factors such as the pleasantness of the experience and overall comfort [12, 13].

Despite the increased interactivity, from a technical point of view, the design of the game is very similar to virtual visits, where scenarios are simulated using hyper-detailed equilateral images, also known as ERP images, at resolutions between 4k and 8k. Apparently, such high resolution may seem excessive, but in VR visualization, it is critical to be able to minimize artifacts such as blur or pixels/texels visible to the naked eye in a virtual session, which can be manifested by using medium resolution images: In a 360° space usable by viewers, the equirectangular image is displayed in spherical form, making the actual pixel density and possible color changes clearly visible. Therefore, an image resolution of no less than 8192 x 4096 pixels is required, which is an excellent starting point for editing a high-quality interactive virtual tour.

It deals with the theme of the water cycle and the importance of proper water use. Technically, it is of lower graphical quality and simpler functionality as it is based on 360 spherical images. It has the same open-question quiz operation, and the answer choice is made in the same way i.e. by pointing the view to the answer.

The difference is that in the case of a wrong answer you pass through a polluted environment ruined by man's misuse of water.

There are many references to the environment and architecture, both ancient and modern. The educational results were excellent. Children showed a lot of interest in using games through VR, both as a form of entertainment and as a new way of learning notions. Data showed that the cardboard-based game was more successful than the other, albeit of lower graphical quality, because it was more intuitive, easier to use without external support, which is necessary when using Oculus (Fig. 1).

3.3 Turris Babel

Project credits - PI: Alessandro Luigini, Research team: Francesca Condorelli, Giuseppe Nicastro, Barbara Tramelli.

In 1679, the Jesuit Athanasius Kircher published a volume in which he offered reflections linking the Tower of Babel to the emergence of modern languages, beginning with the end of the universal Flood. The text, one of the Jesuit's many eclectic works, deals extensively with purely architectural issues, both through careful descriptions of ancient buildings and considerations of construction techniques, to demonstrate the possible untenability of the idea of building the tower. Kircher's presentation of his reasoning

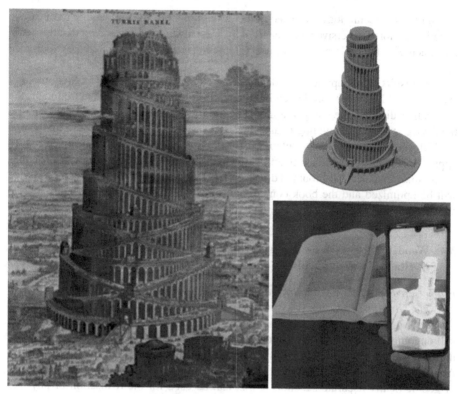

Fig. 3. Turris Babel project: the navigable 3D model of the tower.

and descriptions is accompanied by several illustrations that he had commissioned from Coenraet Decker and Gérard de Lairesse.

Given the importance that the UNESCO attaches to the documentation and valorization of the material cultural heritage, the aim of this project is to show researchers and tourists what they cannot see because they are enclosed by the pages of the book, namely the most significant images of the Tower of Babel and other iconographies of the book such as the Labyrinth. This was made possible by the implementation of a workflow that first involved the reconstruction of the tower model. This is the most difficult part of the entire process, as it involves creating a model of an imaginary architecture that never existed. By combining advanced photogrammetry and 3D modeling techniques, the model was created from the images in the text and compared to other designs for the tower. The second part of the software is the development of an augmented reality application to make the model of the tower navigable in 3D and accessible to the public.

The reconstruction of the tower and the implementation of the application were done using low-cost tools and open-source software.

Augmented reality is undoubtedly an excellent tool not only for visual communication as a knowledge tool, but also for effective interpretation of material cultural heritage.

Markerless technology was used in the development of the application to make the experience more immersive and user-friendly. Recent studies have shown that this technique achieves the optimal levels of user interaction required for this type of experience [14].

The results of AR applications developed for the Athanasius Kircher Archontology are presented below. By implementing the Vuforia tool in the Unity environment, the application displays the navigable model of the tower in real time by simply pointing the device at the corresponding image (Fig. 3).

Vuforia is a cross-platform platform for developing augmented and mixed reality applications with robust tracking and performance across a variety of devices (including mobile devices, head-mounted displays (HMD)). The augmented navigation device will be optimized and the book content narration and illustration descriptions will be enhanced to provide a smooth and immersive experience.

3.4   Wooden Tabernacles – A Research Project to Enhance an Untouchable Heritage of the Capuchins of the Abruzzo

Project credits – PI: Alessandro Luigini; Research team: Alessandro Basso, Daniele Frusone, Giuseppe Nicastro.

The Wooden Tarbernacles research project, which started in September 2022 and is still ongoing, concerns the digitisation of a series of wooden tabernacles made between the 17th and 18th centuries as historical and artistic evidence of the Capuchin order of Abruzzo [15]. The aim of the project is to obtain, through SfM photogrammetry, a series of geometrically accurate 3D models that can be used for the realisation of physical replicas of the objects surveyed through the use of 3D printing. A specially designed Augmented Reality application will make it possible to broaden the experience of using the replica by adding a series of digital information layers (photos, videos, 3D models) that can be activated by framing the replica itself (Fig. 4).

As is well known, in fact, Augmented Reality allows digital elements to be superimposed on a real scene: this feature generates an enhanced vision of reality by applying, through the use of specific devices, a digitised information layer that modifies the real scene in order to deepen its knowledge [16]. By combining this technology with 3D printing, it is therefore possible to associate a physical object with a series of information contents that enrich its fruition.

The progress of the research project is already at an advanced stage but, as already mentioned, not yet concluded: at present, the complete digitisation of a first tabernacle (the tabernacle of the Capuchin friars in Pescara) and the subsequent 3D prototyping has already been carried out. At the same time, the Augmented Reality application has already been created, designed by implementing the Model Target functionalities available with the Vuforia libraries in the Unity software environment. The print prototype turned out to be adequate for the purposes of the project, returning a physical reproduction of the object on a scale of 1:5, capable of accurately reproducing the object's richness of detail. The augmented reality platform was also extensively tested, demonstrating good results in terms of the accuracy of target recognition and thus the correct superimposition between the physical print and the digital layer: in particular, using the

Fig. 4. Wooden Tabernacles project: digital acquisition, 3D modelling, 3D printing and the Augmented Reality APP.

mapped 3D digital model, it was possible to superimpose the colour data of the real object on the 3D print. Further information layers are in progress.

Finally, as far as the overall quality of the physical replica is concerned, the next project steps are to further increase its quality by working on the Layer High value (currently 0.15 mm) and increasing the printing time (currently 61 h) to minimise the printing defects that still remain.

4 Conclusion

Through the development of innovative educational methods that integrate pedagogical knowledge with digital representations, digital applications become useful tools for the transmission of cultural heritage, as they are able to disseminate knowledge and a new awareness through playful and accessible methods.

The 3D models generated will be used to create immersive and interactive experiences, with the aim of bringing users closer to the knowledge of the South Tyrol art site through virtual experiences.

These applications are intended to promote and enhance knowledge about cultural heritage. The use of 3D models for the communication of cultural heritage offers the possibility to use the digital and interactive character of the 3D model to enrich the model itself and thus the applications through the feedback of the end users.

The generated 3D models contain not only three-dimensional information such as measurements, geometries and textures, but also information about the historical phases of the studied site. This type of solution therefore allows data from different sources to be integrated into the digital application in a simplified and intuitive way. The final model will be navigable and searchable in real time. This aspect is crucial for the development of virtual applications and games for teaching and education. It is about making information that is normally inaccessible available and experiential in an attractive way. The virtual learning experience therefore differs significantly from the classic learning experience and allows for greater user involvement.

References

1. Luigini, A.: Proceedings of the 1st International and Interdisciplinary Conference on Digital Environments for Education, Arts and Heritage EARTH 2018, Springer, Cham (2019). https://doi.org/10.1007/978-3-030-12240-9
2. Pellas, N., Fotaris, P., Kazanidis, I., Wells, D.: Augmenting the learning experience in primary and secondary school education: a systematic review of recent trends in augmented reality gamebased learning. Virtual Reality 23, 329–346 (2019)
3. Basso, D., Saracini, C., Palladino, P., Cottini, M.: Travelling salesperson in an immersive virtual environment: experimental evaluation of tracking system device. Adv. Intell. Syst. Comput. 919, 519–529 (2019)
4. Meegan, E., et al.: Virtual heritage learning environments. In: Ioannides, M., Fink, E., Cantoni, L., Champion, E. (eds.) EuroMed 2020. LNCS, vol. 12642, pp. 427–437. Springer, Cham (2021). https://doi.org/10.1007/978-3-030-73043-7_35
5. Paliokas, I.: Serious games classification for digital heritage. Int. J. Comput. Methods in Heritage Science (IJCMHS) 3(2), 58–72 (2019)
6. Hammady, R., Ma, M., Powell, A.: User experience of markerless augmented reality applications in cultural heritage museums: 'museumeye' as a case study. In: De Paolis, L.T., Bourdot, P. (eds.) AVR 2018. LNCS, vol. 10851, pp. 349–369. Springer, Cham (2018). https://doi.org/10.1007/978-3-319-95282-6_26
7. Shih, N.-J., Diao, P.-H., Chen, Y.: ARTS, an AR tourism system, for the integration of 3D scanning and smartphone AR in cultural heritage tourism and pedagogy. Sensors 19(17), 3725 (2019). https://doi.org/10.3390/s19173725
8. Mortara, M., Catalano, C.E., Bellotti, F., Fiucci, G., Houry-Panchetti, M., Petridis, P.: Learning cultural heritage by serious games. J. Cult. Herit. 15(3), 318–325 (2015)
9. Al Zayer, M., MacNeilage, P., Folmer, E.: Virtual locomotion: a survey. IEEE Trans. Visual Comput. Graphics 26(5), 2315–2334 (2018)
10. Luigini, A., Fanini, B., Basso, A., Basso, D.: Heritage education through serious games. A web-based proposal for primary schools to cope with distance learning. VITRUVIO - International Journal of Architectural Technology and Sustainability 5(2), 72–85 (2020)
11. Luigini, A, Parricchi, M., Basso, A, Basso, D.: Immersive and participatory serious games for heritage education, applied to the cultural heritage of South Tyrol. Interaction Design and Architecture(s) Journal - ID&A 43(20), 42–67 (2019)
12. Luigini, A.: Paesaggio Naturale, Paesaggio culturale. Serious Game immersivi e partecipativi per l'educazione al patrimonio. Paesaggio Urbano 4, 79–93 (2019)

13. Luigini, A., Basso, A.: Heritage education for primary age through an immersive serious game. In: Bolognesi, C., Villa, D. (eds.) From Building Information Modelling to Mixed Reality, pp. 157–174. Springer, Cham. (2020)

14. Wu, L.C., Lin, I.C., Tsai, M.H.: Augmented reality instruction for object assembly based on markerless tracking. In: Wyman, C., Yuskel, C. (eds.): Proceedings of the 20th ACM SIGGRAPH Symposium on Interactive 3D Graphics and Games. Association for Computing Machinery, New York, pp. 95–102 (2016)

15. Del Vecchio, L.: Fratelli Marangoni e tabernacoli lignei. Un capitolo di storia cappuccina in Abruzzo, Edizioni Tabula, Lanciano (2001) [First published 1997]

16. Alhejri, A., Bian, N., Alyafeai, E., Alsharabi, M.: Reconstructing real object appearance with virtual materials using mobile augmented reality. Comput. Graph. **108**, 1–10 (2022)

Public Health, Artisanal Activities, Daily Life in Medieval Bologna: Digital Projects as Teaching Tools for Urban History

Taylor Zaneri[1][(✉)] and Rosa Smurra[2]

[1] New York University, 25 Waverly Place, New York, NY 10003, USA
`tlz208@nyu.edu`

[2] Department of Architecture, Alma Mater Studiorum – University of Bologna, Via Saragozza, 8, 40136 Bologna, Italy
`rosa.smurra@unibo.it`

Abstract. This paper will examine how the material from two digital projects, the 1296–7 Estimi online library and the Healthscaping Medieval Bologna webgis, can be used as teaching materials for urban history students. These projects provide students with an interactive means to access primary source material and present a vivid and nuanced picture of how the medieval city of Bologna balanced its vibrant artisanal population and its economic activities, with sanitary and hygiene needs. Instructors can incorporate the material from these two projects into lectures on medieval urban history and pre-modern public health and can also use them to teach specific skills including 1) medieval Latin and paleography, 2) data collection and analysis, and 3) GIS visualization. The data from these two projects is in an accessible form for instructors and this material can be adapted to suit the needs of students. In short, by integrating the data from these two projects, it is possible to present students with a rich case study and at the same time gives them the opportunity to explore the sources themselves, and further their own interests and skills.

Keywords: Medieval Bologna · Urban History · GIS · Public Health · Digital libraries

1 Introduction

The intersection of urban history and digital humanities has resulted in a remarkable reconceptualization of how historical research is conducted and also how these results are presented to an academic audience. From webgis to 3-D modeling to digital archives the last ten years have transformed the field, and it is almost impossible to conceive of a research project without some kind of digital component or output [1]. However the majority of digital outputs have been primarily for a scholarly audience, with much less attention given to how these research products can be used as teaching tools in classrooms [2]. This paper speaks directly to this issue and explores how two different digital history projects which focus on medieval Bologna can be used, not only as

S. Münster et al. (Eds.): UHDL 2023, CCIS 1853, pp. 246–258, 2023.
https://doi.org/10.1007/978-3-031-38871-2_15

repositories of data and sources for future research, but can serve as valuable teaching tools that provide students with an interactive means to access primary source material that would otherwise be beyond their reach.

This paper will examine how these digital projects can be integrated to teach medieval urban history as well as data analysis skills. It will discuss two projects which are large scale repositories for data: the 1296–7 Estimi of Bologna, which has been digitized by the *Centro Gina Fasoli per la storia delle città*, at the University of Bologna [3] and the Healthscaping Medieval Bologna webgis hosted by the University of Amsterdam [4]. In addition to containing large amounts of primary source materials, these two projects are extremely powerful tools for teaching students about daily life, artisanal activities, and public health in medieval Bologna. In addition, they can also be used to teach students data collection, processing, and GIS visualization, along with medieval Latin and paleography. Each project offers different educational possibilities and skills that students can learn, and the data from both websites can be integrated to provide a more holistic perspective on medieval Bologna, and in particular the hygiene risks faced by its citizens.

Contrary to popular thought, medieval governments were highly concerned with maintaining healthy and safe cities, and heavily regulated the urban environment and their large populations of artisans, whose activities were a vital economic part of the city but also produced large amounts of waste that needed to be disposed of and managed [5]. The conditions of medieval Bologna, the enforcement of hygiene and sanitary regulations, and the material consequences of these actions can only be understood by working directly with primary source data [6].

2 Digital History as Medieval History: Overview of Sources

2.1 The Estimi 1296–7 of Bologna

To briefly summarize the digital sources, the first project contains the 1296–7 Estimi of Bologna which is freely accessible on the website of the Centro Gina Fasoli. These estimi are comprised of fiscal sources (tax returns) and contain over 10,000 documents, which recorded the head of each household by the church parish in which they resided, as well as other characteristics such as occupation and financial information [7]. In particular, tax returns were related to chattels and property that Bolognese citizens (both men and women) were required to submit to the city authorities for the purposes of direct taxation [8]. Based on the assessment figure derived from the total value of chattels and property listed in the tax returns, and validated or adjusted by the tax inspectors, the city government determined the *collecta*, a tax with a varying percentage rate depending on the needs of the public finances, especially when the expenses of war were to be met.

The Estimi offer valuable insight into medieval demography and the population distribution in medieval Bologna; to some extent they are relevant to the topographical study of the productive and commercial activities. By provision, heads of household had to specify the quarter and church parish (cappella) not just of the current residence but also of the previous one; the self-declarations were therefore collected and sorted according to these criteria (quarter and cappella) [9]. The Estimi also enable us to identify the social composition of city neighborhoods which is crucial for reconstructing population pressure in a certain district as well as pollution. The core of the Estimi website is a search and browse engine for which metadata describing the tax records of 13th-century citizens of Bologna has been created. The metadata includes textual information (biographical data, professional activity, asset data, etc.) and accompanies the thousands of high-resolution digitized parchment documents.

Since the entire source is online, students can work with the raw material and learn how to read and understand the source. As such it is possible to use the Estimi to teach students medieval Latin and paleography. For example, instructors can choose several of the digitized documents and have students practice doing transcriptions, so they can learn to read medieval texts and understand what kind of information they contain. Figure 1 shows an example of an estimo of one of the parchment makers who lived in San Biagio, along with an accompanying transcription.

1 Dominus Martinus quondam Ugolini de Casaliclo, capella Sancti Blasii
2 qui extimatus fuit tempore domini Pacis et sociorum decem libr. Bon.
3 in quarterio Porte Ravenatis in capella Santi Thome Strate Maioris
4 et nunc vult extimari in predicto quarterio in capella Sancti Blaxii.
5 Denuntiat vobis quod ipse non habet aliquod stabille sed tunc
6 habet in arte chartholarie _____XXV lib. bon
7 item dicit quod habet tantas arnias que valent_____V lib. bon.
8 In primis debet dare Rubeo domini Corradini quindecim lib. bon.
9 et in solido sunt obligati dominus Ugolinus de Monteruçolli et Bertholinus
10 domini Martini ut constat in strumento scripto manu
11 Item debet dare dicto domino Rubeo quattuor lib. bon. ut constat
12 in strumento scripto manu Iohannis Petri Schafari notarii et sunt obligati
13 Bertholinus et Ugolinus eius filii.
14 [adjusted by the tax inspectors] XL lib. bon.

All the Estimi record the church parish in which the head of household lived, but these documents could include more specific locational information such as the street or neighborhood in which the person resided, along with the names of their neighbors. And this information can be used to visualize and reconstruct medieval neighborhoods, as will be seen below. Moreover, as mentioned above, the Estimi also include the individual's financial information such as their debts, credits, as well as the total amount of cash and assets they possessed, and also at times their profession [10].

Learning to read and interpret medieval documents is a fundamental skill for history students and with this project they have the entire source to work with. In a large class, it would be possible to have students work on different Estimi from one or more parishes and then aggregate the data to conduct analyses. For students who do not have paleography skills, the Estimo website offers a searchable database in which the user can search by name, profession or key word. With each search a short summary of every document is returned; in addition it is also possible to browse all the documents, which are organized by church parish. Therefore even students who do not have paleography training can read the short summaries, and these can be used to teach students about the financial realities of the citizens of Bologna, along with the distribution of the population across the city.

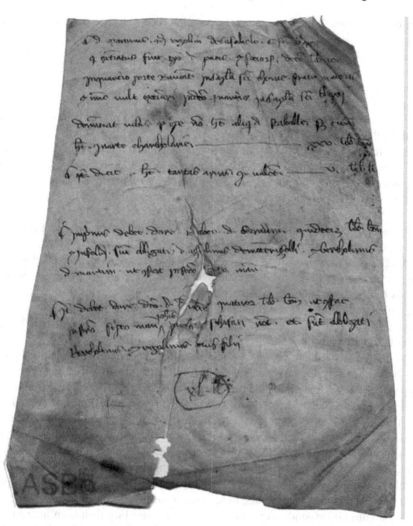

Fig. 1. IT ASBo, Comune, Ufficio dei riformatori degli estimi, s. II, b. 24, 1296–97, Porta Ravennate S. Biagio, 163

2.2 Healthscaping Medieval Bologna

The second source is a webgis, titled Healthscaping Medieval Bologna, which was created as part of the ERC project Healthscaping Urban Europe, directed by Prof. Guy Geltner. This site integrates historical and archaeological information relating to public health, hygiene and infrastructure for Bologna from the 13th and 14th centuries [11]. In particular this webgis provides insight into how officials regulated the artisanal population and managed their infrastructure and environment to promote urban health. The Healthscaping website includes the data in processed form, meaning that it does not have the primary sources available, although some are freely available online. Instead it maps several different sources including: 1) the registers of city officials who were responsible for enforcing hygiene and infrastructure laws – this office was known as the *Ufficio delle acque, strade, ponti, calanchi, selciate e fango* (this is abbreviated in this paper as *Ufficio del fango*), 2) the 1245–67 statutes, which contain the hygiene and infrastructure regulations, and 3) published archaeological evidence of artisanal activities, waste disposal, and infrastructure.

To briefly describe each, the *Ufficio del fango* dataset (which was compiled by Prof. Geltner), is the registers of medieval officials who documented health and sanitary violations that occurred in medieval Bologna. Comprised of 3,500 records from 1287 to 1383, officials described these violations in registers and noted valuable information such as the church parish in which the problem occurred, along with the occupation and gender of the person(s) they deemed responsible; such offenses included a butcher disposing of animal remains in the street or a non-functioning sewer in a neighborhood [12].

The webgis has an interactive interface which allows the user to query the *Ufficio del fango* dataset by demographic characteristics (gender, occupation, church parish), or by type of offense or materials (dung, animals, dirty water) or infrastructure involved (road, canal, well). Instructors can conduct their own queries for specific teaching purposes or students can be allowed to explore the webgis freely. Some queries that can be useful for teaching and discussion could include, which types of artisans were most cited for health violations and where did they live? Or where were women most likely to be cited for health violations?

In addition, the Healthscaping website also includes health regulations from the 1245–67 statutes of Bologna, which have been localized by street, and can also be queried by type of regulation, materials and infrastructure described [13]. Finally the website also includes archaeological evidence of waste disposal, infrastructure and artisanal activities [14]. Therefore it is possible to compare the health regulations, their enforcement by the Ufficio del fango, as well as material realities of daily life in Bologna. In sum this website provides students with the ability to work with multiple different sources and to think about the types of information available in each. From an educational perspective, it would be possible to design a lesson based on a specific artisanal activity or type of infrastructure and query each source to see what kind of data it offers. Presenting data in this medium allows students to conduct analyses based on their own interests and encourages them to reflect on the kinds of questions that can be asked of these sources.

Both of these projects can be used as teaching tools in their own right, or they can be combined together, since each offers different types of information and insights into medieval Bologna, its population, their activities, and the kinds of health problems and risks they faced. In order to do this, students first need to have some grounding in GIS methodology and how to conduct digital history research.

3 Teaching GIS Methodology as Digital History

Now that we have reviewed the sources, this next section will give an overview of how to work with these two projects to teach data visualization and analysis in GIS. In particular this section will review how to translate historical sources into spatially mappable data. And within this broad theme there are four skills which are critical 1) research design,

2) spatial representation, 3) data organization, and 4) data visualization and analysis. Introducing students to methodology is crucial but this can and should be adapted based on the confines of the course, the familiarity of students with GIS and their experience working with historical sources. It is possible to provide a brief overview of these skills in one or two lessons in a general urban history course, or an entire course can be designed focusing on digital history methods. In either case, it is important that students walk away from this experience having a clear understanding of the types of choices that are made when designing a research project and collecting data, and for them to understand how these choices influence outcomes.

Our recommendation is to give students translated material in order to teach these four concepts. This allows them to get direct experience working with the sources and provides them with a foundation for understanding what information is contained in sources and the kinds of research questions that can be asked. Beginning with research design, students can be given some of the Estimi which have been transcribed or some of the published statutes from 1245–67, and be tasked to come up with possible research questions.

The following excerpt is an example of one of the statute regulations which can be used for this activity:

"It is not permitted for anyone to beat skins from the house of the brothers of Lamberti up to the houses of the sons of Beccadelli in strata Santo Stefano, under the penalty of 100 soldi, as to not disturb the religious practices and to avoid polluting the water of the well [15]."

It can be useful to have students analyze multiple statute excerpts and to discuss how to translate this information into spatial data. At this point, it is crucial to introduce some basic GIS concepts. And the most fundamental concept here is establishing the spatial unit – in other words, how information will be represented and analyzed in a GIS environment. And this is going to depend on 1) the research question and 2) the spatial information contained in a source.

To teach a digital history course, ideally students should have at least one lecture introducing GIS data formats – vector and raster – vector is for discrete data types, with fixed boundaries (for example a house or a road), and raster is for continuous data such as elevation or land cover. Typically with historical data, vectors are the most suitable and vectors allow for three geometric representations, points, lines and polygons [16]. It is critical that students understand how their data will be represented before they can do any work or analysis in GIS. It is also critical that instructors stress that the spatial unit must be clear and consistent throughout the historical source in order to work with it in GIS.

For these two projects, 1296–7 Estimi and the data from the *Ufficio del fango* from the Healthscaping webgis were recorded by parish [17]. Therefore they have the same spatial unit. We do not know the confines or territories of parishes, but we do know where the individual churches themselves were, and we can represent these as points. In addition, the Healthscaping webgis also includes some data from the 1245–67 statutes, which can be mapped and identified by street – as such this data was represented as lines [18].

Once students understand what data sources offer, and how it will be represented in GIS, they also must consider how it will be organized. Again we recommend having students work with some of the source material, and based on their research questions or goals, ask them what data they would collect and how they would organize it in a spreadsheet.

It is useful to do this exercise in small groups and then have students come together and discuss with their peers the different approaches they might take. After students understand how to organize data collected from sources and what kinds of information can be obtained, the next step is to teach them how to input this data and visualize it in GIS, and conduct simple queries. Both the Estimi and the Healthscaping project can be used to teach students how to display and analyze data. And the two sources can be combined to provide students with a richer experience with data analysis, as well as provide a deeper understanding of hygiene and public health in the medieval city.

4 Case Study of an Urban Neighborhood: Putting it all Together

To demonstrate how these projects can be used to teach students about public health, artisanal activities, and daily life in medieval Bologna, along with GIS and data analysis methods, this section presents a case study of one neighborhood of Bologna. We will explore an area called *braina Sancti Stephani* (see Fig. 2 circled area) that comprised the area of the churches of Santo Stefano and San Tommaso della Braina (also known as San Tommaso di Strada Maggiore), as well as the nearby church of San Biagio [19]. This area was home to a significant number of parchment makers in the late 13th to early 14th centuries. These artisans were in high demand in a university city such as Bologna where thousands of students stimulated a mass market for textbooks, which were made of parchment. Parchment makers concentrated in *braina Sancti Stephani* because of the abundance of water in this zone, which was particularly clean and suitable for the process of parchment making. However, parchment makers also needed to use chemicals to process animal skins as part of their work, which created toxic waste and therefore pollution risks.

To briefly explain, parchment making was a complex process that required several stages to treat the animal skins, because the skin is made up of several layers and the one used for parchment is the innermost layer. First skins had to be removed from the animals, at which point they had to be preserved in salt or they would decay. The next stage was soaking the skin in a solution of slaked lime (calcium hydroxide) for eight to ten days [20]. From there what remained of the flesh, hair and epidermis was removed manually with a scraper. Then the skin was again soaked in a vat of lime for cleansing. Finally it was stretched and washed and left to dry.

The residences of parchment makers were concentrated in two parishes – San Tommaso della Braina and San Biagio – these two churches were located very close to one another. There are two sources that we can use to identify where parchment makers lived, the first source is the 1296–7 Estimi (recall that these were recorded by heads of households). However, the heads of household did not always list their profession, and we only have twenty who identified themselves as parchment makers; but of those twenty, thirteen lived in San Tommaso and one in San Biagio (See Fig. 3).

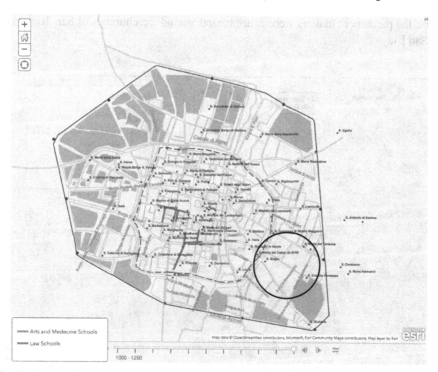

Fig. 2. Topography and layout of medieval Bologna, *Braina Sancti Stephani* circled in black © 2021: Digital Bologna map by R. Smurra from F. Lugli, Cartografia, in *Atlante storico di Bologna* 1995–1998 (ed. F. Bocchi)

But we know from other sources that the population of parchment makers was much larger than that. Another medieval source, the *Liber matricularum societatum artium* from 1294, contains guild matriculation lists – each profession (including parchment makers) kept membership lists which were submitted to government authorities and recorded the names and parish of their member. This source was studied and tabulated by historian Antonio Ivan Pini. According to his study, all of the 152 parchment makers in the guild membership list lived in the parish of San Biagio [21].

Therefore between the two sources we can be confident that a number of parchment makers lived in *braina Sancti Stephani*. This raises another important point for conducting and teaching medieval history – that is – the importance of comparing sources and understanding what kinds of information can be obtained from each source. In this case the 1294 source provides more complete information about the artisans, while the Estimi contain more information about the population and their circumstances.

But we can do better than this, the Estimi are wonderful because they sometimes also contain the street in which the head of household lived, along with the neighbors in houses that were adjacent. Therefore it is possible to visualize where some of these people lived. And in this case, we can reconstruct where some of the parchment makers lived by combining information from the Estimi and the 1294 list (See Fig. 3). As Fig. 3

shows, the parchment makers were concentrated around the churches of San Tommaso and San Biagio.

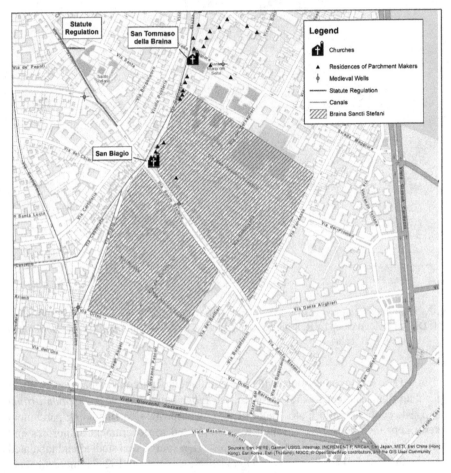

Fig. 3. *Braina Sancti Stephani* neighborhood with residences of parchment makers

The activities of artisans, like parchment makers (along with others such as butchers, cloth dyers, and blacksmiths) were heavily regulated by the medieval government of Bologna, and this was especially true for activities that involved chemicals or burning since these presented immediate health risks to the surrounding population. And we have several lines of evidence that attest to this. The first comes from the 1245–67 statutes, which contain several rubrics aimed at regulating activities involving animal skins or chemicals involved in parchment making. For example, there were prohibitions on the disposal of water that was mixed with lime (recall that lime was used for processing skins), as well as restrictions on where skins could be beaten and processed [22]. In particular, water and animal remains could not be disposed of in public streets, especially in the city center, and it was also prohibited to dispose of these near wells [23].

Sometimes the statutes offer very detailed spatial information in these regulations. For example, the statute excerpt in the previous Sect. 2.2 states that it was forbidden to beat skins in the area from "the house of the Lamberti brothers to the house of the sons of Beccadelli in *strata sancti Stephani.*" In this short sentence, there are several spatial markers and also a street name [24]. We are fortunate that the street names have not changed and *strata sancti Stephani* refers to via Santo Stefano, therefore we can be confident of the road [25]. In addition, it is possible to search both of these family names in the Estimi database and cross reference this information with other historical studies. Often times the statutes used the houses of important families to designate areas, and these have been well studied, making it possible to identify locations at the street level. And this is another useful lesson for students, how to identify areas discussed in medieval sources. In this case we can identify the area that the above statute regulation was referring to with these methods – the regulation applies to a section of via Santo Stefano, not far from the neighborhood, *braina Sancti Stephani* where all of the parchment makers lived (See Fig. 3 for exact regulation location) [26].

In addition to the statutes, the data from the *Ufficio del fango*, the health officials, also provides some insight into hygiene issues caused by the production of parchment. For example, the fango officials cited five parchment makers who were living in San Biagio, for health violations on March 10th 1335 [27]. According to the registers the parchment makers were cited for skinning their hides under porticos, so presumably they were doing this in a private space but nevertheless it was a public problem, which is why they were cited. In addition in January of 1361, another individual living in the parish of San Biagio was cited for a swollen/rotting cow carcass in front of their house – the profession of this person is not recorded; however it is certainly possible that this could have been a parchment maker as well [27].

5 Conclusions

This paper has detailed how these two digital projects, the 1296–7 Estimi online library and the Healthscaping Medieval Bologna webgis can be used to teach a variety of concepts to students, that range from specialized skills such as medieval Latin and paleography, to topical studies of medieval urban history and pre-modern public health, along with data collection, GIS analysis and visualization. Together these two projects offer accessible materials to both instructors and students, and can be incorporated into existing lectures, or alternatively can be the basis for a stand-alone course.

One of the key advantages of the two projects presented here is that they can be adapted as teaching materials to fit the needs of several different types of courses and can be tailored to the abilities and skills of students. We have presented several different ways in which these projects can serve as teaching tools and these digital resources offer several advantages as devices for learning: first, they offer students the ability to work directly with primary source data. In addition, students can conduct queries and explore their own interests through an interactive medium which is easy and familiar. Moreover, students can explore multiple different sources and types of data. Offering students the ability to work directly with primary source data in an accessible format is a huge advantage in that this type of dataset takes years to compile and requires expertise in several languages along with medieval paleography. And it also removes the enormous barrier of processing and analyzing the material and presents students with data that is ready to work with.

In sum, these projects offer students the opportunity to interact directly with a wealth of information about everyday life in Bologna including where people lived, their economic condition, the kinds of activities they were involved in, how this impacted the hygiene and infrastructure conditions, and how this varied across the medieval city. As such the 1296–7 Estimi and the Healthscaping Medieval Bologna webgis offer immense opportunities in the educational realm and are invaluable as teaching sources both for medieval urban history as well as for a range of methodological and GIS skills.

References

1. Dougherty, J., Nawrotzki, K.: Writing History in the Digital Age. Ann Arbor, University of Michigan Press (2013); Blundell, D., Lin, C., Morris, J. X.: Spatial Humanities: An Integrated Approach to Spatiotemporal Research. In Chen, S. (ed.) Big Data in Computational Social Science and Humanities, pp. 263–288. Springer, Verlag (2018); Colson, J.: Reinterpreting space: Mapping people and relationships in late medieval and early modern English cities using GIS. Urban History, 47(3), 384–400. (2020). https://doi.org/10.1017/S0963926820000164

2. Rehbein, M., Fritze, C.: 2. Hands-On Teaching Digital Humanities: A Didactic Analysis of a Summer School Course on Digital Editing. In: Hirsch, B. D. (eds.) Digital Humanities Pedagogy: Practices, Principles and Politics, pp. 47–78. Cambridge, Open Book Publishers (2012); Battershill, C., Ross, S.: Using Digital Humanities in the Classroom: A Practical Introduction for Teachers, Lecturers, and Students. Bloomsbury Publishing, London (2017).

3. Smurra, R.: Progetto Fonti Medievali in Rete. www.centrofasoli.unibo.it. Accessed 1 Jan 2023

4. Geltner, G.: Roads to Health: Infrastructure and Urban Wellbeing in Later Medieval Italy. University of Pennsylvania Press, Philadelphia (2019); Zaneri, T., Geltner, G.: Healthscaping Medieval Bologna, Accessed 1 Jan 2023. https://uvagis.maps.arcgis.com/apps/webapp viewer/in-dex.html?id=98eac4af36ce49cbacb97c167f6dce43

5. For Italy especially see Bocchi, F.: Regulation of the Urban Environment by the Italian Communes from the Twelfth to the Fourteenth Century. Bulletin of the John Rylands Library. 63–78 (1990); Geltner, G.: Roads to Health: Infrastructure and Urban Wellbeing in Later Medieval Italy. University of Pennsylvania Press, Philadelphia (2019); Balestracci, D., The regulation of public health in Italian medieval towns, In: Hundsbichler, H., Jaritz, G., Kühtreiber, T. (eds.) Die Vielfalt der Dinge: Neue Wege zur Analyse mittelalterlicher Sachkultur, pp. 345–57. Verl. der Österreichischen Akademie der Wissenschafte, Vienna (1998)

6. Bocchi, F.: Atlante Storico delle Città Italiane. Bologna II, Il Duecento, pp. 57–71. Bologna, Grafis (1996); L. Sabbionesi, "Pro maiore sanitate hominum civitatis…et borgorum". Lo smaltimento dei rifiuti nelle città medievali dell'Emilia Romagna, pp. 38–77. Florence, All'insegna del giglio (2019)

7. Smurra, R.: Città, Cittadini e Imposta diretta a Bologna alla fine del Duecento. CLUEB, Bologna (2007). For church locations see M. Fini, Bologna sacra: tutte le chiese in due millenni di storia. Pendragon, Bologna (2007)

8. Giansante, M.: Il quartiere bolognese di Porta Procola alla fine del Duecento. Aspetti economici e sociali dell'estimo del 1296–7. Il Carrobbio 11, 123–41 (1985); Micheletti, D.: Gli estimi del comune di Bologna il quartiere di Porta Ravennate (1296–97), Il Carrobbio 7, 293–304 (1981).; Rocca, D.: Gli estimi del Comune di Bologna. Il quartiere di Porta Stiera nel 1296/97, unpublished thesis, University of Bologna, (1984–85); Vallerani, M. (ed.): Il valore dei cives. La definizione del valore negli estimi bolognesi del XIV secolo. In: Valore delle cose e valore delle persone, pp. 241–70. Viella, Rome (2018)

9. Smurra, R.: Fiscal Sources: the Estimi. In: Blanshei, S. (ed.) A Companion to Medieval and Renaissance Bologna, pp. 42–55. Brill, Leiden-Boston (2018)

10. Smurra, R.: Direct Taxation in late thirteenth-century Bologna: the Role of Women as Taxpayers, In: Studies of the Military Orders, Prussia, and Urban History: Essays in Honour of Roman Czaja on the Occasion of His Sixtieth Birthday, pp. 457–69. Print-Art, Debrecen (2020)

11. See note 4 for reference

12. Geltner, G.: Roads to Health: Infrastructure and Urban Wellbeing in Later Medieval Italy. University of Pennsylvania Press, Philadelphia (2019); Zaneri, T., Geltner, G.: The dynamics of healthscaping: mapping communal hygiene in Bologna, 1287–1383. Urban History 49(1), 227 (2022). DOI: https://doi.org/10.1017/S0963926820000541; see also Breveglieri, B.: Il notaio del fango. Atti e Memorie della Deputazione di Storia Patria per le Province di Romagna. 55, 95–152 (2005); Albertani, G.: Igiene e decoro: Bologna secondo il registro del notaio del fango (1285). Storia Urbana. 116, 19–36 (2007)

13. Statuti di Bologna dall'anno 1245 all'anno 1267, 3 vols. Frati, L. (ed) Regia Tipografia, Bologna (1869–1877)

14. See note 6, and also Curina, R., Malnati, L., Negrelli, C., Pini, L. (eds.): Alla ricerca di Bologna antica e medievale. Da Felsina a Bononia negli scavi di Via d'Azeglio. All'Insegna del Giglio, Firenze (2010); Gelichi, S., Cavallari, C., Medica, M. (eds.): Medioevo svelato: storie dell'Emilia-Romagna attraverso l'archeologia. Ante Quem, Bologna (2018); Curina, R., Di Stefano, V., Tassinari, C. (eds.): Un arcipelago di storia: archeologia e isole ecologiche interrate a Bologna.Ante Quem, Bologna (2020)

15. Statuti di Bologna dall'anno 1245 , Vol I. Lib I, Rub XXXIV p. 204 Note A

16. Bolstad, P.: GIS Fundamentals : A First Text on Geographic Information Systems. 6th ed. XanEdu, Ann Arbor MI (2019)

17. See notes 3 and 4 for references

18. Zaneri, T.: The spatial logic of health: managing waste, water and infrastructure in later medieval Bologna. J. Hist. Geogr. 81, 97–109 (2023). https://doi.org/10.1016/j.jhg.2023.02.009

19. Fanti, M.: Le vie di Bologna: saggio di toponomastica storica e di storia della toponomastica urbana, Vol 2., pp. 608. Istituto per la storia di Bologna, Bologna (2000)

20. Ryder, M.: Parchment – its history, manufacture and composition. Journal of the Society of Archivists. 2(9), 391–399 (1964); Reed, R.: Ancient Skins, Parchments and Leathers. Seminar Press, London & New York (1972)

21. Pini, A.: La ripartizione topografica degli artigiani a Bologna nel 1294: Un esempio di demografia sociale. In: Città medievali e demografia storica, pp. 148–79. CLUEB, Bologna (1996). See also Campanini, A., Rinaldi R. (eds.): Artigiani a Bologna: identità, regole, lavoro, secc. XIII–XIV. CLUEB, Bologna (2008); Arnaud, C.: Topographien des Alltags Bologna und Straßburg um 1400. De Gruyter, Berlin (2018)

22. Statuti di Bologna dall'anno 1245, Vol II. Lib. VII Rub. CIX pp.122, Rub. CXXVIII p. 135, Rub. XCVIIf p. 280, Rub. LXXXI p. 268

23. Statuti di Bologna dall'anno 1245, Vol II. Lib. VII Rub. CXLIX p. 158

24. See note 15 for reference

25. Fanti, M. Le vie di Bologna: saggio di toponomastica storica e di storia della toponomastica urbana, Vol 2., pp. 740–1. Istituto per la storia di Bologna, Bologna (2000)

26. See Pini Note 21

27. This dataset was collected by Prof. Geltner and can be downloaded at Ufficio del fango dataset (13th–14th centuries), DANS Data Station Social Sciences and Humanities. https://ssh.datastations.nl/dataset.xhtml?persistentId=doi:10.17026/dans-24x-vyf2; see also Zaneri, T., Geltner, G.: Healthscaping Medieval Bologna, Accessed 1 Jan 2023. https://uvagis.maps.arcgis.com/apps/webappviewer/in-dex.html?id=98eac4af36ce49cbacb97c167f6dce43

Correction to: Towards Querying Multimodal Annotations Using Graphs

Jonas Bruschke⬚, Cindy Kröber⬚, Ronja Utescher,
and Florian Niebling⬚

Correction to:
Chapter "Towards Querying Multimodal Annotations Using Graphs" in: S. Münster et al. (Eds.): *Research and Education in Urban History in the Age of Digital Libraries*, **CCIS 1853, https://doi.org/10.1007/978-3-031-38871-2_5**

The originally published version of the chapter 5 contained the error in Fig. 5. The error in Fig. 5 has been corrected.

The updated original version of this chapter can be found at
https://doi.org/10.1007/978-3-031-38871-2_5

Author Index

Printed in the United States
by Baker & Taylor Publisher Services